1989

JACQUES MARITAIN:

THE MAN AND HIS METAPHYSICS

JACQUES MARITAIN:

THE MAN AND HIS METAPHYSICS

edited by

John F. X. Knasas

AMERICAN MARITAIN ASSOCIATION

The American Maritain Association
Anthony O. Simon, Secretary
508 Travers Circle
Mishawaka, Indiana 46545

This book was formatted and laser printed at:

Desktop Publishing Center
5001 Bissonnett, Suite 101
Bellaire, Texas 77401

TABLE OF CONTENTS

Editor's Preface

EDITOR'S PREFACE

"Woe to me if I do not Thomisticize." On Raissa Maritain's testimony, such were the words chosen by her husband Jacques to express his intellectual vocation. Melodramatic? Perhaps. But the pair were sensational personages.

They met in 1900 as young intellectuals at the Sorbonne. Dismayed with the relativism offered by their professors, they considered suicide. The lectures of Henri Bergson convinced them that knowledge of the absolute was still possible. Yet, it was a chance encounter with the writing and person of Leon Bloy that led them to understand that true knowledge of the Absolute was to be found in the wisdom of the saints. They converted to Catholicism in 1905. Both were not sanguine about Catholicism fulfilling their philosophical desires. Hence, with great joy they discovered the writings of St. Thomas Aquinas. Within Thomism, they perceived a metaphysics of being that perfected the natural capacities of the intellect.

As the above quote indicates, Maritain's introduction to Aquinas was not without responsibilities. In finding Aquinas, Maritain also found his vocation. He would "Thomisticize," i.e., effect an engagement of Aquinas with the 20th century. He would bring Thomism from beyond the seminary walls into the marketplace. Due in no small part to Maritain's witness, intellectuals still feel the call to "Thomisticize." By the publication of this volume, the American Maritain Association initiates a project that will continue to offer to the world men and women animated by Maritain's legacy. The Association also wishes to make itself more widely known as a fellowship that welcomes and engenders the Thomistic vocation.

The volume has three main parts. Articles by noted biographers of the Maritains comprise Part One. The occasion for Part Two is the 50th anniversary (1987) of Maritain's *Existence and the Existent*. The subsections of Part Two come from the chapters of Maritain's book. Articles of the subsections either critically discuss points of the chapter or creatively utilize them to address other issues. Finally, the appendix contains inspiring addresses by the Presidents of the American and Canadian Maritain societies.

On behalf of the American Maritain Association, I convey expressions of sincere gratitude to the following for their financial generosity: Prof. Raymond Dennehy, President, American Maritain Association; the Thomas More-Jacques Maritain Society; the Canadian Maritain Association with Prof. Jean-Louis Allard, President.*

Finally, a special expression of personal gratitude goes to Rev. Leonard A. Kennedy, C.S.B., former Director of the Center for Thomistic Studies, Houston, Texas, for his editorial expertise. And to my wife, Joanne, who word-processed and laser-printed the entire volume.

John F. X. Knasas

*The present book is published in lieu of no. IV (1988) of *Etudes maritainiennes/Maritain Studies*, published annually by the Canadian Jacques Maritain Association.

Le présent ouvrage tient la pace du no IV (1988) des *Etudes maritainiennes/Maritain Studies*, publiées annuellement par l'Association canadienne Jacques Maritain.

PART ONE

JACQUES AND RAISSA

POETRY, POETICS, AND THE MARITAINS

Judith D. Suther

This paper calls attention to the other side of a question now being debated in Maritain criticism and scholarship--the question of what Jacques owed to Raissa. I ask also what Raissa owed to Jacques. In broader terms, I advance the opinion that the entire issue of Jacques' debt to Raissa and Raissa's debt to Jacques, in poetics and, I suspect, in most other matters, is something of a red herring.

The catalyst for my views is a sentence near the end of *Existence and the Existent*. The context of the sentence is Jacques' contention that poetry of the highest order must be granted the element of obscurity proper to human intelligence of the divine. He is referring to the allegedly failed efforts of Kierkegaard and Chestov at understanding the great mystics. "They cruelly and rather shabbily misunderstood them," he says. Their philosophers' understanding was inadequate because--and this is the sentence--"the place towards which [the mystics] journeyed through the shadows was that place where souls possessed and illuminated by the madness of the Cross give their testimony."[1] In other words, potential understanding of the mystics' experience of God lies not in philosophy but in contemplation. And the "madness of the Cross," the generative force of contemplation, is love. Philosophy may be the love of wisdom, but it is not love. It is not madness and it does not testify.

Simplistic as this lexical exercise may seem, it lies at the heart of the opinion I wish to put forward--namely, that we will never know who owed what to whom between Raissa and Jacques, on the matter of poetics or, I am also willing to wager, anything else, because the evidence lies buried in the sanctum of private experience. Further, and more to the point, it lies buried in the mystery of love which transforms all rational, measurable reality into metaphor for everyone but the lover. For all we will ever know, Jacques did gain access through Raissa to kinds of knowledge and levels of understanding which he would not have reached on his own, thus escaping the fate of Kierkegaard and Chestov. I could be cautious and say only "ways of knowing," and thus limit my assertions to the safe arena of process and possibility. But why should I be cautious where he was bold, and not only bold but insistent, reiterative, and tireless in his acknowledgements?

Why should I dilute the actual, if astonishing, record of their interdependence?

I will limit my specific assertions to poetics, since I am not a philosopher, and poetics is the only area of Jacques' work I understand even dimly; I am convinced that he did accede at least to poetic knowledge as a direct result of his experience in love with Raissa. Like Dante at age nine struck dumb and granted access to new awareness by the simple presence of a girl named Portinari, Jacques knew the authority of true poetry and the mystery of being by the simple presence of Raissa Oumansov. And "simple," of course, is the palest of designations for this least simple of privileged experiences: the coming to knowledge through love. If one believes, as Jacques did, that one's partner in love is God's creation and God's direct communicant, then the knowledge flowing through her can only be true knowledge.

As for Raissa, she never ceased to insist that from the age of seventeen, when she met Jacques, she owed everything she knew to him. It was through him that she was able to reach the particular kinds of knowledge that he claimed were uniquely hers: namely, poetic knowledge and the contemplative's knowledge of truth through love. Her deference to him is not surprising. She was a willing heir to two authoritative traditions--the Judaic tradition of Eastern Europe and European Russia, and the resurgent Catholic tradition of anti-positivist, turn-of-the- century France. In what they called their "search for truth," she, at least, never sought to break away from authority, but rather to find and obey the one true authority. Like that of the institutional Church of her and Jacques' time, her thinking was based on a hierarchical model. God, St. Thomas, and Jacques, in that order, were by definition above her in the hierarchy. This arrangement suited her natural disposition; it allowed her to integrate the paternalistic heritage of Judaism into her acquired Christian culture. More to the point of my present topic is that the arrangement locked Raissa into a prescribed intellectual relation to Jacques. He was the active, authoritative partner in their joint endeavors; she was the passive, receptive partner. In her auto-biography, she conveys this relation not only by what she says, but by her very language, as in this representative passage:

> It has been my great privilege to receive, with no merit
> and no effort, to receive from such a dear hand, the fruit of
> his labor, which I could not attain without his help, yet to
> which I aspired with a deep and vital longing. I have been
> blessed in this way; I have lived in an atmosphere of
> intellectual rigor and spiritual righteousness, thanks to St.
> Thomas, thanks to Jacques, and I cannot write these things
> without being overcome with tears and love.[2]

Repeatedly in her autobiography she reveals her conviction that women in general and herself in particular are inherently incapable of taking the active role of artist, scientist--by which term "philosopher" is implied--or scholar: "They do not create," she says of women, "any more in the arts than in the sciences."[3] Women may only study and analyse and appreciate the work of men, who *are* equipped to create.

I lay out this brief exposition of Raissa's self-effacement, not to quarrel with her or deplore her attitude. I only wish to establish the queer complementarity of her deference to Jacques and his deference to her. His is extreme and has often been commented upon, sometimes with annoyance. Hers is as extreme as his, although far more culturally sanctioned. From our present perspective, it is impossible not to be aware of the manipulative and power-shifting strategies that such a definition of roles can lead to. I do not wish to deny that some of those strategies came into play in Raissa and Jacques' case--I think they did. Nor do I wish to dwell on them. I am not interested in amateur psychological analyses, mine or anyone else's, of the Maritains' domestic life or their relative intellectual and spiritual gifts. That is the vicious circle I choose to step out of by accepting the Maritains' own claims at face value. I think Raissa did accede through "the fruits of [Jacques'] labor" to kinds of knowledge she "could not attain without his help." I also think that Jacques' intransigent deference to her was based on the reality of *his* experience, and that he did learn, reach understanding, and gain knowledge through her. And that, of course, is the key to breaking open the vicious circle: we must give up our outsiders' perspective and grant the reality of his experience of her and her experience of him, which was an experience grounded in love.

In the epistemological terms that the couple used in defining their mutual relation, my answer to the question of what Raissa owed to Jacques is straightforward: she owed him everything. In his role as the interpreter of Aquinas and the successor to her grandfathers and her father, he validated whatever she may have reached toward but not grasped on her own. Let me extend a point made by my colleague Deal Hudson in a recent address to a regional meeting of the American Academy of Religion. He argued that Raissa's function as Jacques' Muse was quite literal and continued unabated into Jacques' old age.[4] I trust that Hudson will forgive my reduction of his point to this summary: early in their married life--in October 1912, when they were both still in their twenties--they took the vow as third order Benedictines, pledging themselves to a celibate marriage, at least partially because they understood the enormity of what Raissa represented for Jacques. She represented knowledge through love, divine knowledge that had to be welcomed, honored, served at any cost. It was related to carnal knowledge as Scripture is related to these paltry words I am speaking. I would suggest that the vow was doubly motivated, and that they also understood the enormity of what Jacques represented for Raissa. He represented the authority she needed in order to proceed, in love and obedience, with her own intellectual, spiritual, and artistic growth. If we can move beyond stereotypes of male artist-scientist-scholar and female muse, we can entertain the possibility that Jacques was Raissa's Muse. As indeed I think he was.

In another recent address, this one to last year's American Maritain Association meeting, another colleague, William Bush, also argued the essential part Raissa played in what Jacques knew.[5] As has happened with others, Bush's patience wears thin when assaulted with Jacques' single-minded citing of Raissa on subjects ranging beyond any competence she herself claimed or, for that matter, demonstrated. Bush maintains, I think rightly, that the point lies in Jacques' experience, not ours, and he did experience Raissa as an earthly transmitter of divine knowledge. I apologize also to Bush for this reduction of his comments. I propose a mirroring of them, along the same lines as I proposed with Hudson's: Raissa considered Jacques an authority on subjects on which he himself stubbornly deferred to her, especially contemplation and poetics. I cite Hudson and Bush because I think their comments, or perhaps I should say intuitions, are correct; in order to tell the whole story, or as much of it as can ever be told, the comments require the mirroring, the playing back upon themselves, that I have just proposed.

A readymade example of Raissa and Jacques' own mirroring, in the area of poetics, is provided by the history of the essay "Poetry as Spiritual Experience." It was originally given as a talk by Raissa to a conference on aesthetics in Washington, DC, in 1942, during the Maritains' wartime exile in the United States. A slightly revised version of the talk, under the names of both the philosopher and the poet, was published in a special issue of the journal *Fontaine*, devoted to poetry as spiritual exercise. The English translation, which appeared a year later, also carries both names. Then, when Jacques included the essay in Raissa's *Poemes et essais* (1968), he listed it under her name alone.[6] From this sequence, one can infer at length about who wrote, who revised, and who owed what to whom in the process. Having done that, I can only contend, as I did at the beginning of this talk, that the issue is a red herring. We are asking the wrong question when we insist on trying to figure out relative debts and influences. A more answerable question requires a suspension of control on our part--a leap of faith, of sorts: "How did Jacques owe everything to Raissa and Raissa everything to Jacques?" That is the question I have been attempting to address.

Long before the present debate over who owed what to whom, Henry Bars recognized the current from love to knowledge between Raissa and Jacques. Bars incorporated his recognition into *Maritain en notre temps* (1959), written now almost thirty years ago. In a more recent and more pointed assessment, Bars proposes an intellectual genealogy for Jacques, to supersede the conventional one that situates the philosopher in the lineage of Aquinas. "I have sometimes thought," says Bars, "that one could imagine for [Jacques] a much shorter genealogy, and one that discounts biology: 'Jacques de Raissa'"--Jacques of Raissa, in the manner of John of St. Thomas.[7] Bars' genealogy is somewhat fanciful and certainly affectionate; the rest of us, I think, have lagged behind Bars in recognizing that fancy and affection, not "just" intellect, kept the waters of knowledge flowing between Raissa and Jacques. The ludic communion of lovers was theirs from the beginning and only deepened over the years. Jacques' tireless editing, annotating, and quoting of Raissa's papers after her death reflects not only his determination that "justice be done to Raissa," in his phrase;[8] it also reflects his impossible wish that Raissa be seen through his eyes. As Bars has said, that could not be.

My reason for citing Bars, however--to whom I also owe apologies for reductionism--is that he comes closest to telling, or at least hinting at, the other side of the story: what Jacques would be like seen through Raissa's eyes. Using the central image of her only surviving love poem to Jacques, "Night Letter," Bars suggests that she alone could see into the heart of Jacques the philosopher and Jacques the lover; what she saw was her own small image illuminated there (Bars, 29). The word "small" is hers, and signifies, once again, her experience of Jacques' superior intellect and his transforming power in her life. The fact that the image is there constitutes a poetic admission which Raissa could not make in any other form: without her--more precisely, without the image of her--Jacques would falter.

In the four essays of *Situation de la poésie* (1938), Raissa and Jacques first enunciated together the underlying principles of a poetics they both endorsed throughout their lives as poet and philosopher. Jacques' fullest development of the principles came fifteen years later, in *Creative Intuition in Art and Poetry* (1953), where they are extended to visual art. Raissa worked closely with him on the book. As he says in the Acknowledgements: "Raissa, my wife, assisted me all through my work [on the lectures in this book]--I do not believe that a philosopher would dare to speak of poetry if he could not rely on the direct experience of a poet."[9] Very briefly, the principles laid out in *Situation de la poésie,* and extended in *Creative Intuition,* posit: (1) timeless standards of beauty consonant with the existence of a divine intelligence; (2) contemplation, or at the very least, *recueillement* (recollection), as a condition for release of the artist's creative potential; and (3) the element of mystery that signals the presence of the divine in all true art and links meaning inextricably to form. When Rassa chooses poets whose best work embodies these principles, she aims high; in her most substantive essay in *Situation de la po*ésie, she names Homer, Virgil, Dante, Shakespeare, Racine, Goethe, Pushkin, and Baudelaire. Jacques also aims high, in the exemplars he names in *Creative Intuition*; he chooses, among others, Dante, John of the Cross, Donne, Blake, Hopkins,

Shelley, Mallarmé, and Eliot. The telling choice, however, is none of these--it is Raissa.

Repeatedly, in the company just named, Jacques cites Raissa's poems. And he does not necessarily choose the ones that would best illustrate his (and her) poetics. For example, he does not include "Le Revenant" or "Mirages," easily among her most mysterious and accomplished poems of the contemplative experience. He does include a long and somewhat preachy evocation of an Edenic state of consciousness ("Le Quatrime Jour") and some fragments of other poems that need their original context in order to signify much of anything. There is no doubt that Raissa was aware of what Jacques was appending to the book by way of examples; perhaps she made some of the choices herself. That is a question of the sort that I think can never be answered, and in any case is ill-conceived. The inescapable conclusion, based on the way the Maritains worked together and deferred to each other, is that *they* considered the choices appropriate to the purpose of illustrating the principles of *their* poetics, as outlined briefly above. And they were blind to all that was contingent in each other--which included, of course, anything so incidental, so accidental, as a poem or a choice of illustration for a book. The explanation of this otherwise inexplicable blindness on both their parts now seems obvious to me, after years of obtuseness on my part: Jacques knew what he knew through Raissa, and Raissa knew what she knew through Jacques. The work of each was but a bare extension of the beloved person, and not distinct from that person's bearing of knowledge as God's scribe.

To return to the quotation from *Existence and the Existent* that set off these remarks, I want to close by turning Jacques' claim about Kierkegaard and Chestov onto myself: just as Jacques conceded philosophical analysis as an inadequate means toward understanding the experience of the great mystics, I concede any analysis I could conduct as an inadequate means toward understanding why Jacques thought Raissa was a great poet and Raissa thought Jacques was a great philosopher. In poetics, the only area where texts of his and texts of hers provide a base to work from, I can define a remarkable convergence between his signaling of the mystery essential to true poetry and her enactment of the mystery in a few true poems. Beyond that, I risk the shabby and cruel misunderstanding that Jacques deplored in Kierkegaard and Chestov. I prefer to avoid the risk and opt for a twist of Pascal's wager: I am willing to gamble on Henry Bars' genealogy--"Jacques of Raissa"--and to turn it the other way as well--"Rassa of Jacques." If I am wrong, if they lived an illusion, I will never know. If I am right, someone sometime can mark down another small victory for the difference that one human being can make in the life of another. In the convergence of Raissa and Jacques, pebbles thrown into broader waters than they ever imagined, the circles are still widening.

University of North Carolina

NOTES

1. Jacques Maritain, *Existence and the Existent.* (Westport, CT, 1975) 132-33.

2. Raissa Maritain, *Les Grandes Amitis.* (Paris, 1949) 242.

3. Raissa Maritiain, *Journal de Raissa*, ed. Jacques Maritain (Paris, 1963) 100-01.

4. Deal W. Hudson, "Consummation and Creation: The Meaning of the Muse," Lecture delivered to the Southeastern regional meeting, American Academy of Religion, April 1987. A revised version is published as "'The Ecstasy Which Is Creation': The Shape of Maritain's Aesthetics," in Deal W. Hudson and Matthew J. Mancini, eds., *Understanding Maritain, Philosopher and Friend* (Macon, GA, 1988).

5. William Bush, "RAISSA MARITAIN...et Jacques," Published in *Understanding Maritain* (see note 4).

6. Jacques and Raissa Maritain, "La Poésie comme expérience spirituelle," *Fontaine* 19-20 (Mar.-Apr. 1942): 22-25. Jacques and Raissa Maritain, "Poetry As Spiritual Experience," trans. Julie Kernan, *Spirit* 9 (Jan. 1943): 181-83. Raissa Maritain, *Pomes et essais*, ed. Jacques Maritain (Paris, 1968) 278-84.

7. Henry Bars, "Raissa et Jacques au jour le jour," *Cahier Jacques Maritain* 7-8 (Sept. 1983): 28.

8. Jacques Maritain, "Avertissement" to the *Journal de Raissa* (see note 3) 8.

9. Jacques Maritain, *Creative Intuition in Art and Poetry* (New York, 1953).

LONELINESS AND THE EXISTENT:
THE DARK NIGHTS OF PIERRE REVERDY
AND RAISSA MARITAIN

Bernard Doering

The world of Jean Paul Sartre is filled with a motley mass of beings that exist *en soi*. There is no God to explain their existence; they are simply there and they are *de trop*. In this nauseating multiplicity of objects, there exist certain beings that are conscious of their own existence and of the existence, outside themselves, of objects *en soi*. These conscious beings exist *pour soi*, in a world of pure *subjectivity*. But the conscious existent, the *subject*, can know the existents about him, including other conscious beings, only as objects *en soi*. This leads the subject to the forlorn conclusion that he himself is known to other conscious beings only as an *object*, never as a *subject*; that is, he is never known for himself, in the intimate core of his being. He is never understood completely. He is forever judged unjustly. He is alone. This is the universal human condition, to which, according to Sartre, the typical reaction is the nausea of anguish, loneliness, and despair, a kind of philosophic Dark Night of the Soul.

In his reply to Sartre, *Existence and the Existent*, Jacques Maritain agrees that the conscious subject grasps, in a flash that will never be dimmed, the fact that *he is a self* who is *at the center* of the world. "This privileged subject," says Maritain, "the thinking self, is to itself not object but subject; in the midst of all the subjects which it knows only as objects, it alone is subject as subject."[1] "To be known as object, to be known to others, to see oneself in the eyes of one's neighbor (here Sartre is right)," says Maritain, "is to be severed from oneself and wounded in one's identity. It is to be always unjustly known...."[2] *L'Enfer, c'est les autres*, said Sartre. Hell is other people.

For Maritain, however, God does exist; and as a consequence, the subjective "I", who stands before the tribunal of other subjectivities "accoutered in a travesty of himself," can nevertheless say, "I am known to God. He knows all of me...not as object but as subject in all the depths and all the recesses of subjectivity."[3] This exhaustive knowledge of God is a loving knowledge. "To know that we are known to God is not merely to experience justice, it is also to experience mercy."[4]

But how does the finite conscious self come to know both himself as subject and that Transcendent Self by whom he is known as subject? The knowledge of subjectivity as subjectivity is not a knowledge by mode of conceptual objectization, says Maritain.[5] It is rather a knowledge by mode of "experience." In *Existent and the Existent*, he divides this latter type of knowledge, that is, by mode of experience, into two kinds; first, a formless and diffuse unconscious or preconscious experiential knowledge in which subjectivity is not so much known as "it is felt as a propitious and enveloping night,"[6] and, secondly, an experiential knowledge by mode of inclination, sympathy, or connaturality. This knowledge by connaturality appears under three specifically distinct forms. The first of these is knowlege by affective connaturality which judges by the practical, inner inclination of the subject. The second is knowledge by poetic connaturality *ad extra* by mode of creation. And the third is knowledge by mystical connaturality *ad intra*, by mode of nescience, by possession-giving not-knowing. In his essay "The Natural Mystical Experience and the Void" (published in *Redeeming the Time*) Maritain divides this third knowledge by mystical connaturality into two forms. One is an *affective* experience, a supernatural mystical experience which passes by way of the Dark Night of purgation, loneliness, and abandonment through illumination to the union of love. This is an experience which depends on supernatural charity or grace, and which God, in His inscrutable judgments and unsearchable ways, grants to some souls and refuses to others. The other experience is *intellectual*, a natural mystical experience which passes by way of the Dark Night of the subjective experience of the Void to an intellectual grasp of the Transcendent Self, but no more.[7]

Maritain recognizes that, although singularly exalting combinations (even if they are muddy at times) of the supernatural mystical experience with either poetic experience or natural mystical experience can be found among Christian contemplatives and mystics such as Saint Augustine, and Rysbroeck, and especially Boehme, the distinction between poetic or natural mystical experience on the one hand and supernatural mystical experience on the other must be strictly maintained.[8] In the book which he wrote with Louis Gardet, *L'Experience du Soi, Etude de Mystique comparée*, Olivier Lacombe, a long-time friend and disciple of Maritain, insists, along with Saint John of the Cross and Saint Teresa of Avila, that supernatural mystical experience must pass by way of the infused theological virtues and of the gifts of the Holy Spirit which accompany them.[9] "Christian faith and reflection tell us," he writes, "that God, even though He is more intimate to us than we are to ourselves, nevertheless remains inaccessible in His transcendence to any direct experience that might be the fruit of those spiritual energies which are proper to our nature. The mystical experience of God such as He is in Himself, in the unsoundable depths of His being, can be nothing other than a gratuitous gift, a supernatural grace."[10] Maritain insists that there is no correspondence or parallelism between the nights of the senses and the spirit experienced by St. John of the Cross and the void of the natural mystical experience.[11]

In *Situation de la poésie* Jacques and Raïssa Maritain made a careful distinction between knowledge by poetic connaturality and knowledge by natural mystical experience, even though, they say, there is a "proximity, in the same divine source, in the experience of the poet and that of the mystic."[12] Though poetic experience is indeed, and preeminently, an experience, and is more an experience than it is knowledge, and though it may very well dispose the mind of the poet to mystical experience and is often full of contemplative flashes, it is not properly a mystical experience, particularly not one that is possession-giving. It does not have its goal and its fruit in itself; it does not tend to silence, as mystical experience does. Rather it tends toward utterance *ad extra*. It has its fruit and its goal in an external work which it produces, that is, the poem.[13] When the poet, disposed by poetic connaturality toward contemplation, advances into the mystical experience of the void, the Dark Night of the spirit leads the poet to a radical horror of his own life, to a spiritual death and a despair of *everything* (even of God). Such an experience, in its own special order, says Maritain, is like hell itself. If this Dark Night is a purely natural experience, then for the poet/mystic such a Night, of itself, ends in a catastrophe of the spirit, as it did for Arthur Rimbaud and Lautreamont. In order to survive such a Night, divine grace is necessary. The supernatural night of the spirit, says, Maritain, is the only night from which the spirit can emerge alive, because at the heart of the poet/mystic's radical despair, grace alone maintains a secret hope.[14]

Two poets, contemporary to Jacques Maritain and very close to his heart, both of whom he must certainly have had in mind when he wrote of the natural and supernatural nights of the spirit, were his wife Raïssa and his close friend, Pierre Reverdy. Both were poet/mystics who tried to describe in poetry the mystical experiences they had undergone. They are perfect exemplars, it seems to me, of Maritain's distinction between the Dark Night of an *affective*, supernatural mystical experience on the one hand, and the Dark Night of an *intellectual*, natural mystical experience on the other.

Raïssa Maritain was first and foremost a mystic. Robert Speaight called her poetry "the handmaid of contemplation."[15] In 1912, nine years after their marriage, Jacques and Raïssa took a vow of celibacy so that both of them, and Raïssa in particular, could better devote themselves to a life of contemplation. According to Jacques, it was only fourteen years later that Raïssa began to write poetry.[16] In his preface to the *Journal de Raïssa*, after stating that Raïssa told us everything in her poems, Jacques asks the reader rhetorically if those poems "were not born at the point where, in a very rare encounter, all sources are one and where the creative experience of the poet is but the pure mirror of the mystical experience."[17] On the following page Jacques quotes from the letter which Pierre Reverdy, our other poet of the Dark Night, sent to Raïssa concerning her volume of poetry *Au Creux du Rocher*. "Raising poetry to its highest degree by the simplest of means," he wrote, "you have used it as the step-ladder needed by your sensitivity to follow your soul to the heights of its mystical experience."

But to arrive at the heights of mystical experience, Raïssa had to follow all alone a path that led through the valley of the shadow of death, through the Dark Night of acedia and abandonment, in many ways not unlike Sartre's nauseaous experience of anguish, loneliness, and despair. Her *Journal* is filled with the anguish of this Dark Night. In an entry dated October 27-31, 1924, she writes:

> I have suffered very much. God is absent. My soul is completely crushed. When I feel this horrible emptiness in my heart, I utter terrible cries within me. I seem to have not a scrap of faith left, not a single atom of hope.... No one is there to lift me from the ground, and I am like a bird with broken wings. I drag myself along and everything causes me pain.[18]

And these sufferings become progressively more intense as she advances toward the union of love. A year later she wrote:

> Suddenly I saw myself plunged into an abyss of pain, in the midst of temptations so penetrating and so profound that my heart was absolutely martyrised by them.... My sufferings are indescribable, and I feel that they have taken root in the depths of my soul, at the very springs of my nature.... Poor heart! It has left no resource but tears. Silent tears, so bitter and so hard.... I am at the extremity of distress and I need exterior help since God has abandoned me. I have periods of suffering so terrible that I seem to be losing my mind.[19]

One of the "Feuilles detachées" of her *Journal*[20] contains this poem:

> Tous les moyens se sont avérés impuissants,
> Tous les chemins *trop* courts.
> La nuit divine impénétrable.
> La solitude intolérable, et nécessaire, inévitable.
> Toute parole de consolation paraît mensonge
> Et Dieu nous a abandonnés.

All means have shown themselves powerless,
All roads too short.
The divine night inpenetrable.
The solitude unbearable, and necessary, inevitable.
Every consoling word seems like a lie
And God has forsaken us.

If the sufferings of these Dark Nights are progressively more intense it
is because they are punctuated with periods of consolation, peace, and light
that in their turn are more and more profound. On January 31, 1936, after a
period of intense suffering, she wrote:

> ...a happy surprise awaited me; it was a period of
> recollection immediately very profound and very sweet,
> very peaceful and very restful....[21]

In the beauty of natural phenomena Raïssa found both the consolation
of God's presence and the anguish of His absence. In "Chant Royal" she
wrote:

> Dans le silence éclose voix si frêle
> Et qui dessine un frais ruisseau fleuri.
> Quel doux réveil me font ces notes grêles
> Malgré la neige et le ciel triste et gris.

> A frail voice opens like a blossom in the silence And
> pictures a cool flowery stream.
> What a sweet awakening these slender notes bring me
> In spite of the snow and the sad grey skies.

If God hides behind the veil of his creatures it is a light, diaphanous
veil, "*un léger voile.*" Although it hides her Beloved, the world is "sweet"
because it also reveals Him and brings her the peace of His presence.

> Douceur de monde!
> Jusqu'où monte et descend en mon coeur ta musique!
> Ta magie se donne pour l'éternité....

> O gentle sweetness of the world!
> How your music rises and falls in my heart!
> Your magic is given for all eternity....

Prestiges du printemps, jardin persistant des délices.
Le ciel est limpide et lavé.
Une lumière tendre paraît
descendre du paradis.

Fascination of springtime, enduring garden of delights.
The sky is limpid and washed clean.
A tender light seems to come down from paradise.

Her universe is filled with stars; the world she knows is gentle and kind; she admires its "générosité végétale," the "fécondité miraculeuse du bois"; before the love she sees scattered throughout the world ("épars dans le monde") she cries: "O suavité, plénitude, joie!" (Douceur de monde). Like a ship she rides at anchor on the peaceful waters of the harbor (Chant royal).

But sighs and tears are not excluded from the "orchard" of this world, from this "garden fresh and pure" (Louange de l'epousé). "The gates of the horizon" may still "crumble in the gloom," where souls may still lose their way "in the hellish maze of madness" and cry out their despair (Portes de l'horizon). In the "agony and misery" of its Dark Nights, which the poet calls "those divine throes of death," when God takes back the gift of his presence, the suffering heart is forced by God to "forget the return of those days of peace which love has promised it." (Chant royal)

In the advanced stages of contemplation, the experience of the presence of God, with all His perfections, becomes so very real that, in contrast with the imperfections of the creature, the very intensity of this experience deepens the anguish of the Dark Night, so much so that eventually the pain of abandonment and that sense of distance due to the imperfections of the creature become almost one with the joy of union, as is shown by a poem she entered in her *Journal* on November 11, 1937:

O mort où est ton aiguillon
Le chemin de la mort et le chemin de la vie
Sont un seul chemin si nous allons à pas d'amour....

O death where is thy sting?
The road of death and the road of life
Are one single road if we walk in the steps of love ....

Dans les ténèbres de la vie humaine
Brille une lumière fragile
Comme une étoile qui envoie ses rayons
D'une inimaginable distance:

> C'est qu'il faut monter à pas de mort
> L'échelle de la vie.[22]

> In the darkness of human life
> Shines a fragile light
> Like a star that sends its rays
> From an unimaginable distance:
> It is with steps of death that we must mount
> The ladder of life.

No poem expresses better than "Tout est lumière" Raïssa's characteristic mystical experience of passage from loneliness to union, from anguish to peace, from darkness to light:

> Tout est donné. L'angoisse a passé,
> Et la mort.
> Que mon âme est légère.

> All has been given.
> The anguish has passed,
> And death too.
> How light my soul feels.

> J'ai mis mon esprit entre les mains de Dieu.
> Mon coeur est pur comme l'air des hauts lieux.

> I have placed my spirit in God's hands.
> My heart is pure like the air
> of the mountain tops.

> Tout est lumière.

> All is light.

Pierre Reverdy's experience of the mystical life was very different from that of Raïssa. After his arrival in Paris in 1916, Reverdy dabbled in many of the avant-garde movements: Dada, Surrealism, Cubism, Simultanism, and Futurism. Apart from the enthusiasm of the two years during which he founded and edited the review *Nord-Sud* (March 1917 to October 1918), his writing gives evidence of ever increasing emotional turmoil, psychological uncertainty, and personal fragmentation. At the center of his interior anguish was a profound religious crisis. In 1921, he and his wife converted to Catholicism under the influence of his poet/friend Max Jacob, who, after his own conversion, retired to the Benedictine monastery of

Saint-Benôit-sur-Loire.   In 1925, Reverdy began to frequent the Sunday
meetings in the Maritains' home at Meudon, despite his antipathy toward
most of the intellectuals he met there, and he participated actively in the
Maritains' efforts to bring Jean Cocteau back to the faith.   During the two
years that followed, there is a rather frequent exchange of letters between
Reverdy and the Maritains.   At Jacques' suggestion he made a retreat at
Solesmes where he found an "old abbey wall against which I can lean like a
trellis" (letter of January 22, 1926).[23]   Four months later Reverdy and his
wife moved to Solesmes where they sought seclusion and a life of prayer in
the shadow of the old monastery.   He remained there till his death in 1960.

In 1927, in Maritain's collection "Roseau d'or," Reverdy published
Gant de crin, a book containing his views on aesthetics and some personal
reflections.   It was filled with his admiration of equilibrium and stability and
with his newfound religious enthusiasm.   But in 1928 he underwent another
religious crisis.   Jean Schroeder states categorically that Reverdy lost his
faith completely in 1928.[24]   Gerard Bocholier wonders if he really lost his
faith since he continued to speak of religious matters with a certain monk at
Solesmes[25] who told me once that Reverdy never ceased to struggle to
believe.   John Howard Griffin, in a rare interview with Reverdy in 1946,
quotes the poet, who, speaking "as though he were very tired," said, "it's
hard to believe, you know.   It's very hard to believe."[26]   After Reverdy's
death Griffin received a letter from Maritain concerning his friend's faith in
which he wrote:

> ...Pierre van der Meer (who is now a Benedictine monk in
> Holland) met a monk at Solesmes who saw Reverdy
> frequently, and what he learned from this monk filled him
> with admiration and confidence.   Reverdy believed he had
> lost the Faith.   In reality, God hounded him constantly.
> He hungered for God; this great soul had a passion for the
> Absolute, which even if it never was satisfied, placed him
> always close to the Divine.[27]

Reverdy's letters to Maritain are filled with his hunger for the Absolute.
On January 8, 1925, more than a year before he moved to Solesmes, he
wrote:

> ...I have no other resource than to push on to the very
> end....I must give everything to God or I will risk giving
> him nothing at all or very, very little.... I am extremely
> fragile. I must hold on to the little strength I have. I need
> to die. That's right--to disappear, to become nothing--to
> give myself to God as a religious does, not by abandoning
> my state in life--but by completely leaving behind the

world and the senseless whirlwind of men who still
believe in other things than God and the life beyond this
envelope of nothingness.[28]

He knew, perhaps more deeply than any other poet, what Maritain
called the subjective natural mystical experience of the Void, and though he
tried desperately to fill this Void with something more than a purely
"intellectual grasp of the Transcendent Self," he never seems to have arrived
at, or been granted, the grace of an "affective supernatural mystical
experience" of illumination or of union. His poems are filled with the
forlorn anguish of his loneliness and after the religious crisis of 1928 they
become more and lugubrious.

Poetry, said Reverdy, is made of images. The images that predominate
in his poems are "walls" and "barriers" beyond which the poet cannot
advance, "hedges" through which he cannot see, "rooms" in which he finds
himself enclosed without knowing how he entered there, "curtains" that are
almost drawn, "doors" that are barely ajar, "shutters" that are almost closed,
"thresholds" that cannot be crossed, closed "eyelids" that shut out the light,
"culs-de-sac" with no way out, "cross-roads" where the poet has no idea
which way to turn, "deserted streets" which everyone else has left, passing
by the poet in indifferent silence. The reader is reminded of the empty,
somber city landscapes of the painter Chirico, except that in Reverdy's
poems the poet is always standing there confused, trembling and alone.

Darkness and shadows are everywhere; the poet is frightened by his
own shadow or by others which move furtively along the wall. What lights
there are go out. If there are stars in the sky, the wind passes by and screws
them out like light bulbs. Or stars are like eyes in the sky over which
eyelids open and then close.

And everywhere there is a mysterious unidentified and unidentifiable
presence. "Quelqu'un," someone, is there, behind the curtain, behind the
shutters, behind the door, on the other side of the wall, an indistinct voice in
the other room or behind the bushes. The poet never finds out who this is,
always there, never revealing himself, never responding to a cry for help. In
"Coeur à coeur" the poet writes:

> Je tremblais.
> Au fond de la chambre le mur était noir....
> Comment avais-je pu franchir
> le seuil de cette porte?
> On pourrait crier;
> Personne n'entend.
> On pourrait pleurer;
> Personne ne comprend.

I was trembling.
At the back of the room the wall was black....
How was I able to cross that door's threshold?
I could cry out;
No one hears
I could weep;
No one understands

For Reverdy nature was not the gentle mirror of the Creator, the "léger voile," the diaphanous veil that reveals as much as it hides. At worst it was hostile, at best cold, silent. In his poem "Le Coeur écartelé" (The Quartered Heart) all the elements of nature are indifferent, useless.

Il se ménage tellement.
Il a si peur des couvertures,
Les couvertures bleues du ciel,
Et les oreillers de nuages,
Il est mal couvert par sa foi.
Il craint tant les pas de travers
Et les rues taillées dans la glace.
Il est trop petit pour l'hiver,
Il a tellement peur du froid....
Le temps le roule sous ses vagues.
Parfois son sang coule à l'envers
Et ses larmes tachent le linge....
Sa foi est un buisson d'épines,
Ses mains saignent contre son coeur,
Ses yeux ont perdu la lumière,
Et ses pieds trainent sur la mer
Comme les bras morts des pieuvres.
Il est perdu dans l'univers,
Il se heurte contre les villes,
Contre lui-même et ses travers.
Priez donc pour que le Seigneur
Efface jusqu'au souvenir
De lui-même dans sa mémoire

He takes such care of himself.
He is so afraid of blankets,
The blue blankets of heaven,
The pillows of clouds,
His blanket of faith is not much help.
He is so afraid of missteps

And the streets carved intothe ice
He is too small for winter,
He is so afraid of the cold....
Time rolls him over under its waves.
Sometimes his blood runs backwards
And his tears stain the sheets....
His faith is a bush full of thorns,
His hands bleed against his heart,
His eyes have lost their light,
And his feet drag across the sea
Like the dead arms of an octopus.
He is lost in the universe,
He bumps against cities,
 Against himself, and against his failings.
Pray then to the Lord
That He wipe from his mind
The very memory of himself.

The poem that best pictures for me the *paysage intérieur*, the interior landscape, of Reverdy is his "Son de cloche" (Bell Sound):

Tout s'est éteint
Le vent passe en chantant
Et les arbres frissonnent.
Les animaux sont morts,
Il n'y a plus personne.
Regarde!
Les étoiles ont cessé de briller,
La terre ne tourne plus.
Une tête s'est incliné,
Les cheveux balayant la nuit.
Le dernier clocher resté debout
Sonne minuit.

All the lights have gone out,
The wind passes by singing
And the trees shiver.
The animals are all dead,
There is no one left.
Look!
The stars have stopped shining,
The earth is no longer spinning.
There is a bowed head,
Its hair sweeping the night.

The last belfry left standing
Tolls midnight.

What a contrast in the works of these two poet/mystics, both ardently pursuing the same goal of mystical union, one of whom found "suavit, plnitude, joie" (as she put it), the other, only the black Void. How explain the difference? Maritain's answer to Sartre, that the Transcendent Self is there, One who is more present to us than we are to ourselves, who knows us as subjects and whom we can know as Subject, was spare consolation to Pierre Reverdy. The experience of God's presence and the very faith that makes it possible are both graces which God bestows at his good pleasure.

This was not the first or the last time that Maritain ran up against this ancient and troubling problem of Grace. Georges Bernanos once asked him in a letter: "Why does God refuse Himself to those who desire Him and love Him? This is the problem." Maritain wrote that the grace of a supernatural mystical experience depends on the practice of virtue, especially charity toward one's neighbor.[29] As difficult a personality as he appeared to be, was Reverdy so devoid of virtue? Maritain knew he had no satisfying answer for his friend and could do little more than offer the compassion he showed in his letter to John Howard Griffin. Concerning this same problem, in his book *Christian Perfection and Contemplation*, the famous Dominican theologian Father GarrigouLagrange, Maritain's longtime mentor, and tormentor as well, carefully skirted the issue. He wrote:

> God is not obliged to remedy our voluntary faults,
> especially when they are repeated. The truth of the matter
> is that He often does remedy them, but not always.
> Therein lies a mystery.[29]

Well, I suppose we must leave the question there. If for Raïssa Maritain "Tout est lumière" (all is light) and for Pierre Reverdy "Tout s'est éteint" (all the lights have gone out), with Bernanos we can only wonder why.

University of Notre Dame

NOTES

1. J. Maritain, *Existence and the Existent* (New York, 1948) p. 68.

2. *Ibid.*, p. 76.

3. *Ibid.*, p. 77.

4. *Ibid.*, p. 79.

5. *Ibid.*, p. 71.

6. *Ibid.*, p. 70.

7. J. Maritain, "The Natural Mystical Experience of the Void,"in *Redeeming the Time* (London, 1943) pp. 232f.

8. *Ibid.*, p. 249.

9. O. Lacombe and L. Gardet, *L'Experience du soi, étude de mystique comparée* (Paris, 1981) p. 21.

10. *Ibid.*, p. 28.

11. *Redeeming the Time*, p. 251.

12. J. and R. Maritain, *Situation de la poésie* (Paris, 1938) p. 67.

13. *Redeeming the Time*, p. 231.

14. *Ibid.*, pp. 253-54 *passim.*

15. R. Maritain, *Arbre partriarche* (Worcester, 1965) p. xiii.

16. R. Maritain, *Poèmes et essais (Paris, 1968) p. 12.*

17. R. Maritain, *Journal de Raïssa* (Hors commerce, 1962) p. 11.

18. *Ibid.*, p. 169. All translations are those of the author.

19. *Ibid.*, p. 181.

20. *Ibid.*, p. 241.

21. *Ibid.*, p. 238.

22. *Ibid.*, p. 240.

23. In the Maritain archives at Kolbsheim.

24. J. Schroeder, *Pierre Reverdy* (Boston, 1981) pp. 19-21.

25. G. Bocholier, *Pierre Reverdy, le phare obscure* (Saint- Juste-la-Pendue, 1984) p. 18.

26. J. H. Griffin, "My Neighbor Reverdy," in *The John Howard Griffin Reader* (Boston, 1968) p. 569.

27. *Ibid.*, pp. 569f.

28. In the Maritain archives at Kolbsheim.

29. *Redeeming the Time*, pp. 226, 249, 254.

30. R. Garrigou-Lagrange, *Christian Contemplation and Perfection* (London, 1937) p. 87.

RAISSA, JACQUES, AND THE ABYSS OF CHRISTIAN ORTHODOXY: THOUGHTS ON *"THE FACE OF GOD OR THE LOVE OF GOD AND THE LAW."*

William Bush

In a paper given in Atlanta in 1985 and to appear in the forthcoming volume, *Understanding Maritain*, we examined Raissa impact on her husband's spirituality, as well as what Jacques came to see as Vera's contribution to his spiritual evolution. What we present here therefore is a sort of long footnote to that previous paper, as it were the probing of a rather intriguing text of Raissa which, heretofore, we have pushed aside as being more philosophical than spiritual. It consists in fact of only a few undated pages and is entitled: *The Face of God or the Love of God and the Law.*

Let us begin by observing that not once, but twice after Raissa's death Jacques gave eloquent proof of attaching singular importance to these few undated pages. First of all, in 1963, he imposed them upon the reader as the final statement in *Raissa's Journal* as though they were in fact a summation of all she had said. And, though one may well observe that the placing of this undated text at the end of *Raissa's Journal* might not really be all that important it itself, the fact remains that three years later, in 1966, in summing up his thoughts on man, God and the Church in *The Peasant of the Garonne* Jacques again situated the very same text at the end of his own final chapter, as it were a veritable crowning of his long, closing section devoted to the affairs of the kingdom of God. He even actually integrates it into the last chapter of his own text. Must we not therefore try to see something more in this very special treatment of these few undated pages than a mere whim on Jacques' part to give the last word to Raissa?

In any case, an examination of this short text proves rewarding quite apart from any question of Jacques. Raissa broaches the suject of the divinisation of man in it, giving a very striking presentation of Abraham's willingness to sacrifice his long-desired and only son, and citing this as an example of the transmutation of our fleshly nature into a spiritual one, saying of this great Patriarch that *"he has revealed all the terrible demands of the divinisation of man."*[1]

Now this idea of the divinisation of man is of an impeccable orthodoxy, whether we view it as being the whole purpose of the Incarnation of God and a faithful continuation of the Johannine teaching that God become man in Jesus Christ that men might become sons of God, or from the great and unbroken tradition of Greek Christianity where the divinisation of man--that is, *theosis*--is not looked upon as being an optional goal, but indeed as the only purpose of the Christian life, the only abiding reality in man's mortal state where, apart from belief in the Resurrection of Jesus Christ, man has no option open to him but doom, dust, decay, and oblivion. Could it be then the question of the divinisation of man in these pages which captured Jacques' attention and held it over the years?

Prolonged pondering of the contents of this short text have led me to conclude that such was not, in fact, the case. Indeed, I am convinced that other considerations touched upon by Raissa in these few pages were in the end much nearer Jacques' heart, and that once we have grasped these other considerations, we shall be better able to understand why the greatness of two of France's foremost Christian writers of the twentieth century, Charles Péguy and Georges Bernanos, both friends of Maritian, eluded the philosopher who, at best, regarded their Christianity with a cautious reserve and, at worst, with what one might best describe as a slightly Pharisaical superiority tainted with a bit of rather obtuse priggishness endemic to certain converts.

This observation may appear harsh, yet it is a hard, bitter fact with which I, as a literary critic, have long wrestled, and it has been rendered all the more difficult in that I am fully aware of Jacques' quite extraordinary intellectual gifts and of that far greater degree of Christian charity he and Raissa were capable of exercising toward Péguy and Bernanos than either of the latter two would ever have bothered to exercise towards the Maritains. In fact both Péguy and Bernanos passed quite severe judgements on Maritain. The problem is nonetheless before us. And, though I am not sure how popular the conclusions that we shall draw from Raissa's text may be, I would like to reassure Maritain specialists that my own apprehension in arriving at them--especially for me who am not a Maritain specialist--was no less than theirs may be.

Now a first reading of Raissa's pages leaves us with the impression that everything is fairly straightforward. She argues that, though God is love, man is submitted to the law which God, as the Creator of being, has made and which, in man's eyes, seems opposed to love. Yet, she argues, God could not change the law so he submitted Himself to it in Jesus Christ to show us men that He is with us when we suffer from the law, and that He is actually calling us beyond it into the new law of Christ which has been spread abroad, born from the effusion of His blood. This sacrifice moreover serves as an example for His followers. Furthermore, Raissa maintains, this new law of Christ is much harder than the ancient law. Still, through the love of Christ, one has learned that before all things one must love God, knowing that He is love, and trusting in this love to the end. Finally, in Raissa's closing argument, we find a statement which, to the extent that it could be applied to her and Jacques' own spiritual lives, does indeed confirm their basic orthodoxy. Speaking of the law and of God, Raissa says: "insofar as He is our end and our beatitude, he calls us beyond it."[2]

The disquieting thing is that the very orthodoxy of this statement stands in sharp contrast with what Raissa actually does in this short article. For after such an orthodox statement a Péguy or a Bernanos would have lost themselves in what was well beyond the law where alone is found, they both knew, the dynamism of the ineffable mystery of God. Raissa Maritain however somehow seems to have got grounded by philosophical issues which, I suspect, found an echo within the aging Jacques' philosopher's heart as he compiled her *Journal* and put the finishing touches upon his own testament in *The Peasant of the Garonne*.

Indeed, these pages bear witness to Raissa's innate need to philosophize on questions which, as St. Paul was the first to remind us, can only prove the folly of philosophers when confronted with the cross of Jesus Christ. Raissa, however, resembling Jacques in her intellectuality, boldly forges ahead with her speculations, even talking about the *cause* of God.

Certainly one steeped in the Greek tradition of apophatic theology, whereby one knows that one can never arrive conceptually at what God is but only what He is not, can only tremble at the thought of a God whose cause might be understood. Would He not thereby be reduced to the grasp of man's mind? Respect for the ineffability of God is not however one of the more striking characteristics of philosophers of any ilk, nor is it a characteristic of western Christian thought as a whole after the twelfth century. And it is moreover a fact known to all that the Maritains prided themselves not only on being the most faithful of western Christians but even, more particularly, disciples of St. Thomas Aquinas.

Now if one can, while keeping in view the *whole* of Christianity, look at St. Thomas Aquinas objectively, how can one escape seeing that this great 13th century figure could have come about only in the west, being as it were a local, a regional manifestation? Indeed, Orthodox Christians in a country such as Greece with an apostolic tradition going back to St. Paul, might well ask why a Christian writer should even try to reconcile Christianity with--of all people--their own pre-Christian Aristotle? But such questions were far from Raissa's mind in writing this text where she boldly opposes the *cause* of God to the *cause* of the law. She even views God as being, as it were, trapped by Himself: "He cannot abolish any law inscribed in being,"[3] she maintains.

Once again our Greek Christians might observe that proposing to say
what the Creator can or cannot do is not only risky and dangerous, but also
tends to show a certain intellectual pride in presuming to grasp God's utter
ineffability. Indeed, have Christians, thoughout the centuries, not always
maintained that they know God not by intellectual speculation on His
causes, but rather by personal encounter with the God-Man Jesus Christ
through the Holy Spirit? All Christian saints bear witness to this be they
Catholic or Orthodox. Is this not as true of a great saint of our day such as
Mother Theresa of Calcutta as it was in the last century of that other great
Catholic witness, Thérèse of Lisieux? And is it not also true for the often-
maligned evangelical fundamentalist? All of them speak a common and
essentially Christian language about knowing God, about *experiencing* Him,
though His incarnation in Jesus Christ.

This is not of course to imply, even for a minute, that the personal
encouter with Christ was at all absent from Raissa Maritain's experience.
As we had ample opportunity to point out in our earlier paper, quite the
contrary is true, and is evident in many very moving examples. But such is
nonetheless certainly not the great thrust in these few pages with which
Jacques chose to end both *Raissa's Journal* and his *The Peasant of the
Garonne*. Indeed, the mystery of one's encounters with Christ is singularly
absent with Raissa pushing aside the mystery of the personal and particular
in favour of the generalization of philosophical speculation, rooting it all in
that old Maritainian imperative: "distinguish in order to unite". Mystery
therefore, the fundamental, unseen, and unseeable mystery of how God
works, and why God works, becomes in these pages a matter for
philosophical speculation.

We thus arrive at the two most basic assumptions implicitly, if not
always explicitly, behind Raissa's speculations which, I believe, could not
fail to stir sympathetic vibrations in an aging Jacques' heart. The first
assumption is far-reaching and the second is actually dependent upon it.
Raissa speaks of "the meaning of all human history" as being the
"inexorable Law of transmutation of a nature into a higher nature."[4] She
thus thrusts upon us, as though it were a generally accepted fact, the idea of
progress as well as the idea of the *modern*. The whole business of *moving
ahead*, of *going forward*, and to say it all, of *evolution towards something
higher*, is thus proclaimed by Raissa as being history's essential meaning.

Now such a tenet seems to have been--alas!--basic to Maritain's own
thought, being perhaps a reflection of his notable republican ancestry.
Though the caustic anti-Maritain critic might remark that such ideas of
progress and optimism might be deemed more appropriate coming from a
Marxist or socialist than from a Christian awaiting the second coming of
Christ and the judgement of the world by fire, Maritain did cling to this
tenet which helps explain, I believe, that naiveté he displayed, for example,
in his assessement of America. We realize thus that if, at moments in

reading *The Peasant of the Garonne*, one senses that the author has become aware of a few flaws in the rose-tinted pane through which he viewed the meaning of history, Raissa's essay at the end of this volume nonetheless serves as an antidote to any poison secreted by his pessimistic assessment of some of the fruits of Vatican II.

But a far more dangerous tenet still also lies hidden in these pages. This is Jacques and Raissa's failure to recognize the radical nature of the Fall since both seem to believe, as we have just said, that the meaning of "all human history" is to be found in the "inexorable law of transmutation of a nature into a higher nature," something neither Péguy nor Bernanos would ever have admitted under any circumstances. As their mature works show, neither Péguy nor Bernanos had any illusions concerning man's utter and total inability to speculate on the cause of God and the law, nor upon man's ineptitude to grasp the depths of his own mediocrity, destitution, and twisted nature since losing sight of the Face of God in Paradise.

Certainly the orientation of Péguy and Bernanos was already well defined in French literature not only by Pascal in the 17th century, but brilliantly by the great Baudelaire in the 17th century where, in *The Flowers of Evil*, we are given a panoramic view of man's fall. Péguy, singing in his long masterpiece, *Eve*, not only of man's cosmic destitution, but also of man's cosmic redemption, views Eve not only as the tragic, fallen and humiliated grandmother of the race of men, but also as ancestress of the most holy virgin Godbirthgiver who intercedes for the whole world. Péguy provides us in this most neglected of Christian masterpieces what may some day finally be recognized as the only valid reply not only to Baudelaire's *The Flowers of Evil* but also to Dante's *Divine Comedy*. Moreover in his very first novel Bernanos sees Satan's sun as being manifest whenever man finds his mental lust renewed in the midst of the destruction he has just wrought by his latest attempt to satisfy his intellectual concupiscience-- something so frighteningly relevent for man today as he pigheadedly bashes on seeking salvation through the panacea of nuclear energy and erotic satisfaction in spite of the devastation already brought upon himself by both.

Whatever one may think of Bernanos' sun of Satan, Baudelaire's evil flowers, or Péguy's *Eve*, the fact remains that Jacques Maritian, by giving Raissa the last word in those pages of his own last testament, proved that he remained optimistic about the evolution of the human condition in spite of anything he might have said to the contrary in the rest of *The Peasant of the Garonne*. He moreover obviously agrees with her conclusion that people must be *told* what the difference is between the *cause* of the law and the *cause* of God so that they may be able to understand the love of God. Thus, he no less than she, bases the solution to man's problem upon the imperative of intellectual dissemination.

Of course, salvation by intellectual dissemination hardly startles us who are of a culture canonizing Rousseau and officially recognizing education as the surest scale, after wealth, for measuring civil worth and social nobility. Nonetheless, is it not fair to observe that something quite other than intellecutal dessemination must be regarded as the true measure for the abiding influence of the Maritains' Christian witness?

I am in fact convinced that the Maritain's remarkable impact has come far less from their intellectual witness in their writings than from their own very personal witness of what Jesus Christ was for them, a witness which touched all who came into contact with them. And this relevance of Christ to them was, let us never forget, something they themselves did not get from intellectual stimulation, or even from St. Thomas Aquinas, but rather from their encounter with Léon Bloy, that glorious yet terrible prophet whose soul burned with love for God's ineffable mystery. For the essential greatness of this old genius' personality proved for the Maritains, as for other Christian notables such as the painter, Georges Rouault, a witness to the uncreated Light of God. And Léon Bloy, that great lover of the Holy Trinity as revealed through the incarnation of God in Jesus Christ, was by no means a philosopher--and most definitly not a Thomist.

The amazing thing is that there is in fact a great gulf separating Bloy's Christianity from the Maritain's and it becomes obvious to anyone who bothers to scratch the surface of their respective thought about God and man. For, in spite of Raissa and Jacques' touching fidelity to the memory of Bloy, the abyss separating them is as real as the abyss separating Maritain from Péguy, Bernanos and Baudelaire. And, indeed, is it not the same abyss--the abyss of orthodoxy? For Bloy, let us recall, honoured Baudelaire as a master and, like Baudelaire, he also refused belief in progress, being steeped in a sense of the human race's utter destution since the Fall. In mourning the loss of his little son André, the devastated Bloy prayed that God might forgive us humans our idolatry in seeking Paradise in the face of our children since our exil is so ancient that we have forgotten the true splendour of the face of God, so deeply imprinted on our souls and so abiding in the residual memory of the race that we constantly attempt to replace its loss by the beauty of the face of beings created in God's own image and, more especially, in the faces of our own children.

Certainly it will be for the critics of the next century to assess Maritain's Christianity and compare his spiritual legacy with the legacy left by both Péguy and Bernanos. I suspect though that one will be in for some surprises for, in spite of being viewed in their lifetime as rather suspect Catholics by clerical officialdom, both the latter have left a rich and very orthodox Christian legacy to French literature, a legacy as rooted in the Fall and man's destitution as is the work of Baudelaire or the thought of Pascal, and holding the basic theological tenet that the only meaning to history is found in the Incarnation of God in Jesus Christ.

Yet, in spite of what we all know to be the Maritain's deep identity with Christ, these few undated pages of Raissa entitled *The True Face of God or the Love of God and the Law* clearly demonstrate an implicit denial of the Fall since they hold man capable of reasoning on the *cause* of almighty God Himself, as well as also demonstrating a profound and almost nave optimism concerning human *progress*, maintaining a belief in the inexorability of the "law of transmutation of a nature into a higher nature" as constituting the basic meaning of history.

It is only to the extent that we can apply to Christ Himself what Raissa says about the Creator as "our end and our beatitude" that we can, in fact, implicitly, if not explicitly, bridge the abyss of Christian orthodoxy separating the Christian witness of Jacques and Raissa from that of Péguy, Bernanos, Baudelaire, Pascal and--ironic as it may seem--even from that of their own godfather, Léon Bloy.

University of Western Ontario

NOTES

1. *Raissa's Journal, presented by Jacques Maritain* (Albany, New York: 1974), p. 392.
2. *Ibid.*, p. 394.
3. *Ibid.*, p. 390.
4. *Ibid.*, p. 390.

JACQUES MARITAIN AND THE RISE OF FASCISM

John Hellman

> The Vichy authorities ... vigorously dismantled all the
> structures that had existed for seventy years and
> unhesitatingly demolished all the 150-year-old principles.
> At the end of 1940 a new order was established and
> France changed more radically in a few months than at
> any other time in its history since the summer of 1789[1]

Until quite recently, historical interpretations of France in the 1930's
and under the Vichy regime have been much influenced by the post-war
reversal of alliances and the pressures of the cold war. France needed to put
aside the fratricidal hatreds and achieve national reconciliation after what
had been a de facto civil war in that country in 1944. There was also the
understandable desire of the French to see the period 1940-1944 as a
peculiar aberration without any direct continuity with the creative political
thinking and intellectual effervescence of the thirties in which men like
Jacques Maritain figured so prominently. There has been a marked tendency
to consider Vichy as isolated from the period that preceded Marshall
Pétain's "National Revolution" and to minimize the historical significance of
this period even if it was a time in which "France changed more radically in
a few months than at any other time in her history since 1789".

If Vichy has been downplayed, there has also been a reluctance to see
fascism as more than a simple aberration and to recognize that there existed
home-grown fascist movements in nearly all European countries, and that
the rowdy bands of street fighters were backed by a body of serious political
ideas which could be no less logically defended than those of the democratic
or liberal parties. In fact, merely recognizing that fascist thinking belonged
not only to crackpots but to serious intellectuals, even to brilliant men,
would entail a new way of perceiving the phenomenon.[2] Not long ago, even
suggesting that fascism had been a mass movement possessing an ideology
built upon serious reflection on the realities and contradictions of modern
society led to one's being considered sympathetic to fascism. But most

historians of contemporary France now agree, as one of them put it, that "Fascist influence in France was much deeper, and far more groups were affected than is generally believed or recognized".[3]

Some historians are claiming both that France was far more affected by fascism than has been thought and that "France was ... the country in which fascist ideology in its main aspects came into being twenty years before similar ideologies appeared elsewhere in Europe...."[4] But, if this was the case, it was of particular interest to Catholics for there had to have been considerable overlap between the rise of European fascism and the heyday of that remarkable French Catholic Intellectual Revival which came to have such an important impact on the Catholic Church in both Europe and North and South America. In this regard Maritain's early career is of interest for he is often considered the most important Catholic intellectual of this century and he converted to Catholicism in that same colourful Parisian atmosphere in the first decade of this century in which a protofascist disgust with the Jews and the bourgeoisie seemed to figure at least as importantly as the Sermon on the Mount. It has recently been pointed out, for example, that Maritain's best friend, Ernest Psichari, underwent a "conversion experience" at the same time as Maritain, but to a Christian-soldier mystique which had certain ominous irrationalist overtones.[5]

Like much of modern Catholic thinking in general, and that of the young Maritain in particular, fascism repudiated much of the legacy of the 18th century and the French Revolution. The fascists, like the Catholics, sought to lay the foundations of a new communal and anti-individualist civilization in which all classes of society would be perfectly integrated as in that "New Middle Ages" prophesied by Maritain's friend, the Russian Berdyaev.[6] The revolution embarked on by the Vichy government - "the most important since 1789"[7] - must be understood in relation to the long gestation of an "anti- materialist" mentality among the French elites, and to the immense vogue of antiliberal, antidemocratic, and anti-Marxist thinking, in the half-century which preceded the defeat of 1940.[8] Maritain's Action-Française-phase books, such as *Antimoderne* (1922) and *Trois Réformateurs* (1925), figured importantly in this movement. But so did his important post-Maurrasian efforts such as *Primauté* du spirituel (Paris, 1927), *Religion et culture* (Paris, 1930), and *Humanisme intégral* (Paris, 1936).[9] All of these works execrated the bourgeoisie, particularly the Catholic *bien- pensants*, and the "individualism" of the modern world - the legacy, for Maritain, of the pernicious writings of Luther, Descartes, and Rousseau.[10]

Alongside the successes and reverses of the self-consciously "Fascist" political groupings, there was a more general "drift toward fascism" in France. In the late 1930's there was a milieu in which a kind of sensitization to fascisms occurred which included men of both the Left and the Right who were contemptuous of parliamentary democracy. It included a variety of dissidents, marginals, "non-conformists," many of whom, out of interest in a "spiritual revolution", had frequented the Maritains' at Meudon or the Berdyaevs' at Clamart. We can now see that the aspiration for a total renovation of the country was a factor predisposing all of these men to a reception of fascism - which might, of course, be effected to differing degrees and without necessarily leading to a complete "fascistization."[11] A good example of the complexity in definition lies in the case of Salazar's Portugal. Maritain, despite his growing reputation as the most important French Catholic anti-fascist intellectual, did not find the admiration for his thought in that country incongruous, and he accepted Dr. Salazar's invitation to come and see the Estado Novo (founded in 1933) for himself.[12]

But besides "soft" quasi-fascisms, like that of Portugal, German National-Socialism also exerted a certain attraction in Maritain's milieu. Take, for example, the case of Maritain's young Belgian admirer Raymond de Becker. This young editor of Louvain's influential student newspaper, *L'Avant-Garde*,[13] went from a leadership position in Belgian Catholic action to a long pilgrimage through southern France and the founding of an ascetical community for laymen at the Savoyard Trappist monastery of Tamié, to another sort of "conversion experience" at the Nazis' Ordensburg of Sonthofen in Bavaria. This latter led him to leave the Catholic Church at the end of 1938 and become a major collaborationist figure in occupied Belgium.[14] Maritain soon noted the signs of a disquieting evolution in the "dynamic, charismatic" Belgian but had considerable difficulty in persuading his younger French friends of the danger.[15]

After 1940, in the space of a few months, France drew far closer to its two neighboring countries than had seemed possible a short time before. During the summer and fall of 1940 a sort of revolution took place in the country with a result that very little seemed to remain of the France of 1789. The great French liberal and democratic tradition disappeared before the shocks of crisis, defeat, and the occupation of an important part of the national territory. In the autumn of 1940, the French government, of its own volition, fell into line with Italy and Germany. How could this have happened? Maritain, like his friends in North America such as Yves R. Simon and Paul Vignaux, was shocked and disgusted at the rapid adaptation to the "New Order" of their friends back home, particularly at the sudden political transformation of many of their fellow Thomists.[16] Maritain was particulary shocked, for example, when a man of austere piety such as the great Dominican theologian Reginald Garrigou-Lagrange, former *aumonier* of the Maritain salon at Meudon, simply declared that it would be a mortal sin for a Catholic to support General De Gaulle.[17] But Garrigou-Lagrange was no exception: Maritain and his North American colleagues quickly discovered themselves painfully isolated and alone among the French Catholic intelligentsia in their suspicions about the Vichy regime.[18]

How did Maritain's writings affect events in France during the late
1930's? "Antimaterialism" was the dominant trait of all the movements of
revolt of the interwar period. This brought together, in a single movement of
critical opposition to capitalism and liberalism, schools of thought that had
arisen from right and left but were in conflict with both the Republican right
and left. Inspired by antimaterialism men with very different ideological
backgrounds condemned Marxism, liberalism, and the traditional left and
right in general. Many of the Catholics among them, particularly since the
time of Léon Bloy, Drumont, and Marc Sangnier, professed hating money,
cultural uprootedness, and bourgeois ways. They also condemned the
exclusion of the proletariat from the life of the nation.[19] In an important and
original section of *Three Reformers*, Maritain had condemned the
individualism of the modern world over against the "personalism" he
considered properly Catholic. Eventually a vague "personalist" ideal came to
inspire the general condemnation of materialism of all of these movements
of revolt and helped create the atmosphere of inventive social theorizing, of
readiness for new ideas, characteristic of the 1930's. This language surfaced
again in the major doctrinal speeches of Marshall Pétain in which, after
condemning the individualism and money-mindedness of the modern world,
he outlined the main themes of the "Révolution Nationale" which would
give France a worthy place in the new European order. [20]

We must revise our understanding of Catholic intellectuals such as
Maritain in our new lucidity about the general drift of French thinking in the
interwar period. Maritain was something of the "educator of a generation" in
France before he crossed the Atlantic. Whatever his intentions he must be
seen, in retrospect, as having assisted at the creation of another kind of
"French fascism". Over against the Nietzscheanisms and "paganisms" of
men like Pierre Drieu La Rochelle and Céline, an authoritarian Catholic
social thought came into its own in the early days of the Vichy regime ...
and greatly influenced a host of "antibourgeois" initiatives, from
"progressive" communitarian theological speculation to liturgical innovations
and the worker priests.[21]

Maritain's disciple Yves R. Simon, also self-exiled in America, helped
convince him that there was a dramatic slippage toward fascism among their
closest friends back in France. The two men began to notice disquieting
signs even among men who were adamantly "anti-fascist", even "of the left,"
in the early 1930's. They knew many men who continued to adamantly
criticize important aspects of nazism or Fascism as late as the eve of the war
but who *nevertheless* began adopting what were clearly proto-nazi positions
by the late 1930's.[22]

What had happened to Maritain's hopes for a dramatic spiritual
renovation of society by the late 1930's? His call for moral revolution, "the
primacy of the spiritual" in politics, seemed to have gone beyond what he
imagined, had gone beyond his circle and begun to touch non-believers -

even some of whose political orientations he could not approve. In fact, by the end of the thirties the Belgian "neo-socialist" theorist Henri De Man, the ideologues and planners in the French trade union movement, and even the ex-bolsheviks of Jacques Doriot's Parti Populaire Français, were arguing that the revolution had to be spiritual and "moral" before anything else. The case of Doriot, mayor of the working-class city of Saint-Denis and foremost candidate for the leadership of the French Communist Party just a few years earlier, was illustrative: in his last major speech before the war, in April 1939, Doriot called on the youth of France to abandon "egotism" for the ideal, "materialism" for spirituality. His PPF, whose public political liturgies made it seem the most Hitlerian of French parties, celebrated the feast of Joan of Arc with unprecedented solemnity in May 1939, and in June Doriot went on a pilgrimmage to Lourdes during which he denounced the dechristianization of France.[23]

Self-declared "fascists" were never more than a tiny minority among those Frenchmen who responded in 1940 to the call for youth, dignity, purity, and unity, to the rejection of determinism and materialism, to "this affirmation of the primacy of the spiritual."[24] Far more numerous than the confirmed fascists were the supporters of a new non-proletarian type of revolution, a revolution of the spirit, which Maritain's writings - ironically, given his self-exile in the United States and his support for De Gaulle - had done much to encourage. The popular response to the ideas of the fascist intellectuals who vehiculed these ideas was much greater than is often thought. And even more numerous than the conscious fellow travelers were those who regarded that resurrection of anti-bourgeois values, "the revolution of 1940,"[25] with a benevolent neutrality. Maritain's *Humanisme intégral* had been a prominent and influential anti-bourgeois tract in 1936, in a direct line of inspiration from Léon Bloy, and it played an important role in alerting young Catholics to the mediocrity of liberal and democratic societies, and the Church.

With the collapse of 1940 an ideology that had been spreading through society for half a century rose to the surface and became a significant influence on the holders of political power. Several important figures in the shaping of the ideology of the "National Revolution" had been close to Maritain: his former close friend Henri Massis was in a position of some influence and his protegés of the Esprit group such as Emmanuel Mounier, along with some of the brightest Dominican intellectuals, played decisive roles at the Ecole Nationale des Cadres d'Uriage. In the romantic *Chateau Bayard* in the mountains above Grenoble they helped create an authoritarian, "personalist and communitarian," "spiritualized" replacement for that defunct Ecole Normale Suprieure which had produced "secularized" elites for the Republic before the war.[26]

Vichy could draw its anticapitalism, some of its antisemitism, from Catholic influences because there was a generally recognized "Catholic

Option" for France in 1940 - an alternative economics, culture, foreign policy, ... and, of course, sexual morality (Simone de Beauvoir tells of a female abortionist being guillotined under Vichy). Maritain noted that there was a notion of an authoritarian "Catholic order" even in the progressive Catholic publications to which Maritain contributed, such as *Sept* or *Temps Présent*, which a fascist victory in Europe would be assumed to further.[27]

Whether Vichy might properly be termed a "Fascist" regime, or not, is a matter of semantics: the fact remains that a number of individuals in responsible positions in that regime came to desire a German victory in Europe. And the Vichy government came to promote, more and more, a proto-Nazi life-style, values, and mentality in the young. Many French, when Germany appeared to be winning the war, simply assumed that France would become more and more nazified, more clearly and distinctly "fascist." This, in any case, is how Maritain and his handful of resistance friends came to see things, and they became acutely sensitive to their isolation as Frenchmen as long as the fascist side seemed to be coming out on top. Yves R. Simon was so disillusioned with the political comportment of his fellow Thomists that he concluded that Thomism had not been up to the challenge represented by fascism and nazism. He became determined to rethink, even achieve a "break" with, his philosophical past, and he suggested that Maritain might do the same. In 1943 Maritain wrote *Christianisme et démocratie*, a book which, in Bernard Doering's words, "marked a new stage in Maritain's thought. From this time on he was wholly committed to democracy as a political and social institution."[28] The attractiveness of fascism for the French does not, in itself, explain the French defeat but it helps us to understand the ease, the naturalness, with which an alternative regime was set up in that country and the wide consensus it enjoyed. We now know that Vichy was neither an accident nor an aberration but the logical sequel to a host of imaginative attempts at political renewal in the half-century which preceded the collapse of 1940. Catholic social thinking - on the Left as well as on the Right - contributed to the *Révolution Nationale* and helped promote a distinctive mentality valuing family, chastity, the land, the repression of liberalism and individualism, the primacy of the spiritual dimension, etc. Maritain's case shows how difficult and paradoxical it is to describe that French Catholic "slippage" toward fascism which was so important in those years.

Certainly Maritain contributed to a broad movement of ideas which effected a situation in which "France changed more radically in a few months than at any other time ... since the summer of 1789."[29] His powerful and influential anti-modernist and anti-bourgeois writings made a significant contribution to the ideas of the men who effected that change. But Maritain also came to play an important role in the Resistance movement which would undo those very changes. His intellectual and political itinerary during these years was controversial, instructive, dramatic, principled, and far more unpopular among French Catholics than we tend to think.[30]

McGill University

NOTES

1. Zeev Sternell, *Neither Right nor Left: Fascist Ideology in France* (Berkeley and Los Angeles: the University of California Press, 1986), p. 299.

2. For example, René Rémond, perhaps France's most distinguished historian of the French Right, and of the contemporary French Catholic Church, has largely ignored the existence of a French fascist tradition in his myriad writings despite the fact that important non-French experts on his country's history have documented its importance. Rémond's perspective was also adopted by the leading North American historians of French ideas such as H. Stuart Hughes, and of French political thought, such as Roy Pierce. North American scholars have also tended to follow Rémond, a prominent figure in the French educational establishment amd among the French Catholic intelligentsia, in bending over backwards to avoid tarring Catholic intellectuals with the fascist brush.

3. Sternhell, p. 7.

4. *Ibid.*, p. 27.

5. Robert Wohl, *The Generation of 1914* (Cambridge: Harvard University Press, 1969), pp. 5-41.

6. Nicholas Berdyaev, *Un nouveau moyen âge* (Paris, 1929). During the period in which he wrote this book, Berdyaev kept an intellectual *salon* in his home in the Parisian suburb of Clamart which alternated with that of the Maritains' at Meudon. White Russian emigrants frequented both, and while the Maritains had some differences with Berdyaev's epistemological and metaphysical positions, they were sympathetic with his mystical vision of the Soviet Union's world historical role, and his prophetic announcement of its eventual mass re-conversion to purified, newly "medieval", Christianity. Both *salons* were frequented by the elite of the young Parisian Catholic intelligentsia, clerics and laymen alike.

7. Sternell, p. 29.

8. As in the case of Georges Bernanos, the other prominent Action Française heretic of the time, Maritain's "anti-fascist" activities, notably his refusal to take sides in the Spanish Civil War, did not necessarily bring his numerous admirers, friends, or disciples to an anti-fascist position. Bernanos' "non-conformism" to what seemed *the* Catholic position was often attributed to his irascible temperament, Maritain's to his strong-willed Jewish wife. Even after Maritain was considered an important Free French supporter he received an invitation from occupied Paris to pose his candidature for a position at the prestigious Collège de France.

9. One of Maritain's most important contributions to Catholic intellectual life in the period was his acerbic criticism of "individualism" which he juxtaposed to everything in the mainstream Catholic tradition. Like so many other unsavory things, he blamed it on the Protestants from whom he had come. In *Trois Réformateurs* he juxtaposed "individualism" to the more "Catholic" notion of the person. This distinction had immense subsequent influence in the Catholic world.

10. Only very recently have French social critics begun to question the prevaling assumption among modern French intellectuals that there is something obviously very wrong with modern "individualism." This assumption has been common to intellectuals of both right and left, and Maritain had much to do with it becoming a sort of orthodoxy among Catholics: the "person" was Catholic, the "individual" was not. In his very popular lectures at Harvard during the 1936-37 school year, published as the *Unity of Philosophical Experience* (1937), Etienne Gilson provided an extremely sophisticated and learned

defense of Maritain's earlier charge that Descartes was behind the scourge of modern "individualism." Gilson's celebration of the anti-individualistic medieval epistemology reinforced this all-pervasive anti-individualism among Catholic intellectuals.

11. Cf. Philippe Burrin, *La Dérive Fasciste, Doriot, Déat, Bérgery, 1933-1945* (Paris, 1986), p. 94. This well-documented study shows how important personalities of the French Left gradually, almost imperceptibly, evolved toward fascism. It convincingly demonstrates that fascism and nazism had far more appeal for French intellectuals of the 1930's, of both the left and right, than has been assumed. But, like so many of his contemporary historians, Burrin is extremely discrete in dealing with the Catholic dimension of his three subjects.

12. Maritain wrote at least one letter to Yves R. Simon about his Portugese experiences. Salazar claimed inspiration from Catholic social thought in general (notably the "Social Encyclicals"), and Jacques Maritain in particular. Most historians shy away from calling Salazar's regime "fascist."

13. This newspaper had been made influential in this period by the famous Catholic youth leader become fascist, Léon Degrelle.

14. Cf. Raymond de Becker, *Le live des vivants et des morts* (Brussels, 1942), p. 229. De Becker expressed a certain respect for Maritain even when he had become contemptuous of his own Catholic past and most of the other prominent Catholics who figured in it.

15. The correspondence *Maritain/Mounier, 1929-1939*, ed. Jacques Petit (Paris, 1973), contains an interesting exchange of letters between Maritain and his French protégé Emmanuel Mounier over de Becker in which the older man's warnings largely fell on deaf ears. The French *Esprit* group kept trying to maintain joint projects with the mercurial Belgian.

16. This is a major theme of the unpublished Maritain-Simon correspondence during the years 1941-1942. Maritain's bitter feelings about, and harsh judgements upon, his friends at Vichy were, for several understandable reasons, hushed up after the war.

17. A copy of a letter from Maritain to Garrigou-Lagrange in late 1946 in which this fact is recalled remains in the Yves R. Simon papers.

18. The entry of the United States into the war and, particularly, the ill-fated German invasion of the Soviet Union, altered matters by the end of 1942. But even at that date militant anti-*Pétainistes* were a relative rarity among the French Catholic intelligentsia and were often considered traitors to "the Catholic side." French Catholics were prepared for non-cooperation with the German occupants much sooner than for working against a regime in which they had far more influence than under any government of the Third Republic.

The only major study of French Catholics under the Vichy regime, Jacques Duquesne's *Les Catholiques français sous disproportionate importance to a handful of Catholic "resisters." There is still no study of Vichy's intellectuals, and Catholics figured prominently in their number.*

19. The role of Bloy's vituperative polemic in shaping Maritain's thinking is well known and Maritain himself published *Quelques pages sur Léon Bloy* (Paris, 1927). Far more influential than Bloy in the 1930's was Edouard Drumont whose left-wing, anti- capitalist, and anti-bourgeois anti-semitism was considered "Catholic socialism" at the turn of the century. In 1932 Georges Bernanos, frustrated with the footdragging bourgeois conservatism of his friends in the Action Franaise, published a vibrant celebration of the ideas of his "vieux maitre" Drumont (*La Grande Peur des Bien-Pensants*), and in 1938 was dissuaded by his publisher, Grasset, from publishing a book of excerpts from Drumont - whose nationalist and socialist tendencies he admired. See my article "Drumont, Bernanos, and the Rise of French Fascism" in the forthcoming special Bernanos centenary issue of *Renascence*.

20. Several of the individuals considered to be Pétain's speechwriters, or the most important sources of his social ideas, such as René Gillouin, Gaston Bergery, François Perroux, Gustave Thibon, frequented "Personalist" circles before the war.

21. In his studies of the birth of progressive Catholicism in general, and the worker priests in particular, the distinguished scholar Emile Poulat simply avoids giving the larger Vichy context in which many of the initiatives which he described in great detail such as the Mission de Paris, which he describes in great detail, were born. So does the post-war anglo-american celebrator of these same movements and personalities, Maisie Ward. Cf. Emile Poulat, *Naissance des prêtres-ouvriers* (Paris, 1969); Maisie Ward, *France Pagan? The Mission of Abbé Godin* (London, 1949). Ward does not tell us that her hero, the Abbé Godin, was enthusiastic about Vichy's social and economic initiatives, which he analyzed in his book *La Charte du Travail* (Paris, 1943). In his lively and critical portrait of his parents, whom he describes as firm anti-fascists, Wilfrid Sheed does not allude to his mother's apparent indifference to the ambiguous origins of some of the "progressive" ideas she helped import from France into the English-speaking world. Cf. *Frank and Maisie: A Memoir with Parents* (New York, 1986).

22. Cf. Philippe Burrin, *op. cit.*

23. Cf. Lanoux, "Le discours de Lourdes," *L'Emancipation Nationale*, 9 June 1939, p. 2. On Doriot see Jean-Paul Brunet, *Jacques Doriot* (Paris, 1986), and Burrin, *op. cit.*

24. Sternhell, p. 272. Whether or not Maritain was originally responsible, the phrase "primacy of the spiritual" became a commonplace to describe the shared aspirations of the French in a new European order by the late 1930's and during the period of the occupation.

25. The phrase is Maurice Duverger's as cited by Sternhell, *op. cit.*, p. 272.

26. On Uriage, see my *Emmanuel Mounier and the New Catholic Left, 1930-1950* (Toronto and London, 1981), Chapter VIII. For decades, the French Catholic intelligentsia had demanded proportionate influence in the French Republic's educational and cultural institutions. The Uriage school is an instructive instance of these Catholics, suddenly, in power. Its numerous graduates steadfastly maintain that it was a "Resistance" institution (against the Germans) and, at this writing, they constitute a mafia sufficiently powerful to dissuade young French historians from saying anything too critical about it. It was clearly anti-individualistic, anti-liberal, anti-democratic, anti-communist and anti-american. Cf. *Pierre Dunoyer de Segonzac, Le vieux chef: Mémoires et pages choisies* (Paris, 1971). One of the instructors claimed it was modeled after the Nazi Ordensburgen. Cf. Gilles Ferry, *Un expérience de formation des chefs* (Paris, 1945), p. 33.

    Poet Pierre Emmanuel wrote Maritain (27 September 1941) about "great movements" in France, "rich in hope and promise," of "the same spirit of enthusiasm in discipline and hope in the future" in the Ecole des Cadres d'Uriage which is "forming true men, in whom the feeling for spiritual reality is not stifled but rather exalted". Cited and translated in Bernard Doering, *Jacques Maritain and the French Catholic Intellectuals* (Notre Dame, 1986), p. 201.

27. The unpublished Maritain-Simon correspondence reveals how remarkably isolated these two men felt in the Catholic world for adopting a global anti-fascist position in the late 1930's and during the first two years of Vichy. Even in the United States they were delighted to find the odd maverick like Dorothy Day. One need only study the attitude toward the European conflict in very Catholic Québec during those years to realize the extent to which, as Maritain and Yves R. Simon were shocked to find, pro-fascism was the generally perceived "Catholic" position. *The Commonweal* later claimed to have been firmly antifascist in this period but Maritain and Simon saw it as, with the exception of C.G. Paulding, "a nest of pacificism" at the time.

28. Bernard Doering, p. 179.

29. Sternhell, *op. cit.*

30. In interviewing a host of French Catholic intellectuals of Maritain's generation, I found an almost complete lack of interest in, or appreciation for, his resistance activities. Could they

have been expected to welcome him home then after the war with open arms, as North Americans rather naively assumed they would?

JACQUES MARITAIN AND CHARLES PÉGUY: A REASSESSMENT

Pierre L'Abbé

Since the untimely death of Charles Péguy (1873-1914) in the first weeks of the First World War in the Battle of the Marne, numerous writers have been preoccupied with his life. All of the major accounts have dealt with Péguy's relationship to Jacques Maritain (1882-1973) and the influence of the Maritains on Péguys attitude toward Christianity.

The account by Jean and Jérome Tharaud may be, as some have said, sensationalist; nevertheless, the many pages which this early account devotes to our topic demonstrates that the young Maritain was an influential figure for Péguy in the eyes of contemporaries.[1] Another first-hand account by Daniel Halévy shows Maritain's importance in Péguy's spiritual struggles. Indeed, in an Addendum to his book, Halévy makes an appeal to Maritain to tell his side of the story.[2] This response was made, seemingly to the satisfaction of Maritain, by his wife Raissa as part of her autobiographical work *Les grandes amitiés*. Here Maritain is portrayed as highly apologetic for any misunderstandings between himself and Péguy to the point of taking all responsibility for the breakdown of their friendship and for any pain which Péguy may have suffered as a consequence. Péguy scholars today accept this stand as a point of fact and moreover extend Maritain's "responsibility" into the sphere of his being the cause of certain of Péguy's spiritual and even familial strifes. Pie Duployé's *La religion de Péguy* represents such a view. The conversations Duployé held with Maritain around 1964 did nothing to change this view; rather they reiterated and strengthened the stand found in *Les grands amitiés*. Maritain in the preface and annotations to the Péguy-Maritain correspondence published in 1972 once again upholds a view of himself as "responsible" and "to blame."

The full correspondence and Maritain's journal, *Notebooks*, were not available to Duploy in 1965. These, along with a considerable number of other sources, can significantly reshape the debate over the Péguy-Maritain relationship. Henry Bars has given a short response to Duployé;[3] however, much remains to be done in terms of presenting an account which does not take at face value Maritain's acceptance of blame.

The first known letter between Maritain and Péguy is one addressed to the latter on March 13, 1901. Here Maritain compliments Péguy on his article "Casse-cou," but suggests that Péguy was too hard on Jean Jaurès. Maritain politely chastises Péguy: "You know very well that he [Jaurès] does not 'demand for the present day that one be a materialist and an atheist'....Did he not say...'With respect to my concerns, I have never taken sides against or disdained high religious aspirations, which under the diversity of myths, symbols, and dogmas have supported the human spirit"?[4]

Also at this time, as part of the activities at Péguy's shop, Raissa and Jacques began attending the Bergson lectures at the Collège de France in the fall of 1901: "One day, having seen that our disillusionment was complete, he [Péguy] took us to hear Bergson." Raissa goes on to describe how the great hall could not hold the crowd, so with Péguy, George Sorel, and Psichari they came early to get seats. Not long after, the Maritains would credit Bergson's philosophy as being an influence which led to their conversion. Later Bergson himself would be at the centre of a controversy not only in the Church, but also between Maritain and Péguy.[5]

Soon after, Maritain began working for Péguy; the first certain date of his employment is October of 1904. Letters between Péguy and Maritain deal with Maritain's work in finding source material for the *Cahiers*, although his major task was that of a proof-reader.

As for Maritain's marriage, his mother recounts that Péguy and Jeanne, Jacques' sister, pleaded with her for the prompt marriage of Maritain. Favre wanted a delay of two years while Maritain could get his *agrégation* in philosophy. She even went so far as to say that "the surprise was, for her, very jolting."[6] The marriage occurred without her cooperation as this letter of Thursday, November 24, 1904, from Maritain to Péguy on the eve of the Maritains' wedding, shows: "You know that my mother is leaving for Brittany tonight....I hope to be able to replace you this afternoon for the ceremony on Saturday."[7]

Favre's account skips this fact and shows her anti-religious bias once again: "November 1904, marriage of Jacques: civil marriage, like that of Jeanne: something very natural for Péguy, who also had a civil wedding."[8]

The first record of Maritain's financial assistance to the *Cahiers* is a letter from Péguy to Maritain on the day of the latter's wedding: "Therefore, can you give Bourgeois one thousand francs cash Wednesday morning at nine?"[9]

Later Maritain and Péguy concocted a scheme to win Favre's approval for a loan of 10,000 francs to Péguy; Maritain had come into the money through the death of his father. A first letter sent to Favre by Péguy on May 15, 1905, spoke generally of his financial difficulties and hopes. The second arrived a few hours later:

"Dear Madame,
Jacques has thought up and is completely convinced,
without my having given him the least suggestion, a
solution which will be in every respect perfect and
definitive; do you approve of this solution?"[10]

It is unclear whether it was only Favre's moral approval which they
were seeking, or, since another letter also refers to the need for her approval,
if she in fact controlled a certain financial trust for her son; it should be
remembered that as yet Maritain was under twenty-five years of age.

Maurice Reclus believed that the loan was for 10,000 francs and adds
that the money was "evidently lost" to Maritain. Later letters suggest that
some sort of repayment schedule was in effect, but it is unclear as to how
much of this was towards Maritain's wages which were in arrears or how
much was towards the loan.[11]

A letter of a few months later, in August of 1905, shows that Favre had
loaned Péguy an additional 10,000 francs and that the sum was being repaid
with interest. The most important religious development in this period was
the Maritain's relationship with Léon Bloy. The first communication
between them took place after the Maritains read about Bloy in a newpaper
article in June of 1905. Bloy then received a letter from them containing 25
francs.[12] In a few months the Maritains were attempting to republish Bloy's
Le salut par les Juifs. Initially, Péguy was also to be involved by having the
work appear in the *Cahiers*. But the issue is clouded by Bloy's urging that
he wanted it understood that the money he was receiving was an advance on
the edition of *Salut* which Péguy truly intended to publish. Maritain tried to
obtain money from Péguy to this end.[13] By January of 1906, the project
was underway with the cooperation of Péguy's printer who would in part
finance the deal.[14]

By the end of 1906 Péguy's cooperative attitude toward Bloy was
beginning to erode. As Raissa recounts, with obvious reference to the
Maritains' growing attachments to Bloy, "unhappy differences grew up
between Péguy and ourselves: and we came to know how easily he could be
unjust (a thing very natural in a temperament like his), and how jealously he
could wish to keep his friends for himself alone."[15]

The next period of interest, before turning to Maritain's trip to Péguy's
home, is that of June, 1906, through May, 1907, the period of the
conversions of Maritain and Péguy. Maritain's conversion was definitely
decisive in that he broke with a former way of life and immediately took up
new activities. Péguy's conversion, however, did not involve any immediate
or radical changes in behavior; changes were largely attitudinal. And
whereas Maritain found a home in the established Catholic Church, Péguy
never lost his anti-clerical bend.

On June 11, 1906, the Maritains along with Raissa's sister, Vera, were baptized in the Church of Saint-Jean l'Evangeliste in Montmartre, Paris, by Abbé Durantel.[16] The ceremony took place one year after the Maritains met Bloy, and he, although apparently not an insistent proselytizing character, was definitely the effective cause. After some initial hesitations concerning the truth of religious values, the Maritains were by April, 1906 decidedly eager to convert. Raissa's family was shocked by the conversions of their only two daughters when they eventually learned of them; although the family had been influenced by France's cultural milieu and by a popular scientific positivism since moving to Paris, they had observed pious Jewish practices while in Russia approximately ten years earlier.

As for Maritain's family, his mother was not informed of the conversion. This fact in itself bespeaks an anti-religious pressure. As for Maritain's only other immediate family member, his sister Jeanne, soon she too would convert to Catholicism.

The date of Péguy's conversion is most often given as March 5, 1907. Yet this is not the record of any conversion experience; rather it is the first of a number of confidences Péguy made that he had returned to the faith; and this first confidence was to Maritain.

Maritain returned to Paris on his own for a visit in March of 1907. The reaction he got from Péguy on this trip, however, was somewhat different, as his journal entry shows: "Lunched with Péguy at my mother's. Overwhelmed with joy at what he tells me about himself (he has made the same journey as us). 'The body of Christ is larger than one thinks.'"[17] Because Péguy requested secrecy, Raissa testifies: "After his confidence to Jacques, Péguy's secret had been strictly kept by us and by Dom Baillet, and by Péguy himself...." That was the case until Péguy broke the secrecy to Joseph Lotte.[18]

Given that after Péguy's confidence to Maritain the two had a new understanding of their friendship in terms of a mutual faith, three important letters of the spring of 1907 show how they tried to work out an even stronger friendship. Péguy writes on May 15, 1907 that he needs Maritain to work during the summer and goes on to say:

> "I also need for us to talk regularly during this time. You are an essential part of my system and I very much need, in order to complete the eighth series, a general examination. "I have not overwhelmed you with demands this year. I am sure that you will not refuse me this."[19]

Later that month, May 24, 1907, Péguy expanded on these ideas:

> "During this time we can chat and discuss as much as it becomes necessary. Not because I would like to return to

the decisive conversation that we had while you visited us in Paris. On the contrary, I want to push all that ahead and henceforth organize our friendship in detail. To give you a particular example of what I intend by this, I have friends who for several years have taken refuge on the Isle of Wight and since that time I have had almost no news of them, except one thing which I will show you. It seems to me that it should fall on you to finally re-establish with them my spiritual communication."[20]

Maritain's response to all this is curiously cautious, given that he said he was "overwhelmed" to have heard Péguy's news. Considering that a letter of January, 1907, implies that Péguy was in considerable financial debt to Maritain, the latter may have been wary of any further business dealings with Péguy.

Péguy's attitude toward religion was definitely not settled. He told Maritain that he wanted secrecy in order, as he later said, to be able to prepare his readers for the new Christian direction of his journal. Indeed, the concern was not unfounded since he was to lose a large number of subscriptions in later years as a direct response to the explicitly Christian material he wrote.

Two events figure prominently after Maritain's return from Germany: first, the trip by Maritain to the exiled monks of Solesmes on the Isle of Wight to see Père Baillet on behalf of Péguy; and second, Maritain's visit to Péguy's family in Lozère.

The origin of the first of these missions was Péguy's request that Maritain establish a "spiritual" contact with his old classmate Baillet. After describing the state of affairs to Baillet, however, Maritain was charged with the counter-mission of telling Péguy to have his children baptized. It seems that much was made of Maritain's "embassadorial" role, as this term and such language as "to represent Baillet among you" was used by Maritain and Péguy until 1910.

The second event, which was orginally to have been carried out by Maritain's sister, Jeanne, was a far more critical one since it occurred after heightened tension had set in between Maritain and Péguy. As Duployé's account of the incident goes, which he said he confirmed with Maritain around 1964, when Maritain arrived in Lozère he said that if the Church meant nothing to Mme Beaudouin, Péguy's mother-in-law, and Charlotte, his wife, then why not let Péguy baptize his children? Mme Beaudouin answered that she told Péguy that she herself had been baptized and that since one apostate in the family was enough, she could not allow her grandchildren to live through such a drama. Moreover, the Beaudouins had honoured Péguy by allowing him into their republican family. In marrying Charlotte, he had married the revolutionary cause and to become a Catholic would be quite simply to apostasize.[21] Maritain's journal entry from this date, July 22, 1909, confirms this in more straightforward terms: "Visit to Mme Beaudouin and Mme Péguy. Complete failure."[22] In the days that followed, Péguy twice sent Favre to Lozère in order to calm his family.

At this point I would like to draw a number of conclusions which I feel substantially challenge the traditional interpretation of the Péguy-Maritain relationship.

First, Favre maintains throughout her article on Péguy that the strained relations between herself and her son were caused by his religious beliefs, and so far scholars have assumed this to be the case. If, however, Favre's statements are accurate, they reveal that a strong break with her son first came about because of his marriage.

Second, contrary to the perception that the Péguy-Maritain disagreements lay purely in the spiritual realm, I believe they had a strong financial undercurrent. Raissa recounts that Péguy was hurt by Maritain's letters from Heidelberg which "savored of anxiety and criticism."[23] Péguy's requests, however, were not only that Maritain should help him put his spiritual life in order but that Maritain should also work with him constantly at the *Cahiers*.[24] Maritain's response is most unexpected and amounts to his more or less saying that he would prefer to remain at an arm's length.[25] The only explanation for this is to be found in previous letters between Maritain and Péguy's secretary which show that Maritain was owed not only the 10,000 francs but also back wages.[26] Since this sum was never repaid and Maritain had to work at editing jobs which he avowedly disliked, it must be concluded that this financial factor remained an irritating undercurrent throughout their spiritual disputes.

Third, concerning Maritain's trip to Lozère, Raissa, Favre, and virtually all of Péguy's many biographers depict this visit as having pushed Péguy's evolving spiritual orientation into a critical confrontation with his family. The conversions of Péguy's entire family after his death give the impression that they too were in a spiritual evolution. Yet, this was clearly not the case. Shortly before the trip in question, while Maritain was dining in Lozère Mme Péguy announced that her husband was "suffering a violent attack of Catholicism."[27] Even the most partisan of biographers reveal a familial situation of tension in which Péguy's brother-in-law had assumed the position of father. Maritain walked into an explosive situation at Lozère, one Péguy felt he himself was no longer capable of facing.

Fourth, although the two men did have at least one congenial meeting in later years, a certain bitterness did arise. Péguy's bitterness can be seen in this report of Maritain: "Péguy told...[Psichari], as he told my mother, that he had sent me to the Isle of Wight in order that I might get in touch with Catholics of better quality that Léon Bloy. Sad double game."[28] Raissa's account suggests that the Maritains accepted this as true.[29] If indeed they did, then their interpretation of Péguy's entire spiritual awakening of the years 1907-1910 would have changed radically. All of Péguy's vacillations, including investigating a *sanatio in radice*, having his children baptized without the consent of their mother, and Maritain's trips and many letters to the Isle of Wight on Péguy's behalf must then have appeared as a sort of cat-and-mouse game. The Maritains thought they were leading Péguy to the Church while Péguy was attempting, at the instigation of Maritain's mother, to lead the Maritains away from the Church. Only the Maritains' extreme frustration at Péguy's waverings could have made them consider this a possibility, since Péguy's letters to Maritain in May of 1907 show that at least at the beginning Péguy was sincerely seeking the Maritains' spiritual support.

University of Toronto

NOTES

1. J. and J. Tharaud, *Notre Cher Péguy* (Paris, 1943).

2. D. Halvy, *Péguy*, transl. R. Bethell (London, 1946) p.224.

3. H. Bars, "Remarques sur l'ouvrage de Pie Duployé," *Cahiers Jacques Maritain*, III (1981) 9-15.

4. A. Martin, "Correspondence Péguy-Maritain," *Feuillets de l'Amitié* Charles Péguy, 176 (1972) 11-12.

5. J. Maritain, *Notebooks*, transl. J. Evans (Albany, 1984) p.75.

6. G. Favre, "Souvenirs sur Péguy (1903-1914)," *Europe*, 182 (15 février 1938, 15 mars 1938, 15 avril 1938) 149.

7. A. Martin, 20.

8. G. Favre, 149.

9. A. Martin, 20.

10. G. Favre, 152; M. Reclus, *Le Péguy* que j'ai connu: avec 100 lettres de Charles Péguy 1905-1914 (Paris, 1951) p. 136.

11. A. Martin, 34.

12. J. Maritain, p. 75.

13. A. Martin, 38.

14. J. Maritain, 30-31; R. Maritain, *We Have Been Friends Together* and *Adventures in Grace*, transl. J. Kernan (New York, 1961) p. 132.

15. R. Maritain, p. 55.

16. J. Maritain, p. 30, p. 76.

17. J. Maritain, p. 39.

18. R. Maritain, p. 210.

19. A. Martin, 34.

20. A. Martin, 35.

21. P. Duployé, *La religion de Péguy* (Paris, 1965), p. 386.

22. J. Maritain, p. 53.

23. R. Maritain, p. 210.

24. A. Martin, 34-36.

25. A. Martin, 36-37.

26. A. Martin, 34.

27. R. Maritain p. 215.

28. J. Maritain, pp. 57-58.

29. R. Maritain, p. 208.

PART TWO

EXISTENCE AND THE EXISTENT

A. Introduction

REFLEXIONS SUR l'INTELLIGENCE

Thomas De Koninck

Summary

Jacques Maritain's concern for the intellect and everything it implies is evident everywhere in his work from the very outset. It would be presumptuous and in any case impossible to sketch in one short talk even an outline of such a fundamental theme of his thought or indeed of philosophy. Still, it has become probably more vital today than ever before to awake to what intellect means. This brief paper attempts merely to indicate a few questions worth pursuing anew in the spirit both of Maritain and the chief sources of his thought on the matter.

The questions include the following. Why invariably link together human dignity and intellect, as our tradition, no less theological than philosophical, undoubtedly seems to? Objections to this are, *prima facie*, rather obvious: an excessive cult of rationality; an implicit neglect of other, far more important, values; apparent scorn for the ignorant or the uninstructed; most plainly, forgetting love and the human heart. We face again the question: whence the dignity of intellect? What light can we expect the neurosciences and similar disciplines to shed on the nature of the mind? Are reason and intellect quite the same thing? What *is* intellectual knowledge; its relation to existence and the existent; its relation to beauty and to the transcendentals; and its role in creativity?

In a word, how is one to interpret Augustine's *Intellectum vero valde ama*? Or to face the greatest interpretive challenge of all, the famous saying of St. John of the Cross: "One thought alone of man is worth more than the entire world; hence God alone is worthy of it"?

***

Qui contesterait la justesse des propos suivants de Francesco Viola: "(...) Toute la réflexion maritainienne est pénétrée par la découverte de la richesse et de la diversité des formes de vie de l'intelligence. C'est là le fil d'Ariane qui relie les thmes les plus divers, de l'ontologie à la morale, de l'esthétique à la politique"? Ou encore l'insistance du même auteur que jamais Maritain "ne sépare l'esprit de l'être des choses. L'esprit, en effet, n'est pas autre chose qu'ouverture à l'être. Dans cette ouverture Maritain voit toute sa richesse et son mystre"?[1] Peu sans doute se seront-ils donc étonnés qu'on choisisse de parler de l'intelligence dans un congrès sur Jacques Maritain et sur, aussi bien, l'existence et l'existant .

L'embarras est plutôt celui du choix, face à cette richesse, cette diversité et ce mystère de l'intelligence, non moins marqués à vrai dire dans l'oeuvre de Maritain que dans toute la tradition, grecque ou chrétienne, dont il se réclamait. Quoi élire en vingt minutes touchant un aussi grave et grand sujet?

La tâche se complique en outre du fait qu'aujourd'hui tant de disciplines revendiquent "l'intelligence." On sait l'essor récent des neurosciences, par exemple, ainsi que des sciences dites cognitives, la fascination qu'exerce depuis plusieurs décennies "l'intelligence artificielle," le débat sans cesse renaissant autour de la raison humaine qu'alimentent des domaines aussi diversement autorisés que la paléanthropologie, l'éthologie, la psychologie, la linguistique et quantité d'autres, pour ne rien dire de l'art, de l'éthique, des diverses écoles philosophiques mêmes. "L'intelligence n'est que"..., "Mind is nothing but...", la formule est éprouvée et nous n'en sommes gure à un réductionnisme près. Pour peu toutefois qu'on les mette bout à bout, ces points de vues exclusifs, quelle abondance de vérités! Combien merveilleuse déjà la réalité susceptible de tant de théories diverses, à vrai dire complémentaires!

Cela étant, j'ai pris le parti de tenter d'énoncer rapidement ici quelques-uns des points et des questions paraissant toujours les plus dignes de considération, en vertu justement de leur portée fondamentale. Tous ont leurs attaches dans l'expérience commune, de même que leurs antécédents en des sources grecques, chrétiennes, contemporaines, de l'ordre de celles qu'invoquait Jacques Maritain. Il est aisé de retracer ces thèmes dans son oeuvre propre, et je me contenterai ici de ses premiers ouvrages où les jalons essentiels sont d'emblée posés. Cette oeuvre montre au reste comment par l'approfondissement des interrogations décisives, permanentes, urgentes en ce sens, on peut seul espérer progresser de façon authentique.

1/ S'agissant d'intelligence, de pensée, chacun est mis en face de son être personnel le plus intime. On se souvient de Pascal: "Pensée fait la grandeur de l'homme,"[2] "Toute la dignité de l'homme consiste en la pensée."[3] Pourtant, que faut-il comprendre par là et comment l'entend-t-on de fait aujourd'hui? Je vois s'élever déjà les protestations. Excluerait- on le coeur? Omettrait-on les ignorants, ceux qui n'ont pas eu la faveur d'une instruction appropriée, voire les infirmes "mentaux"? N'existe-t-il pas d'autres sources de grandeur humaine, plus adaptées à notre temps, à notre sensibilité?

Et cependant, l'accord des sages, potes, philosophes, maîtres spirituels, marquant la dignité particulire de l'intelligence humaine, ne laisse pas d'étonner. "In apprehension how like a god!" dit Hamlet de l'etre humain.[4] Et encore ceci: "Sure he that made us with such large discourse,/ Looking before and after, gave us not/ That capability and god-like reason/ To rust in us unused./"[5] On croit réentendre la sentence d'Euripide: *ho nous gar hêmôn estin en hekastô theos*, "L'intellect est Dieu en chacun de nous".[6] D'après des pages platoniciennes bien connues, il n'est "rien dans l'âme de plus divin (*theioteron*) que cette partie où résident la connaissance et la pensée".[7] Aristote abonde dans le même sens: "(...) Que pourrait-il y avoir de supérieur et à la science et à l'intellect, écrit-il, sauf Dieu?"[8] Le paradoxe de notre condition, selon Platon et Aristote, est que ce qui nous définit le plus proprement en tant qu'humains se découvre en même temps ce que tous deux dénomment notre "partie la plus divine".[9] Pour Aristote, ce qui pense (*to nooun*) n'en est pas moins chacun de nous (*hekastos*) soit purement et simplement, soit au plus haut point.[10] Les maîtres chrétiens, y compris les mystiques, sont tout aussi admiratifs de l'intelligence. Me contentant d'évoquer ici le mot de saint Augustin, *Intellectum vero valde ama*[11], je terminerai ces trop rapides citations par la plus remarquable, à mon sens. On sait l'estime de Maritain pour son auteur, saint Jean de la Croix: "Une seule pensée de l'homme est plus précieuse que tout l'univers: d'où vient que seul Dieu en est digne"[12] Qu'est-ce-à-dire? N'y a-t-il pas là un vaste programme de réflexion?

2/ Il convient de s'interroger, tout à fait d'autre part, sur l'apport possible, quant à l'intelligence de l'intelligence, de la neurophysiologie, par exemple, des progrs de la biologie moléculaire ou des analogies tirées des ordinateurs? Dans un texte récent, le philosophe britannique Thomas Nagel constate qu'en réalité "the more we learn about the brain the clearer it is how little we understand its embodiment of the mind".[13] Lui-même un objet physique éminemment complexe (douze milliards de cellules, chacune d'entre elles à son tour une structure complexe ayant jusqu'à soixante mille boutons synaptiques de connexion avec d'autres cellules), notre systme nerveux a ceci de tout à fait particulier qu'il est en même temps une portion du monde physique que nous connaissons pour ainsi dire du dedans, dans la mesure en tout cas où nous avons l'expérience interne de vivre. Nous éprouvons en nous-mêmes, en effet, l'exercice d'un certain nombre -- pas toutes -- d'activités vitales qu'il rend possibles; par exemple toucher, voir, entendre, sentir que nous sentons, imaginer, nous souvenir, nous mouvoir, aimer ou vouloir et leurs contraires, nous réjouir et nous attrister, nous apercevoir à l'oeuvre et discerner, penser ceci ou cela, nous demander ce que sont ces multiples activités, y inclus celle même de penser. "Les manifestations extérieures de la vie d'autrui ne sont reconnues comme vitales qu'autant que je les vois semblables aux miennes -- aux miennes que j'aperçois par cette expérience externe dont j'ai en même temps l'expérience interne."[14]

Il est vrai que nous sommes de mieux en mieux renseignés eu égard aux frontires externes du système nerveux -- stimuli sensoriels, contractions musculaires -- cependant que les processus centraux demeurent obscurs.

Nous en savons de plus en plus sur les neurones, leur interaction, la propagation des impulsions électriques nerveuses. L'observation de cas pathologiques a permis un commencement de géographie du cerveau: des lésions d'une aire (Broca) de l'hémisphre gauche entraînent des troubles de langage (aphasie motrice), celles d'une autre aire (Wernicke) du même hémisphre cérébral affectent la compréhension du langage (aphasie sensorielle); la perte de l'hippocampe empêche la constitution de nouveaux souvenirs; et ainsi de suite. Mais relativement à la compréhension du langage, de la mémoire, il est évident que cela ajoute bien peu. "It is [écrit Nagel] like trying to understand how the US political system works by locating the public buildings on a map of Washington DC."

On le voit, nous ne sommes guère plus avancés aujourd'hui touchant le problème fondamental de la relation entre l'expérience purement externe et cette expérience interne qui, elle, suscite toutes nos questions relatives à la vie comme telle. Peut-on espérer jamais accorder la vue de nous-mêmes du dehors et celle du dedans? Il y a plus de cinquante ans, Husserl avait dit l'essentiel à propos de l'ambition d'étudier la *psychê*, l'âme, en prenant "le chemin qui passe par le dehors, le chemin de la physique et de la chimie." "Si donc [déclarait-il] on cherche la source de toutes nos détresses, la réponse s'impose: cette conception objectiviste ou psycho-physique du monde, bien qu'elle parût aller de soi, était naïvement unilatérale; sa propre partialité était demeurée incomprise. Il est absurde de conférer à l'esprit une réalité naturelle, comme s'il était une annexe réelle des corps, et de prétendre lui attribuer un être spatio-temporel à l'intérieur de la nature."[15] Le savant, dit-il, a oublié le principal, à savoir lui-même, les psychologues "ne remarquent aucunement que même eux n'ont pas accès à eux-mêmes (...) ils ne remarquent pas qu'ils se présupposent eux-mêmes à titre préalable (...) son objectivisme interdit absolument à la psychologie d'inclure dans son thème de réflexion l'âme, le moi qui agit et souffre, pris en son sens le plus propre et le plus essentiel."[16] Karl Popper prend une direction analogue, *mutatis mutandis,* dès les premières pages de *The Self and its Brain*, ayant trait au dépassement nécessaire du matérialisme.[17]

3/ A supposer toutefois que l'on concède à Husserl que "partout à notre époque se manifeste le besoin pressant d'une compréhension de l'esprit,"[18] comment parvenir à cette dernière? Ceci suggère une troisime réflexion.

Les lecteurs assidus d'Aristote auront souvent rencontré le mot *kenos*, "vide", associé au mot "logique" ou à un de ses synonymes; en des formules comme *logikôs kai kenôs*, par exemple, ou *dialektikôs kai kenôs*.[19] Quel sens donner à ces connotations péjoratives du mot "logique" (de noble extraction, si on songe à *logos*) sous la plume pourtant de celui qu'on considère comme le fondateur de la discipline de ce nom? C'est un thème qui appelle une longue discussion. Pour nos fins actuelles le court texte suivant devrait suffire: "Un aveugle de naissance peut raisonner (*sullogisaito*: "syllogiser") sur des couleurs; pour de telles gens, nécessairement, il y a raisonnement (*logos*) sur des mots, mais il n'y a pensée de rien (*noein de mêden*)."[20] Voici donc une opposition très nette entre "raisonnement" ou "discours" (*logos*) et "pensée" ou "intelligence" (*Nous*). Qu'est-ce-à-dire?

Je ne sais si c'est une semblable distinction que vise la célèbre remarque de Heidegger: "La pensée (*Denken*) ne commencera que lorsque nous aurons appris que cette chose tant magnifiée depuis des siècles, la Raison (*Vernunft*), est l'ennemie la plus acharnée de la pensée".[21] Mais à mon avis le premier chapitre d'*Antimoderne*, de Maritain, offre un commentaire remarquable de cette distinction,[22] annonçant à vrai dire *Réflexions sur l'intelligence*, *Les Degrés du Savoir* et quantité d'autres textes plus mûrs. Maritain y prend soin au préalable de rappeler qu'Intelligence et Raison ne sont pas deux facultés différentes mais bien deux aspects ou opérations d'une seule et même aptitude humaine.[23] A quoi peut incliner toutefois la "*raison purement discourante*" (italiques de Maritain; l'expression reviendra tout au long de l'étude) "sinon au raisonnement vide et au discours vain (...) elle ne peut plus que travailler sur soi-même, dominée par l'automatisme des combinaisons logiques (...)". Elle "tend à n'être plus qu'un mécanisme d'aspect intellectuel au service de l'imagination verbale."[24] Peut-on mieux caractériser certaines formes de "logique" que tous auront reconnues? Combien proches de ceux qui, à l'instar de l'aveugle-né d'Aristote syllogisant sur les couleurs, discourent sur des mots sans aucune pensée. Leur *Nous* est "vide;" "présents ils sont absents", dirait Héraclite.[25]

Que se passe-t-il donc? En fait, explique Maritain, "le raisonnement doit tout ce qu'il a d'être à l'Intelligence."[26] Omettre "seulement ce petit point que l'intelligence saisit l'être même, et s'ordonne à l'être, conduit forcément l'esprit humain à chercher sa fin en lui-même, non dans l'être."[27]

4/ Nous voilà reconduits à une nouvelle interrogation, toujours jeune pour qui a une véritable disposition philosophique (dans les excellents termes de Thomas Nagel: "the essential capacity to be mystified by the utterly familiar"[28]): qu'est-ce que connaître? C'est, nous disent les *Réflexions sur l'intelligence* de Maritain, "la question plus profonde"[29] même que celle de la vérité. Considérons-là un bref instant.

Dès les premières pages de cet ouvrage, concernant la vérité, Maritain renvoie à la parole bien connue de Parménide: *tauton d'esti noein kai houneken esti noêma*, qu'il traduit: "la pensée, et ce dont il y a pensée, c'est tout un."[30] Plus littéralement, on pourrait traduire, comme Beaufret: "Or c'est le même, penser et ce *à dessein de quoi* il y a pensée ,"[31] ce qui ajoute un accent téléologique au propos semblable du fragment non moins célèbre *to gar auto noein estin te kai einai*:[32] "Penser et être sont en effet le même". "(...) Où que l'intelligence se tourne, c'est toujours l'être qu'elle voit. Partout elle est en sa présence; chaque fois qu'elle connaît, elle tient de l'être. L'idée de l'être est l'étoffe commune de la pensée."[33] Et plus loin, après les distinctions indispensables entre "la *chose* et son *existence*, la chose elle-même et *le mode d'exister* de la chose"[34] puis entre "l'*essence* ou *nature* abstraite par l'esprit, et l'*existence* de cette nature soit dans l'esprit, soit dans la chose"[35] il insiste que "*le terme immédiatement atteint par l'intelligence au moyen du concept, (...), c'est la chose même, c'est la nature même qui est à la fois dans la chose pour exister et dans le concept pour être perçue*," qualifiant ceci de "thèse absolument fondamentale."[36]

Il ne s'agit donc pas de rejeter "le principe de Parménide" mais de le nuancer. Maritain renvoie pour cela aux "sages précisions aristotéliciennes, où l'intelligence des anciens avait mis toute sa délicatesse de toucher": "L'acte du senti et celui de la sensation, disait Aristote, est un seul et même acte; mais l'être propre diffre en l'un et en l'autre."[37] "(...) Au point précis où porte purement le connaître, il n'y a nulle diversité entre la connaissance et la chose, entre la pensée et l'être; si bien que le connaissant et le connu, sans que l'être propre de l'un se mêle en rien à l'être propre de l'autre, sont un et le même sous le rapport précis de l'acte de connaître."[38]

On peut confirmer cette lecture maritainienne d'Aristote par des énoncés frappants de ce dernier, certains d'entre eux peut-être insuffisamment connus, ou médités, touchant l'intelligence elle-même cette fois, l'*epistêmê* et enfin l'âme, ce qui permettra au surplus de répondre une première fois à la question de la dignité de la pensée. Après avoir répété à deux reprises *to d'auto estin hê kat'energeian epistêmê tô pragmati*, "la science en acte est identique à la chose,"[39] Aristote affirme même: *holôs de ho nous estin ho kat'energeian ta pragmata*, "D'une manière générale, l'intellect en acte est identique aux choses,"[40] au point que "l'âme est en quelque sorte tous les êtres", *hê psuchê ta onta pôs esti panta.*[41]

D'aucuns se souviendront des développements pleins d'esprit de *Théonas*, où Maritain parle plaisamment du "surhomme selon Aristote", retraçant l'usage du mot "surhomme", *suprahomines*, bien avant Nietzsche, dans les *Moralia in Job* de saint Grégoire le Grand.[42] "Ce par quoi l'homme est le plus vraiment homme, c'est l'intelligence, qui est en lui chose divine, et par laquelle il participe à la nature des esprits."[43] Voilà bien ce qu'avançaient déjà Platon et Aristote dans les textes précités. Mais comment l'expliquer?

Peut-être est-ce dans *les Degrés du Savoir* que se trouve exprimée sur le mode le plus élaboré la réponse de Maritain à cette question, qui revient à vrai dire à celle du "mystère lui-même de la connaissance,"[44] du "plus important de tous les problmes de la noétique."[45] Il aura eu en tout cas le mérite d'y revenir patiemment chaque fois que s'en présentait l'occasion. Après les passages des ouvrages antérieurs cités plus haut, on ne s'étonne pas de lire maintenant, par exemple: "C'est dans la pensée même que l'être extramental est atteint, dans le concept même que le réel ou métalogique est touché et manié, c'est là qu'il est saisi, elle le mange chez elle, parce que la gloire même de son immatérialité est de n'être pas une chose dans l'espace extérieur à une autre chose étendue, mais bien une vie supérieure à tout l'ordre de la spatialité, qui sans sortir de soi se parfait de ce qui n'est pas elle (...)."[46]

Si, comme on a raison de l'affirmer, connaître consiste à devenir l'autre dans son altérité, ce qui s'y oppose dès lors le plus radicalement, c'est la possessivité de la matire. La matière a en effet la propriété évidente d'accaparer les déterminations qu'elle reçoit *une à une* comme *sienne*. Ce n'est pas le refroidissement de mon doigt (quelque nécessaire qu'il soit) dans l'eau froide qui constitue la sensation du froid; c'est le fait que par mon toucher je sois moi-même et le froid *de cette eau-ci*; le bâton refroidi n'est toujours que lui-même. Or, loin qu'elle n'appréhende que le tangible, l'audible, le visible, etc. voire que le sensible tout court, l'intelligence est en mesure de connaître d'une certaine manire *toutes choses*. Sartre avait raison d'écrire que le "je ne sais rien" de Socrate "désigne par ce *rien* précisément la totalité de l'être considéré en tant que vérité".[47] Quelque imparfaitement que ce soit, sous l'aspect d'être et de non-être, notre intelligence embrasse tout. Sous ce rapport exact, l'être humain est par conséquent exempt de toute matire, totalement dégagé des conditions de celle-ci.

Autrement dit, si le dedans, l'*intus*, de l'intelligence était le moindrement matériel, il rendrait impossible son être même. Si le dehors, l'extérieur matériel connu, constituait la nature de l'intelligence, celle-ci ne connaîtrait rien. Si son dedans était tel que le dedans des êtres matériels qu'elle connaît, il obstruerait, empêcherait l'être de l'autre. Même la chose matérielle la plus subtile est opaque, car elle ne peut être que soi. *Intus apparens prohibet extraneum.*[48]

Ainsi donc, pour autant que notre âme, selon le mot d'Aristote, est d'une certaine manière toutes choses, étant naturellement apte à toutes les connaître, "selon ce mode-là de perfection, il est possible que dans une seule chose particulire, existe la perfection de l'univers tout entier."[49] Quel prodige déjà, dont nous aurions tort de ne pas nous étonner: "(...) Par l'espace, l'univers me comprend et m'engloutit comme un point; par la pensée, je le comprends."[50] L'univers certes, son ordre, ses origines et ses causes, mais n'y a-t-il pas aussi l'au-delà, obscurément pressenti et conçu par mode de convenance, d'analogies et de négations pour le moment?

5/ En conclusion, je voudrais suggérer que ce qui précède n'offre encore qu'un commencement de réponse aux questions posées au début, y inclus celles que provoque la sentence de saint Jean de la Croix. Je le ferai en m'inspirant surtout cette fois de saint Augustin, non sans avoir fait appel au préalable à un thème central de l'esthétique de Maritain et à quelques-unes de ses sources.

Ce thème, on l'aura deviné, est celui de la beauté, dont la perception nécessite l'intelligence, même si ses premières manifestations sont sensibles.[51] Maritain y insiste ds *Art et Scolastique*,[52] pour y revenir avec vigueur dans *Creative Intuition in Art and Poetry*.[53] Il n'est pas possible d'en articuler ici les raisons. Je relverai plutôt un aspect de l'expérience du beau qui est admirablement rendu par Baudelaire, cité dans *Art et Scolastique*[54]: "c'est cet immortel instinct du beau qui nous fait considérer la terre et ses spectacles comme un aperçu, comme une *correspondance* du ciel. La soif insatiable de tout ce qui est au delà, et que révèle la vie, est la preuve la plus vivante de notre immortalité. C'est à la fois par la poésie et *à travers* la poésie, par et *à travers* la musique, que l'âme entrevoit les splendeurs situées derrière le tombeau". Les larmes qu'amène "un poème exquis" sont le témoignage "d'une nature exilée dans l'imparfait et qui voudrait s'emparer immédiatement, sur cette terre même, d'un paradis révélé". La même idée se trouve dans une page non moins splendide de Marcel Proust.[55]

Platon avait déjà dit l'essentiel concernant le beau, distinguant ses différents sens principaux, depuis le beau sensible, moral, intellectuel, jusqu'au beau transcendental,[56] mais surtout en ces deux mots du *Phèdre*: *ekphanestaton* et *erasmiôtaton*: la beauté est "ce qui se manifeste avec le plus d'éclat" et "ce qui le plus attire l'amour."[57] Lumière et clarté d'une part, attirance amoureuse de l'autre. Les deux composantes essentielles de la contemplation.

En parlant plus haut de prodige, s'agissant de l'intelligence, de sa capacité d'embrasser l'univers et de percer au delà, je ne faisais pas usage d'hyperbole. Saint Augustin ne craignait pas de dire, par exemple, "ce monde est même assurément un miracle plus grand et plus beau que tous ceux dont il est plein."[58] Ou encore: "Peut-être le miracle des natures visibles a-t-il perdu de sa vertu à force d'être vu: il n'en est pas moins, à le considérer sagement, supérieur aux miracles les plus extraordinaires et les plus rares. Car l'homme est un plus grand miracle que tout miracle fait par l'homme."[59] Plus miraculeux que le changement de l'eau en vin aux Noces de Cana sont l'eau et le vin eux-mêmes, prodiges qui se renouvellent constamment sous nos yeux. Plus merveilleuse encore est la "puissance d'un seul grain de n'importe quelle semence (...), l'esprit attentif en est saisi d'effroi." Il y a plus extraordinaire encore: "Un mort est ressuscité, les hommes sont étonnés; il y a tant de naissances chaque jour, et nul ne s'étonne! Pourtant, si nous y regardons avec plus de discernement, il faut un plus grand miracle pour faire être ce qui n'était pas que pour faire revivre qui était."[60]

Que dire même de l'âme humaine qui ne se voit pas, mais qui est manifeste partout par ses oeuvres; il n'est que de penser à ce qui advient du corps aprs la mort, quand elle ne le contient plus. Que dire de l'intelligence, qui discerne bien et mal, juste et injuste. "Et pourtant (...), cette âme, si merveilleuse par sa nature et sa substance, demeure invisible et ne peut être saisie que par l'intelligence."[61] Sans l'intelligence, en d'autres termes, rien de cela ne serait connu. Point de prodige ni de beauté.

Le plus étonnant, enfin, c'est qu'une âme voie en elle-même ce qu'elle ne voit nulle part ailleurs: ainsi la justice, au moins sous la forme de l'idéal à l'aune duquel elle juge qui est juste et qui l'est moins;[62] grâce auquel, aussi bien, nous protestons chacun contre les injustices; idéal que nous aimons dans la mesure exacte où nous nous efforçons de l'atteindre.[63] A bien examiner à son tour la nature du véritable amour, celui qui anime notamment la recherche, le désir de savoir, il est tout de suite évident que nul ne saurait aimer ce qu'il ignore totalement.[64] Si nous n'avons dans l'esprit, à l'état d'ébauche, une idée déjà de cette science que nous brûlons d'acquérir, du sens de ce mot que nous tentons d'élucider, nous ne chercherions pas. La connaissance provoquant l'amour, nous cherchons ardemment le sens. C'est dire à quel point nous *aimons* l'intelligence et sa quête.

Qu'aime donc de son côté l'intelligence elle-même lorsqu'elle cherche à savoir et en particulier à se connaître elle-même?[65] Ne serait-ce pas pour commencer toutes les valeurs qu'elle permet elle-même d'aimer en nous les faisant connaître? Non pas seulement la beauté du savoir lui-même, celle de la justice elle-même, déjà resplendissante, mais l'amour lui-même, qui n'est pas visible, et que j'aime nécessairement avant tout, quand j'aime le prochain, car il m'est intérieur.[66] J'entends bien l'amour authentique et non la convoitise.[67] L'amour lui-même du vrai et des autres transcendantaux en même temps. Condition de possibilité de tout ce qui est proprement humain, dans l'ordre pratique, l'art et l'éthique d'abord, puis théorique, l'intelligence ne l'est pas moins de l'amour humain lui-même en tout ce qu'il peut avoir de plus noble, autant que du désir des réalités éternelles qui ne passent pas. Car sans elle rien de tout cela ne nous serait d'aucune façon accessible.

Platon déjà déclarait que l'union de l'âme et de l'être véritable (*to onti ontôs*) par le savoir "engendre l'intelligence et la vérité."[68] L'enfant aura les traits de ses parents. Leur l'affinité réciproque, ou connaturalité (*suggenês*), est, partant, essentielle. Semblablement, c'est la partie de l'âme la plus proche par nature de l'être véritable qui peut seule s'unir à l'être de manire féconde. Or il s'agit évidemment de l'intelligence elle-même.

En cette insistance sur l'image de l'enfantement, si nette dans la maïeutique, on aura pressenti, bien entendu, l'idée du verbe, du *logos*. De même que celle, plus générale -- si centrale pour peu qu'on réfléchisse à la nature de l'intelligence -- de génération, conception, naissance, à entendre au sens propre avant de passer au figuré.[69] Penser, c'est découvrir, donc reproduire en soi-même, concevoir, enfanter un concept qui se traduira en parole, c'est-à-dire un *logos*. Le premier modèle afin de comprendre l'activité de l'esprit est forcément la vie même, dans ses manifestations les plus concrètes et les plus profondes. Les artefacts au contraire présupposent l'intelligence.

Quoi qu'il en soit, on aura compris que cet amour de l'être, du vrai, du bien et des autres transcendantaux, est en vérité amour de Dieu, de qui l'intelligence désire jouir comme l'oeil de la lumire.[70] Ne serait-ce pas là le plein sens de la phrase de saint Jean de la Croix: "seul Dieu en est digne"?

de l'Université Laval

NOTES

1. Francesco Viola, *La connaissance de la loi naturelle dans la pensée de Jacques Maritain*, in *Nova et Vetera*, LIXe année, no. 3, juillet septembre 1984, pp. 204-205.

2. Blaise Pascal, *Pensées*, fr. 346 Brunschvicg; 759 Lafuma.

3. *Ibid.*, fr. 365 Brunschvicg; 756 Lafuma; cf. 347 Brunschvicg; 200 Lafuma.

4. Cf. William Shakespeare, *Hamlet*, II, ii, 323-328.

5. *Ibid.*, IV, iv, 36-39.

6. Euripide, fragment 1018 (Nauck).

7. *Premier Alcibiade*, 133 c.

8. *Ethique à Eudème*, trad. Vianney Décarie, VIII, 2, 1248 a 28-30.

9. Cf. respectivement *République*, IX, 589 e: *to heautou theiotatou* et *Ethique à Nicomaque* X, 7, 1177 a 16: *en hemin to theiotaton*. De Platon, voir en outre *Théétète*, 176 b et *Timée*, 90 c. D'Aristote: *De Partibus Animalium*, IV, 10, 686 a 28-29; *Eth. Nic.* X, le chapitre 7 en entier; *De Anima*, I, 4, 408 b 25; III, 4, 429 a 15; 429 b 23; 430 a 18; 430 a 24 sq.; *De Generatione Animalium*, II, 3, 737 a 9-10; *Ethique à Eudème*, VIII, 2, 1248 a 26-30.

10. Cf. *Ethique à Nicomaque*, IX, 4, 1166 a 16-23; IX, 8, 1168 b 35 et 1169 a 2; X, 7, 178 a 2-7; *Protreptique*, fr. 6 (Ross). On trouve une abondance de textes autour de ce thème dans Jean Pépin, *Idées grecques sur l'homme et sur Dieu*, Les Belles Lettres, Paris, 1971, notamment pp. 80-94.

11. Ep. 120 ad Consentium, iii, 13. Cf. *De Trinitate*, XV, ii, 2; et xxviii, 51.

12. "Un solo pensamiento del hombre vale mas que todo el mundo; por tanto solo Dios es digno de el" (San Juan de la Cruz, *Dichos de luz y amor*, 34; trad, P. Cyprien, *Les Maximes*, 51).

13. Thomas Nagel, *Is that you, James?*, London Review of Books, vol. 9 no. 17, 1 October 1987, p. 3.

14. Charles De Koninck, *Introduction à l'étude de l'âme*, in *Laval théologique et philosophique*, vol. III, no. 1, 1947, p. 14.

15. Edmund Husserl, *La crise de l'humanité européenne et la philosophie*, trad. Paul Ricoeur, Edition bilingue, Aubier Montaigne, Paris, 1977, p. 83.

16. *Ibid.*, p. 89.

17. Cf. Karl Popper and John C. Eccles, *The self and its Brain*, Springer International, London, 1977, pp. 3 sq.

18. *Loc. cit.*, p. 91. Les derniers mots de cette conférence de Husserl, prononcée à Vienne en 1935, sont: *Denn der Geist allein ist unsterblich* (p.104), "car seul l'esprit est immortel" (p. 105).

19. Cf., par exemple, *Ethique à Eudème*, I, 6, 1216 b 40-- 1217 a 4, et I, 8, 1217 b 21; *Génération des animaux*, II, 8, 748- a 8; *De anima*, I, 1, 403 a 2, puis 24 sq.; voir aussi *Métaphysique* A, 9, 991 a 20-22; 992 a 28; Z, 4, 1029 b 13; *Lambda* 1, 1069 a 26-28; M, 4, 1089 b 25; *Ethique à Nicomaque*, II, 7, 1107 a 30.

20. Aristote, *Physique*, II, 1, 193 a 8-10.

21. Martin Heidegger, *Holzwege*, 5e édition, Klostermann, Frankfurt am Main, 1972, p. 247; *Chemins qui ne mènent nulle part*, trad. Wolfang Brokmeier, Gallimard, Paris, 1962, p. 219.

22. Jacques Maritain, *Antimoderne*, Nouvelle édition revue et augmentée, Revue des Jeunes, Paris, 1922, ch. 1, *La science moderne et la raison*, pp. 29-68. Cette étude est en réalité de 1910. Son "ton oratoire (...) ne me plaît guère aujourd'hui", écrit Maritain au début de son Avant-Propos (p.13); mais il ajoute plus loin (p. 14) qu'elle est "apte encore, malgré ses imperfections, à rendre service" et qu'il garde "une certaine indulgence à son égard".

23. Cf. *loc. cit.*, pp. 30 sq. Maritain renvoie ici à saint Thomas, *Ia Pars*, q. 89, art. 8; aussi art. 10 et *Q. D. De Veritate*, q. 11, art. 1: Ratio comparatur ad intellectus ut generatio ad esse. Cette distinction correspond, *mutatis mutandis*, à celle qui oppose *Nous* et *dianoia*; voir l'excellent résumé de H. H. Joachim, *The Nicomachean Ethics*, Oxford, 1955, pp. 289-291.

24. *Ibid.*, p. 35.

25. Cf. Héraclite, fr. 34: DK 22 B 34.

26. Ibid. p. 34. cf. P. 31: "le noble nom d'Intelligence".

27. *Ibid.*, p. 64.

28. *Loc. cit.*, p. 5.

29. Réflexions sur l'intelligence et sur sa vie propre, Nouvelle Librairie Nationale, Paris, 1926, p. 11. Les *Oeuvres complètes*, volume III (1924-1929), Fribourg, 1984, en contiennent une nouvelle édition préparée par l'auteur lui-même.

30. *Ibid.*, p. 13. Le texte cité de Parménide se trouve en DK 28 B 8, 1. 34.

31. Cf. *Le Poème de Parménide*, présenté par Jean Beaufret, coll. "Epiméthée", P.U.F., Paris, 1955, p. 87. C'est moi qui souligne.

32. DK 28 B 3.

33. Réflexions..., p. 14.

34. *Ibid.*, p. 17.

35. *Ibid.*, p. 18.

36. *Ibid.*, pp.19-20. Comme dans les citations précédentes les termes soulignés le sont tous par Maritain.

37. *Ibid.*, p. 24. La note correspondante cite le texte grec de *De Anima* III, 2, 425 b 26 et 426 a 15.

38. *Ibid.*

39. Aristote, *De Anima*, III, 5, 430 a 19-20; et 7, 431 a 1- 2.

40. *De Anima*, III, 7, 431 b 17.

41. *De Anima*, III, 8, 431 b 21.

42. *Théonas*, Nouvelle Librairie Nationale, Paris, 1925, p. 24 et p. 206. Les trois premiers chapitres de cet ouvrage s'intitulent respectivement *La Liberté de l'Intelligence*, *La Théorie du Surhomme*, *L'Intelligence et le Règne du Coeur*.

43. *Ibid.*, p. 215.

44. Jacques Maritain, *Les Degrés du Savoir*, Desclée de Brouwer, Paris, 1932, p. 215.

45. *Ibid.*, p. 217.

46. *Ibid.*, 201-202.

47. Jean-Paul Sartre, *L'être et le néant*, Gallimard, Paris, 1943, p. 51.

48. J'ai exposé tout cela davantage dans *L'intelligence et les contraires*, in *Les Etudes Philosophiques*, octobre- décembre, 1971, pp. 449-460.

49. *Ibid.*, p. 215. Maritain cite ici saint Thomas, *Q. D. De Veritate*, q. 2, a. 2.

50. Pascal, *op. cit.*, fr. 348 Brunschvicg; Lafuma 113.

51. Voir saint Augustin, *De Civitate Dei*, VIII, 6, 330.

52. Jacques Maritain, *Art et Scolastique*, La Librairie de l'Art Catholique, Paris, 1920. Voir surtout le chapitre V, *L'art et la beauté*, pp. 35-57 et *passim* dont les abondantes notes.

53. Princeton University Press, 1953; Paperback, 1977. Voir ch. 5, pp. 160 sq.

54. pp.48-49

55. "Il n'y a aucune raison dans nos conditions de vie sur terre pour que nous nous croyions obligés à faire le bien, à être délicats, même à être polis, ni pour l'artiste athée à ce qu'il se croie obligé de recommencer vingt fois un morceau dont l'admiration qu'il excitera importera peu à son corps mangé par les vers, comme le pan de mur jaune que peignit avec tant de science et de raffinement un artiste à jamais inconnu, à peine identifié sous le nom de Ver Meer (*La Prisonnière*, in *A la recherche...*, Pléïade, 1954, III, p. 188).

56. Cf. le discours attribué par Socrate à Diotima dans *Le Banquet*, 210 e à 212 a.

57. Cf. *Phèdre*, 250 d 5-8. Je me suis expliqué davantage sur tout cela dans un article de la revue *Communio*, tome VII, no. 6, novembre-décembre 1982, pp. 31-40.

58. *De Civitate Dei*, 21, 7, 11. "Miraculum" signifie d'abord "prodige", "merveille"; "nomen miraculi ab admiratione sumitur", rappelle saint Thomas: *Ia Pars*, q. 105, a. 7, c.; "sunt simpliciter mira, quasi habentia causam occultam (...);" "(...) universaliter omne opus quod a solo Deo fieri potest, miraculosum dici potest": *Ia-IIae*, q. 113, a. 10, c. Ces propos d'Augustin et les développements qui suivent ne devraient donc pas faire difficulté.

59. *De Civitate Dei*, 10, 12, trad. G. Combès.

60. *In Joannis Evangelium*, Tractatus VIII, 1, trad. M. F. Berrouard. Cf. *Sermo* 242, 1; P. L. 38, 1139: "Les naissances de tant d'hommes qui n'existaient pas sont chaque jour des miracles plus grands que les résurrections de quelques morts qui existaient".

61. *Ibid.*, 2.

62. Cf. saint Augustin, *De Trinitate*, VIII, vi, 9.

63. *Ibid.*, 9.

64. Cf. *De Trinitate*, X, i, 1 et sq.

65. Je paraphrase ici, mais en d'autres sens, ce que saint Augustin développe de manière extraordinairement éloquente en *ibid.* X, iii, 5 sq.

66. Cf. *Ibid.*, VII, vii, 10 et 11.

67. Cf. *Ibid.*, VIII, vii, 10

68. Cf. *République* VI, 490 a-b.

69. Voir les travaux de J. L. Le Moigne rapportés par Edgar Morin dans *La connaissance de la connaissance*, 1/ *Anthropologie de la connaissance*, Seuil, Paris, 1986 et les propres idées d'Edgar Morin pp. 185 sq. Les mots trahissent constamment l'importance de ce thème pour qui veut comprendre l'activité de l'esprit: génie, ingénieux, ingénieur, genre; ou encore le lien entre l'impossible et l'"inconcevable," l'inengendrable.

70. Ce qu'ont bien vu Platon et les Platoniciens. Cf. *De Civitate Dei*, VIII, 8, 333. Ainsi philosopher c'est *amare Deum*, "aimer Dieu". On lit d'autre part dans les *Retractationes* (I, 1, 3) que "dans les réalités incorporelles et suprêmes," l'amour de la beauté et la philosophie sont la même chose.

PART TWO

EXISTENCE AND THE EXISTENT

B. Being

THE INTUITION OF BEING: METAPHYSICS OR POETRY?

John P. Hittinger

I. THE "INTUITION OF BEING"

In *Existence and the Existent* Maritain says that an "intuition of being makes the philosopher.[1] In the *Peasant of the Garonne* his words are more emphatic. He says "The intuition of being is not only, like the reality of the world and of things, the absolutely primary foundation of philosophy. It is the absolutely primary principle of philosophy." The intuition of being is really the key to Maritain's work; to his mind it is the key to St. Thomas and philosophy as such.

We must try to re-capture that germinal insight which bears so much weight in Maritain's philosophy. He is fond of recounting numerous ways or roads to the intuition of being. In *Existence and the Existent* he merely lists some of these. For example, he mentions the way of Thomas Aquinas who grasped the being of things through an "imperial intelligence serenely relying on its limpid strength." He mentions also a "natural grace" at the sight of a blade of grass; the sudden perception of self; the sense of the contingency of the world; the inner experience of duration, anguish, or fidelity. Many of these concrete ways are fleshed out in other works.[2] He was fond of recounting his wife's vivid experience of self-awareness. He often elaborated upon the sense of contingency in his proof for God's existence. The writings of Bergson, Marcel, and Heidegger he used for the way of inner experience. And we cannot fail to mention his praise of poets like Wordsworth and Hopkins for their appreciation of singular beauty.

The following is Maritain's own attempt to render in metaphoric terms the intuition of being:

> What I then perceive is like a pure activity, a consistency, but superior to the whole order of the imaginable, a vivid tenacity, at once precarious (it is nothing for me to crush a gnat) and fierce (within me, around me, mounts like a clamor the universal vegetation) by which things surge up against me and triumph over possible disaster, stand there,

and not merely there, but in themselves, and by which they
shelter in their thickness, in the humble measure meted out
to what is perishable, a kind of glory demanding to be
recognized.[3]

The act of existing in things is a "glory to be recognized." In each case
of the concrete approaches, including his own metaphorical description, the
intellect must "release in one authentic intellectual intuition, the sense of
being, the sense of the value of the implications that lie in the act of
existing."[4] *Existence and the Existent* is an attempt to release this intuition
and to unfold its implications through various metaphysical issues like
act/potency, causality, and evil.

What are we to make of this claim to an "intuition of being"? Any
claim based on intuition is immediately suspect to philosophers. Perhaps it
is nothing more than "mere poetry." It bespeaks vague feeling or easy and
gratuitous assertion. It is a term more suited to poetry, not the stern stuff of
metaphysics and logic. Moreover, for Thomist philosophers, the question
arises as to Maritain's faithfulness to the master. Is this notion of an
intuition of being derived from or compatible with St. Thomas?

In this paper I shall assess Maritain's intuition of being by examining its
Thomistic origins and by noting the similarities and differences between
poetry and metaphysics in Maritain's philosophy. I shall argue that the
charge of "mere poetry" is formally incorrect; that the "intuition of being" as
a fundamental habit of mind is essential to any Thomistic philosophy, as
well as to any realistic metaphysics; and lastly, that the charge ironically
displays a dissociated sensibility that Maritain sought to overcome.

II. THOMISTIC ORIGINS

The Thomistic context and warrant for the "intuition of being" is well
laid out in *Existence and the Existent*. As a preliminary to the intuition,
Maritain goes over the familiar ground of the role of judgment in Thomistic
epistemology.[5] Simple apprehension abstracts an intelligible note from
things and forms a concept. But the act of knowing must return through
judgment to the sensible being in order to judge the truth of things. The
intellect does more than contemplate the picture of essences in ideas: it must
restore them to existence through judgment. The concept, the universal,
exists only in the mind; what actually exists is a "subject," a being. The
reality known derives from a "trans-objective subject." Thus the function
of judgment is "existential": judgment "transposes the mind from the plane
of simple essence of the simple object of thought, to the plane of the thing,
of the subject possessing existence."[6] Judgment is fundamentally an
affirmation of existence.

But, since existence is of another order than essence, existence is not an
intelligible or object-like essence. It cannot be grasped conceptually, but
only in judgment. The concept of existence cannot be visualized apart from

being. Being contains within itself the two-fold valence of essence and existence, a notion of "what something is" and the judgment "that it is." In the intuition of being, the mind surges beyond the grasp of essence to the existence of things. But the existence of the being draws the mind to consider something more than brute facticity or a dark surd. The intuition of being grasps the formality of existence, a "super-intelligible" datum for the mind.

A difficulty in assessing Maritain's intuition of being comes in the interpretation of the nature of metaphysical judgment. As he acknowledges in a long footnote in *Existence and the Existent*, metaphysical judgment is a judgment of "separation." That by virtue of which a thing is what it is, is different from that by which a thing is said to be as such. Thus, the intelligibility of being is seen to be free from the intrinsic determination of matter; that is, being need not be material. There is dispute among Thomists as to the conditions necessary for this judgment. Does it require prior knowledge of immaterial substances such as angels or God? Or does it require merely an understanding of intellectual immateriality? Or can it be derived from the distinction of essence and existence as separate intelligibilities?[7] Maritain seems to think that the last is true, and this has drawn some criticism, which has been directed also at many existential Thomists, who are accused of seeking to pull being out of a chair, somehow short circuiting the long arduous path to metaphysics. Others may reject this approach because it operates in the sphere of naive understanding without critical awareness. The notion of being must be derived, they would say, from a transcendental analysis of the structure of human knowing. Others may even argue that the notion of being is derived from the Christian distinction between God and creatures, and thus the intuition is sensible only within the ambiance of faith. Although Maritain did intend the intuition to constitute the entry into metaphysics, he also considered it the formal habit of mind that must constitute the basis for any Thomistic philosophy.

The intuition of being is the beginning of philosophy; it is a "beginning" in both senses of the word, genetically and formally. It is the *arche* of philosophizing, as Socrates considered wonder to be, calling it "the beginning of philosophy." Indeed, the intuition of being is the experience of wonder at the "inexhaustibility" of the real and the "super- intelligiblity" of being. The intuition of being is first and foremost a habit of mind, a disposition towards the world, that envelopes the entirety of the intellectual life, giving it a certain tone. Maritain does not mean to suggest that all of reality can be seen at a glance or deduced from this simple but profound intuition, thereby obviating the need for any science or logical analysis. Maritain is not guilty of such romantic or apriori excess. Rather, the intuition of being is a testimony to the integrity and wholeness of things, the depth of reality that will always elude our final grasp, which yet gives the thinker a reason to inquire further, as he strives for greater integration of knowledge of the real. It is the source and inspiration of "Thomistic realism."

As a habit of mind, the intuition of being is the proper "dwelling place" or "modus" for any type of Thomistic metaphysics, and, as Maritain would argue, for any realistic metaphysics. By whatever process one deems metaphysical judgment to be legitimately effected, the effect in the knower is a habit of mind by which the intelligibility of being in "its full amplitude" is acknowledged. In the *Preface to Metaphysics*, Maritain speaks about the intellectual virtue of the metaphysician. In addition to the objective light constituted by the degree of immateriality which specifies a science, there is a "subjective light perfecting the subjective activity of the intellect, by which the intellect is proportioned to a given object, fitted to apprehend it."[8] I believe that this is a key to the importance and relevance of Maritain's notion of the "intuition of being." By a habit one is disposed to think or to act in a determinate and stable way; in this case one becomes disposed to recognize and acknowledge the presence of being and the full amplitude of being as such. Thus by whatever means one comes to the judgment of metaphysics the effect is the same acknowledgement of the intelligibility of *esse* as the act of all acts and the perfection of all perfections.

And the intuition of being should be appreciated in the order of the formality, as much as in the order of the genesis, of metaphysics. That is, even if one is uncomfortable with the attempt to base metaphysics in an intuition of being, without the steps of natural philosophy or other discipline, the result of any Thomistic metaphysical system must be the return to the intuition as the stable habitual center of the intellectual life. We must begin with the "sense of the value of the implications that lie in the act of existing."

We have a further clue concerning the intuition of being in the distinction between "ratio" and "intellectus," or reason and intellect.[9] In Maritain's account "intellectus" is rendered as "intuition." There is textual warrant for translating in this way.[10] Perhaps however this term is misleading and should be replaced by "vision" or "understanding". Maritain would have philosophy begin with a vision, acknowledgement, or awareness of the being of things.

At the heart of the distinction is Thomas's insistence upon a non-discursive moment in intellection. In addition to the complex apparatus of dialectic and abstraction, demonstration and reasoning, the human knower must be said to "see" simply. In fact Thomas says that reason begins and ends with intellection; "ratio" is related to "intellectus" as motion is related to rest, as the imperfect is related to the perfect, and even as time is to eternity. The process of reasoning terminates in vision of what a thing is or the truth of some conclusion. Reasoning without some terminal insight, at least in aspiration, is non- intelligible in Thomas's scheme. All human knowledge, all human science, aspires to fruition in metaphysical knowledge. The labor of reason aspires to the intuition of being. Hence we arrive again at the dynamic character of the intuition of being as a habit of mind. For Thomas describes the relation of "ratio" to "intellectus" in terms of a power specified by a habit. Reason and intellect are not two distinct powers in man, he argues, because the intellect functions as a habit specifying the rational power.[11] Philosophy as a function of "intellectus" is a contemplative act; the mind must be receptive. Maritain says: "It is difficult to arrive at the degree of intellectual purification at which this act is produced in us, at which we become sufficiently disengaged, sufficiently empty to hear what all things whisper and to listen, instead of composing answers."[12]

Thus, as much as Maritain insisted upon a "rational confirmatory analysis" of the intuition of being, he equally insisted that logical analysis alone would not yield the intuition.[13] Philosophy can neither begin nor end with the confirmatory analysis: intellect is related to reason as motion to rest. Analysis by itself lacks insight. Maritain admits that the intuition is beyond technical manipulation. The rational confirmation is a part of a way of judgment, a "via judicii," whose function is to go over the discovered truth and affirm its validity. It does not replace the original intuition or deductions. The explicit rational confirmation, as well as any sophisticated epistemological defense of realism, must finally come to the simple moment of vision. The mystery predominates over the problem. Being remains an object for "enraptured contemplation."[14]

Maritain warns of the two dangers of the average functioning of the intellect in our time, "mental productivism" and the "primacy of verification over truth."[15] Mental productivism elevates the sign over the reality known, as we take more interest in the conceptual apparatus than the real being made manifest by it. Similarly, the mania for an external process of verification and proof could also nullify the vision of being which comes from common experience. Maritain says: "We take more interest in verifying the validity of the signs and symbols we have manufactured than in nourishing ourselves with the truth they reveal." The intuition of being is first and foremost a habit of mind in which the encounter with being is fully appreciated and "suffered." It is a habit of mind rooted in pre- scientific experience. The contemplative moment is a habit alien to a scientific/technological bent of mind. Thus, the intuition of being is an antidote for misplaced abstraction. Whitehead speaks of philosophy as "the critic of abstractions," which completes them "by direct comparison with more concrete intuitions of the universe."[16] As Whitehead apppeals to the evidence of pre-scientific experience and poetry, as found for example in Wordsworth, to refute modern subjectivism, Maritain would similarly find in the poet a great support for the recovery of a sense of being.

III. POETRY AND METAPHYSICS

Maritain is quite adamant in preventing a confusion of poetry and philosophy. In *The Range of Reason* he remarks that, "if one confuses the planes or orders of things, if poetic knowledge claims to become philosophical knowledge," then both are spoiled.[17] On a number of points poetry must be rigorously distinguished from philosophy. First of all, they are entirely different orders of rationality: poetry is ordered to making, not to knowing. Its good is a work produced "ad extra," not a concept or judgment produced within for speculative knowledge. It is axiomatic for Maritain's poetic theory that poetry be held within the genus of making. When freed from this restraint, the poet loses his way. The very object of poetic knowledge is non-conceptualisable. Thus, poetic intuition is a type of "divination," a knowledge of the heart; the intuition of metaphysics is an "abstractive visualization." Again, the poet engages his subjectivity and emotion as he grasps the world; the philosopher is more purely intellectual. Finally, the poet is engaged more directly with the things of sense, with singularity and particular things. Metaphysics is more universal and abstract. In *Creative Intuition* Maritain gathers these ideas into a memorable passage:

> Poetry is a divination of the spiritual in the things of sense --which expresses itself in the things of sense, and in a delight in sense. Metaphysics also pursues a spiritual prey, but metaphysics is engaged in abstract knowledge, while poetry quickens art. Metaphysics snatches at the spiritual in an idea, by the most abstract intellection; poetry reaches it in the flesh, by the very point of sense sharpened through intelligence. Metaphysics enjoys its possession only in the retreats of eternal regions, while poetry finds its own at every crossroad in the wanderings of the contingent and the singular.[18]

Maritain sharply distinguishes poetry from metaphysics. However, we should not "run the risk of forgetting that though poetry cannot be confounded with metaphysics," Maritain says that "it yet responds to a metaphysical need of the spirit of man, and is metaphysically justified."[19] Poetic knowledge of the world is allied to metaphysics; Maritain says that the poet aims at "being." This is manifest in a number of ways. The poet is existential precisely because he must be directed to the good of the work; a concrete work to be made and "posited in existence." Further, poetic knowledge is existential because it must attend to the sensible particulars; it is less apt to be lost in a cloud of abstraction. By affective connaturality there resonates "that which is most existent and most concrete in things in that which is most existent and concrete in the subject." Although

Maritain's poetic is known most of all for the epistemological notion of the connatural knowing of the self and the world, his theory actually culminates in the metaphysical notion of the superabundance of being. The work of art opens out onto the world of being and presses to the infinitude of being itself:

> Poetic intuition does not stop at this given existent; it goes beyond, and infinitely beyond. Precisely because it has no conceptualized object, it tends and extends to the infinite, it tends toward all reality which is engaged in any singular existing thing. . . . As grasped by poetic knowledge, things abound in significance, and swarm with meanings. Things are not only what they are. They ceaselessly pass beyond themselves, and give more than they have, because from all sides they are permeated with the activating influx of the Prime Cause. . . . I would think that this mutual communication in existence and in the spiritual flux from which existence proceeds . . . is perhaps in the last analysis what the poet receives and suffers.[20]

This passage from *Creative Intuition*, similar to a passage contained in *The Situation of Poetry*, corresponds very closely to a section of *Existence and the Existent*.[21] Maritain explains that the metaphysics of Thomas Aquinas is not essentialist, not centered upon static essences, but rather upon the dynamic reality of existence, grounded in a superabundant divine being. Maritain has discovered here not only the diffusive nature of the good, but also the relevance of process, context, and relation, to our understanding of the being of things in the world.[22] Maritain exhibits in his poetic theory a notion that finds some affinity with Whitehead's use of Wordsworth. In *Science and the Modern World* Whitehead points to Wordsworth's awareness of "that mysterious presence of surrounding things, which imposes itself on any separate element that we set up as an individual for its own sake. He always grasps the whole of nature as involved in the tonality of the particular instance."[23] Maritain and Whitehead both see a positive value in the sheer self-assertion and endurance of things and the relation of one to another. Granted, the two thinkers conceptualize the insight in very different ways. Whitehead uses the notion of "event" to name the actuality that emerges against the flux; Maritain, of course, retains the perennial notion of "being." But, as mentioned above, both would agree that the "poetic rendering of our concrete experience" must not be omitted from a metaphysical account of the real. Time does not permit analysis and judgment as to whose account is truer to concrete experience.

For its existential mode of knowing and for its grasp of the superabundance of being, poetry is salutary for philosophy, given its present state. Although in its essence philosophy is free of the poetic mode of knowing, the state of philosophy is another consideration. Maritain says that "to philosophize man must put his whole soul into play, in much the same manner that to run he use his heart and lungs."[24] And poets can enliven the metaphysical habit. The intuition of being may receive a deep confirmation, for example, in the works of Wordsworth, Hopkins and Eliot; a similar concern may be found in the writers of the American South with whom Maritain was familiar: Tate, Gordon, and Ransom. These poets are enraptured with being; they recognize that there is indeed ensconced in the humble things of the world "a glory demanding to be recognized." They give this glory expression through their verses and stories. Maritain remarks in *A Preface to Metaphysics* that the metaphysician must be a sensitive man and "keenly and profoundly aware of sensible objects. And he should be plunged into existence, steeped ever more deeply in it by a sensuous and aesthetic perception as acute as possible so that aloft in the third heaven of natural understanding he may feed upon the intelligible substance of things."[25]

In light of that remark allow me to end with a reading from Nathaniel Hawthorne, surveying his garden at the Old Manse:

> Speaking of summer squashes, I must say a word of their beautiful and varied forms. They presented an endless diversity of urns and vases, shallow or deep, scalloped or plain, moulded in patterns which a sculptor would do well to copy, since Art has never invented anything more graceful. A hundred squashes in the garden were worthy -- in my eyes, at least -- of being rendered indestructible in marble. . . . There was a hearty enjoyment in observing the growth of the crook-necked winter squashes, from the first little bulb, with the withered blossom adhering to it, until they lay strewn upon the soil, big round fellows, hiding their heads beneath the leaves, but turning their great yellow rotundities to the noontide sun. Gazing at them, I felt that, by my agency, something worthwhile living for had been done. A new substance was born into the world. They were real and tangible existences, which the mind could seize hold of and rejoice in.[26]

Hawthorne surely has the germ of Maritain's intuition of being in this appreciation of the squash's "victorious thrust over nothingness." An abstractive leap is required to form terms like the "diversity and autonomy of being," "the superabundance of being," and so forth. But I have learned from the Southern poet and critic, Marion Montgomery, whose work *Why Hawthorne was Melancholy* I commend to you very highly, that Hawthorne was quite aware of the issue of being and the tragic presumption of men who elevate their mind to a point of denying the givenness of things and the common plight of humanity.[27] Hawthorne faced the specter of Emersonian transcendentalism, a form of idealism or "ideosophy," which seemed to be premised on the denial of the fundamental intuition of being. Emerson viewed nature as a "subjective phenomenon," an "apparition" or shadow cast by the knowing mind. "Perhaps there are no objects," Emerson opines. "Once we lived in what we saw; now, the rapaciousness of this power, which threatens to absorb all things, engages us."[28] After witnessing the loss of the world in abstraction, Hawthorne attends to the lowly squash and savors the glory of its being.

Maritain, I think, would be delighted to have these prophetic poets return us to the savor of being as they call forth that intuition. They will strengthen that habit of mind, the habit of being. Ironically, the turn to poetry might bring us around to a more demanding metaphysics of being and a greater appreciation for Thomas's strict logic. The intuition of being --metaphysics or poetry? It is both; but let us distinguish in order to unite.

College of St. Francis

NOTES

1. Jacques Maritain, *Existence and the Existent*, transl. Lewis Galantière and Gerald B. Phelan (New York, 1966), p. 42. See *A Preface to Metaphysics* (New York, 1939) "It is this intuition that makes the metaphysician" (p. 44). *The Peasant of the Garonne: An Old Layman Questions Himself about the Present Time*,. translated by Michael Cuddihy and Elizabeth Hughes (New York, 1968), pp. 110-111. See also, *The Range of Reason* (New York, 1960), p. 9.

2. *Preface to Metaphysics*, pp. 47-51; *Approaches to God* (New York, 1942), chapter one.

3. *Peasant*, p. 111.

4. *Existence*, p. 21.

5. See, for example, Joseph Owens, *An Interpretation of Existence* (Milwaukee, 1968).

6. *Existence*, p. 17.

7. See John Wippel, "Metaphysics and *Separatio* in Thomas Aquinas," in *Metaphysical Themes in Thomas Aquinas* (Washington, 1984), pp. 69-104.

8. *Preface*, p. 45.

9. Thomas Aquinas, *De Ver.* XV, 1; *In Boeth. de Trin.*, VI, 1, pt. 3. See J. Peghaire, *Intellectus et Ratio selon s. Thomas D'Aquin* (Paris, 1933) and my unpublished M.A. dissertation, *Reason and Intellect in Two Texts of St. Thomas Aquinas*, The Catholic University of America, 1978.

10. See *De Ver.*, I, 12; *In II Sent.*, d. 9, 1, 8, ad 12.

11. *De Ver.*, XV, 1.

12. *Preface to Metaphysics*, p. 48.

13. See *Preface*, pp. 54-57.

14. *Preface*, pp. 3-7, 56.

15. See *The Range of Reason*, p. 27.

16. Alfred North Whitehead, *Science and the Modern World* (Macmillan Free Press, 1967), p. 87.

17. *Range*, p. 29.

18. *Creative Intuition in Art and Poetry* (New York, 1963), p. 236.

19. *The Situation of Poetry* (New York, 1955), p. 59.

20. *Ibid.*, p. 127.

21. *Situation*, p. 79; *Existence*, p. 42: "Being superabounds everywhere; it scatters its gifts and fruits in profusion. This is the action in which all beings here below communicate with one another and in which, thanks to the divine influx that traverses them, they are at every instant . . . either better or worse than themselves and than the mere fact of their existence at a given moment. By this action they exchange their secrets, influence one another for good or ill, and contribute to or betray in one another the fecundity of being."

22. See for example, Thomas Langan, "Substance, System, and Structure," *New Scholasticism* LXI (1987) 285-306.

23. *Science in the Modern World*, p. 83.

24. On the distinction between nature and state, see Maritain's *An Essay on Christian Philosophy* (New York, 1955), pp. 11- 33. 25. *Preface,* p. 23.

25. *Preface,* p. 23

26. Nathaniel Hawthorne, "The Old Manse," in *Tales and Sketches,* "The Library of America," edited by Roy Harvey Pearce (New York, 1982) pp. 1132-1133.

27. Marion Montgomery, *The Prophetic Poet and the Spirit of the Age,* Vol. III *Why Hawthorne Was Melancholy* (New York, 1984). See also *Possum: and Other Receits for the Recovery of "Southern" Being* (Athens, 1987).

28. See Emerson's essay "Experience." Irving Howe, in his *American Newness* (New York, 1987), says: "To confront American culture is to feel onself encircled by a thin but strong presence: a mist, a cloud, a climate. I call it Emersonian." In this mist, consciousness becomes "the beginning and end of existence . . . swallowing the very world in its pride."

HOW THOMISTIC IS
THE INTUITION OF BEING?

John F. X. Knasas

I propose to evaluate Maritain's approach to Thomistic metaphysics as presented in *Existence and the Existent*. I conclude that, pruned of an excess, the approach is sound.

I

In prose that is at once incomparable and frustratingly elusive, Jacques Maritain presents the intuition of being, *l'intuition de l'être*, as the entry into metaphysics. The initial difficulty in understanding Maritain lies in a hard-to-pin-down ambiguity in the word *être*.

On the one hand, *être* can mean the subject of metaphysics--*ens commune* or *ens inquantum ens*. He writes:

> A philosopher is not a philosopher if he is not a metaphysician. And it is the intuition of being [*l'intuition de l'être*]. . . that makes the metaphysician. I mean the intuition of being in its pure and all-pervasive properties, in its typical and primordial intelligible density; the intuition of being *secundum quod est ens* [*l'intuition de l'être secundum quod est ens*].[1]

As the last line makes evident, Maritain employs *être* in the sense of the Latin *ens*.

Earlier, in *The Degrees of Knowledge*, Maritain describes *ens*. He is commenting upon Aquinas' discussion of *ens* at *De Veritate* I, 1c. Maritain makes three points. First, *ens* designates an intelligible object that "is not the privilege of one of the classes of things that the Logician calls species, genus, or category. It is universally communicable."[2] The scholastics called such objects transcendentals. Second, *ens* is an analogous commonality. By an analogous commonality, Maritain understands a *unum in multis*, a one in many, that implicitly but actually contains the differences of the instances of the *multa*.[3] It makes only an incomplete abstraction from its analogates, or instances. Third, though the data in which *ens* is spied are sensible things, the data release an understanding of *ens* that includes possible immaterial instances. The point will prove to be Maritain's Achilles' heel. He himself acknowledges surprise at it:

> Such objects [e.g., *ens*] are trans-sensible. For, though they are realized in the sensible in which we first grasp them, they are offered to the mind as transcending every genus and every category, and as able to be realized in subjects of a wholly other essence than those in which they are apprehended. It is extremely remarkable that being, the first object attained by our mind in things . . . bears within itself the sign that beings of another order than the sensible are thinkable and possible.[4]

Hence, in one sense the intuition of being refers to the intellectual perception of *ens*, a transphysical analogous commonality. On the other hand, there is another sense. Now *être* refers to Aquinas' basic metaphysical principle of *esse*. The intuition of being becomes the intuition of *esse*. In *Existence and the Existent*, Maritain remarks:

> This is why, at the root of metaphysical knowledge, St. Thomas places the intellectual intuition of that mysterious reality disguised under the most commonplace and commonly used word in the language, the word *to be* [*être*]; a reality revealed to us as the uncircumscribable subject of a science which the gods begrudge us when we release, in the values that appertain to it, the act of existing [*cet acte d'exister*] which is exercised by the humblest thing - that victorious thrust by which it triumphs over nothingness.[5]

Maritain identifies être with *acte d'exister*. Later Maritain says that the act of existing is what Aquinas calls *esse*.[6]

II

In sum, the "intuition of being" has two senses. The intuition refers to the intellectual perception of a trans- physical and analogous commonality. "*Être*" in this sense is what Aquinas calls *ens* when he speaks of the subject of metaphysics. Maritain's intuition of being also refers to the *esse* of things.

Different as these senses are, a connection between them exists. The second sense is the basis for the first. A heightened appreciation of *esse* produces the realization that a being is not necessarily a body. After insisting that the concept of existence (*esse*) cannot be cut off from the concept of being (*ens*, that-which-is, that-which-exists, that whose act is to exist), Maritain says:

> When, moving on to the queen-science, metaphysics, . . .
> the intellect disengages being from the knowledge of the
> sensible in which it is immersed, in order to make it the
> object or rather the subject of metaphysics; when, in a
> word, it conceptualizes the metaphysical intuition of being
> . . . what the intellect releases into that same light is, here
> again, first and foremost, the act of existing.[7]

Something about the existence of a sensible thing informs the intellect that to have existence is not necessarily to be a body. To have the intuition of *ens* is to have the intuition of *esse*. The insight into the immateriality of *ens* is rooted in an insight into the intelligibility of *esse*.

At this point in *Existence and the Existent*, Maritain provides a footnote containing the most striking assertion of his thesis. The footnote is also important for the liaison made between the thesis and the Thomistic texts. Maritain refers to *In De Trinitate*, V, 3c as

> confirm[ing] the thesis that the metaphysical concept of
> being [*le concept m*taphysique de l'être] . . . is an eidetic
> visualisation of being [*lêtre*] apprehended in judgment, in
> the *secunda operatio intellectus, quae respicit ipsum esse
> rei*.   This doctrine shows indeed that what properly
> pertains to the metaphysical concept is that it results from
> an abstraction (or a separation from matter) which takes
> place *secundum hanc secundam operationem intellectus*. .
> . . If it can be separated from matter by the operation of
> the (negative) judgment, the reason is that it is related in
> its content to the act of existing which is signified by the
> (positive) judgment and which over-passes the line of
> material essences - the connatural object of simple
> apprehension.[8]

Ens is separated from matter thanks to a confrontation with the act of existing - an act that "over-passes the line of material essences."   The immateriality of *ens* is squarely rested upon the immateriality of *esse*. Maritain notes that Aquinas prefaced his discussion of metaphysical separation, or negative judgment, with a discussion of the grasp of *esse* in the composing mode of the mind's second act - positive judgment. Maritain is confident, then, that for Aquinas also an appreciation of *esse* is the key for an appreciation of metaphysical *ens*. The judgment negating matter from *ens* has its justification in a positive judgment whose content includes the act of existing.

In an earlier section Maritain describes the intellect's act of judgment. Characteristic of judgment is that it reintegrates with its existing subject a previously abstracted object of thought. In accomplishing this reintegration, judgment does not merely apprehend existence but lives it intentionally.[9]

But in his *Approches sans Entraves*, written at the end of his life, Maritain emphasized that the intuition of *esse* does not occur in all judgments. By the word *est* some judgments link the subject to a predicate expressing an idea previously abstracted. Other judgments, for example of the type "I exist," "Things exist," affirm in the mind the subject as in extra-mental reality. In these judgments the intellect intuitively knows the extra-mental *esse* of the subject.[10] The intellect produces an affirmative judgment of existence on the occasion of some individual reality known in its singularity by an external sense, e.g., sight.[11] Unfortunately, Maritain is unclear on the specifics of the production.[12]

In conclusion, what is Maritain's approach to the subject of Thomistic metaphysics? Maritain's approach to the transphysical commonality of *ens inquantum ens* is through one of its components, *esse*. A heightened judgmental appreciation of the *esse* of sensible things leads us to realize that *esse* itself is not necessarily confined to actuating bodies. Hence, *ens*, or that-which-*exists*, need not be a body.

III

The difficulty in Maritain's presentation of the entry into Thomistic metaphysics has long been noted. Maritain's approach claims more from experience than experience can give. From a number of judgments, I can see that *esse* is an act that need not actuate this body or that body. Nevertheless in every case, *esse* is still presented as the act of some body. From the data no indication yet exists that *esse* possesses an ability to actuate more than bodies. From judgmentally grasped *esse*, Maritain draws an object too great for the data to bear. In general, the apprehension of a transphysical commonality presupposes some knowledge of an immaterial being.[13]

Aquinas shares this reservation. Aquinas understands abstraction to be determined by the data. For example, animality does not include rationality because the former is *found* without the latter. Hence, in the *De Ente et Essentia* Aquinas remarks:

> If plurality belonged to [humanity's] concept, it could never be one, though it is one when present in Socrates. So, too, if oneness belonged to its concept, the nature of Socrates and of Plato would be identical, and it could not be multiplied in many individuals.[14]

In light of a reflection upon the *facts*, one realizes that an absolutely considered nature is neither one nor many. Likewise, in the commentary on Boethius' *De Trinitate*:

> But finger, foot, and hand, and other parts of this kind are outside the definition of man. . . . For whether or not he has feet, as long as he is constituted of a rational soul and a body composed of the elements in the proper mixture required by this sort of form, he will be a man.[15]

Noteworthy is that this text is from the very article to which Maritain appeals for the intuition of transsensible *esse*. But later in the commentary, Aquinas also remarks:

> We say that being and substance are separate from matter and motion . . . because it is not of their nature to be in matter and motion, although sometimes they are in matter and motion, as animal abstracts from reason although some animals are rational.[16]

The comparison with animal indicates that *ens* is abstracted as immaterial from data that include some immaterial instances. Just as one would never abstract animal from rational if one knew it only in humans, so too one would never abstract being from matter if one grasped it only in bodies. Aquinas is not drawing *ens commune* simply from sensible things.

IV

The standard neo-Thomist critique of Maritain is unassailable. Nevertheless, Maritain's position remains basically sound. For Aquinas *ens* means *habens esse*, and *esse* is grasped in judgment.[17] Maritain is, then, correct to begin Thomistic metaphysics with the judgmental grasp of the *esse* of sensible things. The defense of Maritain consists in correcting an overstatement on his part. Like most neo-Thomists, Maritain assumes that Thomistic metaphysics begins with the apprehension of a transphysical commonality. The assumption is not arbitrary. Aquinas specifies transphysical *ens* as the subject of metaphysics, and it seems only fair to initiate a science with its subject. Fairness aside, the assumption is the reef upon which neo-Thomistic ventures into metaphysics come to ruin. In this respect, neither the natural philosophy nor the transcendental Thomist approaches to Thomistic metaphysics do any better than Maritain's.[18] Nevertheless, there is an indication that transphysical *ens* is not the entry point of Aquinas' metaphysics. Transphysical *ens* characterizes the subject of metaphysics at a later and mature stage of reflection. The metaphysician formulates the notion after he alone, according to Aquinas, demonstrates an immaterial being in the form of a separate substance or the rational soul.[19]

Prior to that stage, the consideration of the metaphysician is targeted upon the *esse* of simply sensible things.

What is the Thomistic indication I am speaking of? Question 44, 2c, of the *Prima Pars* catches Aquinas in the act of initiating metaphysics simply from the judgmental grasp of the *esse* of sensible things. Simply *habens esse* specifies the consideration of the metaphysician. In the *responsio* Aquinas presents a three-fold breakdown of the history of philosophy. In Aquinas' eyes, philosophy has done more than spin on its heels. Little by little (*paulatim*) and step by step (*pedetentim*), philosophers advanced in a knowledge of the truth. Especially to be noted is what distinguishes the three stages. The principle of distinction is not increasing immateriality but increasing penetration of the sensible given.

At the first stage the given is analyzed into the components of substance and accident. The first of these is regarded as eternal. Progress to the second stage is made from the recognition of substantial change. Substances themselves transmute. Change in this zone of the sensible given leads to understanding substance itself as a composition of substantial form and matter--the latter being uncreated. This deeper penetration of the sensible given allows reasoning to a more encompassing cause. In Aristotle's hands, matter/form reasoning went as far as the oblique circle--a reference to the celestial sphere responsible for the movement of the sun.

Finally, advance is made to a third consideration--*ens inquantum est ens.* The nature of this third consideration is not delineated. By extrapolating from the first two stages, however, one can understand the third consideration--at least in a rudimentary way. The consideration of the first stage is denominated *ens inquantum tale ens.* As noted, the object of the consideration is composite--a substance in the light of its accidental determinations. The consideration of the second stage is denominated *ens inquantum hoc ens.* Again, the object characterizes the consideration; the object is a composite--the thing in the light of its substantial form. With this procedure in mind, *ens inquantum ens* should signal a consideration marked by the discovery of a still more profound region in the sensible given. Will this region not be the thing's *esse*? Such is a safe bet. Earlier at 8, 1c, *esse* is described as what is most intimate (*magis intimum*) and deeply set (*profundius*) in creatures. Also at *De Potentia* III, 5c - a parallel text to 44, 2c, the third stage of the history of philosophy is said to be marked by a "*consideratio ipsius esse universalis.*" Every indication is that the consideration of *ens inquantum ens* is a consideration of the sensible given as *habens esse.*

For my purposes four points can be taken from 44, 2c. First, in the third stage, Aquinas finds a distinct philosophical consideration of the sensible given. This consideration is not specified in terms of accidental and substantial form but in terms of *esse*--existential act.

Second, the third stage is described in terminology otherwise used to characterize the subject of metaphysics. The terminology of 44, 2, is *ens inquantum est ens*; in *In De Trin.*, V, 4c, the subject of metaphysics is identically expressed.

Third, Aquinas' 44, 2, portrayal of the history of philosophy as it rises to the metaphysical stage is not marked by increasing immateriality but by increasing profundity. Each succeeding viewpoint goes deeper into the given. Only the causes, not the considerations, become more universal. The third stage reaches the most universal cause because it deals with the most basic principle in the sensible given. Fourth, Aquinas gives no indication of how the third stage is reached. As the basis for the second stage, he mentions substantial change. In the background, then, is Aristotle's trenchant analysis of *Physics* I, 7, for the intrinsic principles of change. The third stage contains no similar indication. Yet in the the *Prima Pars* and scattered in earlier writings are texts that argue for God on the basis of *esse*.[20] These texts should be explicating the third stage reasoning for the most universal cause. But, most importantly, they indicate how the consideration of *habens esse* is reached. According to the texts, to understand *esse* so that *esse* leads to God, *esse subsistens*, is to understand the *esse* of the thing as *praeter essentiam eius*: as besides its essence. This understanding immediately calls to mind Aquinas' doctrine of the two-fold operation of the intellect.[21] In its first operation the intellect spies the essence of the thing; in its second operation the intellect grasps the thing's *esse*. The consideration of the third stage would have been reached by reflection upon the intellect's two-fold operation.

In sum, the third stage of 44, 2, shows Aquinas presenting metaphysics simply in terms of *habens esse* rather than *ens commune*. To move to a consideration of *ens inquantum est ens*, it suffices to grasp the sensible real as *habens esse*. The text shows no preoccupation with understanding *ens* as able to be in matter as well as apart from matter. The sole concern is with *ens* as *habens esse*. In the formulae for the three various considerations, the first *ens* seems to be consistently just the *sensible* existent.[22]

V

In conclusion, *Prima Pars* 44, 2, catches Aquinas in the act of presenting metaphysics simply in terms of *habens esse*. No Thomistic need exists to burden Maritain's intuition of being with the intellectual perception of a transphysical commonality.

The first mentioned sense of the intuition of being can be dropped and the second retained. Pruned of that excess, Maritain's position avoids the major philosophical criticism directed against it. In that light, Maritain's intuition of being is an enduring contribution to metaphysical reflection.

University of St. Thomas

NOTES

1. Maritain, *Existence and the Existent*, trans. by Lewis Galantiere and Gerald B. Phelan (New York: Vintage Books, 1966), p. 19. Other references to this sense of *être* are: *A Preface to Metaphysics* (New York: Mentor Omega Books, 1962), p. 49; *The Degrees of Knowledge*, trans. by Gerald B. Phelan (New York: Charles Scribner's Sons, 1959), p. 215.

2. *Degrees*, p. 210.

3. *Ibid.*, pp. 212-213.

4. *Ibid.*, p. 214. By way of clarification, not contradiction, Maritain subsequently acknowledges that this grasp of possible immaterial beings is as yet "entirely undetermined." One is not yet talking about possible human souls, pure spirits, or subsistent being.

5. *Existence*, p. 19. Other references include: *Preface*, p. 51; *Approaches to God*, trans. by Peter O'Reilly (New York: Collier Books, 1962), p. 18; *The Peasant of the Garrone*, trans. by Michael Cuddihy and Elizabeth Hughes (New York: Holt, Rinehart and Winston, 1968), p. 134.

6. In *Existence*, p. 36, Maritain remarks that *l'acte d'exister* is the act and the perfection of all form and all perfection and then quotes to this end Aquinas' *De Pot.*, VII, 2, ad 9m, mention of *esse*.

7. *Existence*, p. 26. See also p. 20.

8. *Ibid.*, p. 28, n. 14. Cf. "There is finally a concept of being which the mind forms in itself upon a judgment of existence sufficiently penetrating and sufficiently spiritual to read through the empirical conditions of the existing given. . . ." Olivier Lacombe, "Jacques Maritain Metaphysician," *The New Scholasticism*, 46 (1972), p. 22.

9. *Existence*, p. 18. Also, *Degrees*, p. 97.

10. *Approches sans Entraves* (Paris: Fayard, 1973), p. 264. In his "Maritain's Three Concepts of Existence," *The New Scholasticism*, 49 (1975), pp. 298-9, Joseph Owens notes that in Aquinas the situation is more complicated. Every use of the copula bears upon *esse*, substantial or accidental.

11. *Approches*, p. 271.

12. Just how the mind is led to make an affirmative existential judgment remains a mystery in Maritain. This is especially true given Maritain's earlier presentation of judgment as essentially copulative. As noted, judgment reintegrates the abstracted nature or essence with its extra-mentally existing subject. How does this analysis elucidate affirmative existential judgments?

13. This criticism is found in Joseph Marechal, *Le Point de départ de la métaphysique*, V, as partially edited and translated by Joseph Donceel, *A Maréchal Reader* (New York: Herder and Herder, 1970), p. 146. For a list of neo-Thomists who require a proof of immaterial being to grasp transphysical *ens*, see my "*Ad Mentem Thomae* Does Natural Philosophy Prove God?",forthcoming in the 1987 *Proceedings of the American Catholic Philosophical Association.*

14. *De Ente et Essentia*, ch. 3; as trans. by Armand Maurer, *On Being and Essence* (Toronto: Pontifical Institute of Mediaeval Studies, 1968), p. 46.

15. *In De Trin.* V, 3c; as trans. by Armand Maurer, *The Division and Methods of the Sciences* (Toronto: Pontifical Institute of Mediaeval Studies, 1963), p. 32.

16. *Ibid.*, V, 4, ad 5m; Maurer, *The Division*, pp. 48-49.

17. See Gerald B. Phelan, "A Note on the Formal Object of Metaphysics," in *G.B. Phelan Selected Papers* (Toronto: Pontifical Institute of Mediaeval Studies, 1967), as edited by Arthur G. Kirn, pp. 64-66; "The Existentialism of St. Thomas," *ibid.*, pp. 74-55, 80-81. On the judgmental grasp of *esse*, see *infra*, n. 21.

18. For problems in these other approaches, see my "Immateriality and Metaphysics", forthcoming in the 1987 volume of *Angelicum*.

19. At *In De Trin.*, V, 4c, the natural knowledge of God and separate substances is exclusively reserved to the philosopher who reasons from being as being. The latter is the subject of metaphysics. At *In VI Meta.*, lect. 1, n. 1159, Aquinas also reserves to metaphysics the knowledge of the human soul as separable from matter.

20. *S.T.*, I, 3, 4c, first arg.; *S.C.G.*, I, 22, *Amplius. Si*; the Marietti ed. of *De Ente*, ch. V, n. 4, p. 17. For texts in the commentary on the *Sentences*, see Joseph Owens, "Quiddity and Real Distinction in St. Thomas Aquinas," *Mediaeval Studies*, 27 (1965), p. 18, n. 32.

21. *In I Sent.*, d. 19, q. 5, a. 1, ad 7m; d. 38, q. 1, a. 3, Solut. Also *In De Trin.*, V, 3c.

22. Why does Aquinas so often present the subject of metaphysics in terms of the transphysical commonality of *ens*? A plausible answer is provided by Joseph Owens. From a study of the texts, Owens sees the Thomistic presentation as motivated by the need to launder Aristotelian metaphysical terminology for Christian theological purposes. For Aristotle, metaphysics dealt with the "separate" in the sense of immaterial beings. In a Christian context this understanding of metaphysics would make revealed theology a branch of metaphysics--something intolerable. To safeguard the autonomy of revealed theology yet permit continued use of Aristotle's "separate" terminology, Aquinas made metaphysics bear upon common notions that were separate from matter in the sense that they could be found outside of matter as well as within matter. See Owens' "Metaphysical Separation in Aquinas," *Mediaeval Studies*, 34 (1972), p. 306; "Aquinas as Aristotelian Commentator," as edited by John Catan, *St. Thomas Aquinas on the Existence of God* (Albany: State University of New York Press, 1980), pp. 4-12.

L'intuition de l'être chez Maritain

Bertrand Rioux

Summary

Maritain often treats of intuition: the intuition of being, creative intuition in art and poetry, the experience of the self, affective knowledge through moral experience. He has explored all the avenues leading to the mind. In contradistinction from Kant, for whom intuition can be only sensible, Maritain speaks of an abstractive intuition of the human intellect, which apprehends directly reality, not concepts.

Perception of being on the metaphysical level takes place in a judgment of existence. It is an immediate grasp of the act of being, a grasp which appreciates being as analogous. It is not something simply of the psychological or the moral order; it is deeper, the most primordial of all experiences. Its object is the intellect's object *par excellence*. It is also not mystical; it can be explicated by concepts.

***

L'intuition de l'être est au coeur de la philosophie de Maritain. Il écrit en effet: "Il ne suffit pas de rencontrer le mot être, de dire "être," il faut avoir l'intuition, la perception intellectuelle de l'inépuisable et incompréhensible réalité ainsi manifestée comme objet. C'est cette intuition qui fait le métaphysicien."[1] Ce thème de l'intuition déborde le domaine de la métaphysique puisqu'il est omniprésent dans l'oeuvre du grand philosophe français qu'il s'agisse de l'intuition eidétique de l'être ou de l'intuition du moi-agent en tant que l'intelligence perçoit par une réflexion spontanée sur son acte concret et singulier l'existence même de l'âme qui connaît,[2] mais aussi d'une connaissance par connaturalité ou par sympathie et non-conceptuelle qui regroupe des expériences très différentes comme celle de l'homme vertueux, de l'expérience mystique du Soi ou l'expérience mystique surnaturelle issue de l'amour et, enfin, de la connaissance poétique. Toutes ces voies royales de l'esprit en source, Maritain les a explorées avec une profondeur inégalée. Nous nous en tiendrons à l'intuition de l'être, au fondement même de la métaphysique. Cette thèse capitale ne se comprend bien cependant que si l'on reconnaît que l'intelligence *voit*. C'est pour n'avoir pas reconnu l'intuitivité de l'intelligence que le positivisme et le Kantisme n'admettent pas que la métaphysique et la philosophie soient authentiquement des sciences et des connaissances capables de certitude démonstrative, universelle et nécessaire et c'est parce qu'il a compris que l'intelligence voit et qu'elle est faite pour l'être que Maritain est thomiste.[3]

Il nous faut fixer brièvement le sens du mot intuition. C'est dans le chapitre III de *La Philosophie bergsonienne* portant sur l'intuition et la durée qu'il établit les divers sens du mot "intuition". Le sens étymologique est "très voisin du mot vision" et se rapporte en premier lieu à la perception visuelle, qui restera toujours le type sensible et l'exemple le plus commode de toute intuition.[4] C'est par analogie que nous l'étendons aux autres sens comme à d'autres fonctions de connaissance. Au sens philosophique et selon une acception très large, l'intuition est "une connaissance ou une perception *immédiate*, une connaissance ou une perception *directe*, où la chose connue termine l'acte de connaissance sans intermédiaire, sans intermédiaire d'un moyen terme, où elle est *vue* en un mot."[5] Une connaissance immédiate sans aucun intermédiaire subjectif comme l'est une similitude intentionnelle ou objectif comme dans la connaissance chronologique ne se réalise que dans la connaissance que Dieu et l'ange ont d'eux-mêmes ainsi que dans la vision béatifique. En ce qui concerne une connaissance immédiate qui use toutefois d'une similitude de l'objet dans le sujet, on peut distinguer la *perception sensible* qui atteint la chose comme *physiquement présente* et la perception des choses par l'intellect angélique, l'intuition du moi-agent ou la perception introspective du moi et la perception intellectuelle dont l'objet direct et immédiat n'est plus un existant, mais un objet abstrait rendu présent à l'intelligence par un concept. C'est cette intuition que Maritain appelle intuition abstractive. Cette affirmation que l'intelligence jouit dans son ordre d'une intuition rejoint la position de saint Thomas.[6] Si Maritain parle d'une intuition eidétique de l'être au niveau métaphysique, c'est parce qu'il défend d'abord le droit de parler d'une intuition intellectuelle.

Par cette thèse fondamentale de l'intuition abstractive, Maritain veut mettre en relief la nature proprement intuitive de l'intellect ainsi que le caractère immédiat de la connaissance intellectuelle. Il s'agit de réconcilier dans l'homme la raison et l'intelligence, l'intuition et le discours et, plus particulièrement, l'intuition et l'abstraction en surmontant les deux positions extrêmes d'un intuitionisme purement rationaliste ou purement antirationnel. La position intermédiaire qui colle à "la condition charnelle de l'esprit" est celle d'une intuition intellectuelle qui ne s'exerce qu'en s'appuyant sur la connaissance sensible et qui use de l'abstraction comme passage de phantasme élaboré de la connaissance sensible au concept pour donner lieu à une intuition qui est la saisie ou la vision directe et immédiate d'une essence présente à l'intelligence grâce à un concept. Les expressions utilisées par saint Thomas peuvent nous convaincre qu'il s'agit bien d'une intuition intellectuelle. *"Intelligere dicit nihil aliud quam simplicem intuitum intellectus in id quod sibi est praesens intelligibile."* (I Sent. III, 4, 5.) *"Illa praesto esse dicuntur intellectui quae capacitatem ejus non excedunt, ut intuitio intellectus in eis figatur."* (Ver. 14, 9; cf. id., 15, ad 7.) *"Dicitur intellectus ex eo quod intus legit, intuendo essentiam rei"* (Ethie, VI, 5, n° 1179).[7]

Mais il faut ajouter que l'intelligence humaine ne voit qu'à condition d'abstraire et de discourir. Maritain écrit à cet effet "l'intelligence voit en concevant, et ne conçoit que pour voir."[8] Si l'intelligence voit en concevant, c'est que le concept ne s'oppose pas à une saisie immédiate du réel lui-même. Il n'est qu'un pur signe *quo* ou *in quo* par lequel ou dans lequel l'intelligence saisit le réel. La connaissance abstractive se termine à la chose même connue directement et non pas à l'idée ou à des objets-phénomènes. La philosophie moderne avec Descartes a séparé l'objet de la chose en sorte que la chose est devenue l'absurde chose en soi cachée derrière l'objet. On ne s'est pas aperçu que le phénomène ne peut être pensé que postérieurement à l'être et que nous arrivons toujours trop tard pour réduire le réel au connu puisque le connu est en prise directe avec le réel qui se révèle à nous comme ce qui est, ce dont l'acte est l'exister. C'est la même chose qui existe pour elle-même dans la réalité et pour moi dans le sujet connaissant grâce à l'existence intentionnelle qu'elle revêt en moi. Et il en est ainsi parce que l'intelligence a été informée par une similitude intentionnelle venant de l'objet sous l'action de l'intellect illuminant. L'intelligence connaît le réel même dans le concept qu'elle produit parce qu'elle était déjà devenue l'objet en acte premier. On voit bien que l'intuition intellectuelle humaine est une intuition rationnelle, elle n'est pas comme celle de l'esprit pur qui voit directement et immédiatement le réel lui-même à sa source dans des idées infusées par le créateur. Ce n'est pas l'intuition cartésienne qui porte sur des natures simples, ni l'intuition d'intelligibles séparés comme chez Platon, ni l'intuition hégélienne obtenue au terme d'un procès dialectique, ni l'intuition supra-intellectuelle de la durée chez Bergson. C'est une saisie intellectuelle d'un intelligible tiré du sensible. Cependant, parce que la raison est faculté du réel, l'intuition intellectuelle doit s'achever dans le jugement. En effet, écrit saint Thomas: *"Prima quidem operatio respicit ipsam naturam rei, secunda operatio respicit ipsum esse rei."*[9] L'intelligence ne se saisit pas des intelligibles qu'elle dégage de l'expérience des sens "pour contempler seulement dans ses idées le tableau des essences," mais bien pour les restituer à l'existence par l'acte en lequel s'achève et se consomme l'intellection, je veux dire par le jugement qui déclare: *ita est*, il en est ainsi.[10] Dans le jugement, l'intelligence ne fait pas que composer des concepts, mais elle affirme l'identité dans le réel de deux concepts distincts et eu égard à l'existence exercée par la chose. Le jugement ne construit l'énonciation que pour percevoir ce qui est uni ou distingué dans le réel et se saisir de l'exister

exercé par le réel.[11] Tout jugement, directement ou indirectement a une
fonction existentielle parce que le propre du jugement est d'affirmer
l'existence elle-même et de restituer les essences à l'existence.
L'intelligence se prononce sur le réel en rapport avec l'existence qu'il
exerce et situe tout sur le fondement super- catégorial de l'être. Il achève
l'intellection en composant l'objet de pensée avec l'exister qui est "la
perfection et la gloire de l'être et de l'intelligibilité." Le jugement fait
passer l'esprit du plan de l'*objet* présenté à la pensée au plan de la *chose* eu
égard à l'existence qu'elle détient ou exerce (actuellement ou
possiblement).[12] Cette unité que le jugement restitue au réel se trouvait
d'abord posée dans l'existence détenue par la chose. Cette existence dont se
saisit l'intelligence par et dans l'affirmation et non plus par l'abstraction à la
manière d'une essence est l'existence détenue par la chose. L'existence
n'est plus seulement appréhendée et signifiée, elle est affirmée comme
détenue à même l'acte de juger. L'intelligence se saisit de cet acte d'exister
que la chose exerce hors de l'esprit et qu'elle exprime par l'acte de juger qui
lui est propre.[13] L'acte d'affirmer de l'esprit répond à l'acte d'exister
exercé par les choses. L'intelligence vit l'intelligibilité propre de cet acte
d'exister d'une manière implicite et occulte car il demeure caché et
dissimulé. Il faudra l'intuition de l'être "au sommet de l'abstraction" pour le
dévoiler pleinement. Je ne connais pas beaucoup de philosophes qui,
comme Maritain, aient fait cet effort de réflexion pour donner au jugement
toute sa valeur du point de vue de la connaissance de l'être. Heidegger a
reculé devant la tâche en définissant le jugement comme un acte secondaire
et dérivé, enfermé dans la sphère de l'ontique alors que Maritain en
montrant que le jugement achève le dévoilement de l'étant du point de vue
de l'être, c'est à dire de l'acte d'exister, rendait possible le fondement de la
métaphysique de même qu'un discours sur l'être qui utiliserait l'analogie et
la participation.

C'est au plan métaphysique que Maritain parle d'une intuition de l'être
qui seule ouvre la porte à une métaphysique authentique. Par ailleurs, si le
jugement situe la saisie de l'être au plan de l'exister, cela ne signifie pas que
nous avons accès d'emblée à l'exister comme l'acte des actes et la
perfection des perfections, antérieur et supérieur à tout l'ordre des essences
qui deviennent alors des puissances d'exister et qui sont comprises comme
une *proportio ad esse* d'où dérivent leur être même et leur intelligibilité.[14]
Comment parvient-on à l'être comme acte, voilà ce qu'il faut décrire avec
attention. Maritain est conscient d'avoir été le premier philosophe thomiste
à chercher à faire la lumière sur cette question qui engage les ressources
secrètes de l'esprit. Il écrit en effet dans *Réflexions sur la nature blessée*:
"L'intuition de l'être a été vécue in *actu exercito* par saint Thomas et par les
thomistes (les bons thomistes), mais je ne connais pas (c'est peut-être dû à
mon ignorance) de traité de la *disquisitio* où elle ait été étudiée par eux in
actu signato."[15] Il semble que la meilleure façon de mettre en lumière

l'intuition de l'être au sommet de l'abstraction métaphysique, est de prendre conscience que nous avons deux concepts d'existence au moins, sinon trois. Le malheur est que nous utilisons un même mot pour signifier deux intelligibles différents, celui d'être-là et celui d'être, celui de *Dasein* et de *Sein*. Ces deux concepts diffèrent quant à l'origine: l'un a une origine abstractive et est saisi par mode d'essence au moyen d'une idée issue de l'abstraction du sensible alors que l'autre a une origine judicative en tant qu'il est consécutif à l'intuition de l'être. Ils diffèrent aussi quant au sens: le premier appartient au registre de l'être-là, de la présence à mon monde, du *Dasein*, le second à un sens purement existentiel en tant que l'être est pris absolument dans son universalité sans limites et intrinsèquement variée. Alors que le premier est limité au monde sensible, le second est un concept transcendantal et analogue. En regard de l'intuition de l'être, le concept d'existence ordinaire vient avant et ne fait pas partie intégrante de l'intuition de l'être. Il ne joue aucun rôle dans l'intuition de l'être et lui reste parfaitement étranger.[16] Au contraire, le second concept de l'*esse* vient après l'intuition de l'être "par retour de la simple appréhension, ou de l'intelligence comme formatrice d'idées, sur cette intuition." L'intelligence produit ce concept à partir de l'intuition de l'être et par retour sur elle. Ce concept n'a pas été tiré des phantasmes par l'opération abstractive comme c'est le cas des autres idées, mais il suit et provient d'un jugement d'existence. Il faut noter qu'il ne s'agit pas d'un jugement d'existence ordinaire puisque l'existence est comprise plus souvent et explicitement dans un substitut de l'être, celui d'être-là. Si j'affirme qu'il y a une rose, je comprends que *cette rose* est *là*. Le prédicat n'est pas l'existence dans son actualité absolue comme si je disais: cette rose *est*, mais bien cette rose m'est *présente*. Il s'agit d'une assertion copulative de présence à mon monde dans laquelle le "est" n'est pas un verbe-prédicat mais a une fonction de liaison du sujet et du prédicat "présent". C'est une proposition à trois termes où le verbe être est distinct du prédicat *présent à mon monde*. C'est bien pourquoi une philosophie qui ne résout pas l'être (*ens*) dans l'acte d'être reste ouverte à l'idéalisme. Seul le réalisme métaphysique qui fonde l'étant sur l'acte d'être peut échapper complètement à toute tentative de phénoménalisation du monde par la mise entre parenthèses de son existence. L'intuition de l'être a lieu dans un jugement affirmatif de l'exister: je suis et les choses sont. Elle concerne donc le jugement et non pas la simple appréhension abstractive. En affirmant l'exister comme tel et non pas un autre prédicat, l'intelligence voit que le "est" a un sens propre qui ne se dissout pas dans le sens de copule ou d'actualité empirique. Ce sens est unique parce qu'il fonde tous les autres actes d'ordre formel qui n'en sont qu'une participation et qu'il est donc l'acte ultime pour tout ordre de réalité en même temps que l'acte le plus intime à un être puisqu'il le fait être réel. L'intelligence voit que l'*ens* se prend de l'acte d'être - *ens sumitur ab actu essendi* - comme ce qui a pour acte d'exister. L'acte d'être est ainsi ce qu'il y a de plus formel en ce que l'essence elle-même bien que déterminée en elle-même reçoit l'exister comme un acte sans lequel elle ne serait rien. L'intelligence voit directement que l'acte d'exister est exercé en proportion de l'essence et qu'il est donc lui-même varié. Il n'est pas seulement un fait à constater, mais nous le pensons comme un acte. Le "est" est dégagé de son rapport au monde sensible et vu dans son amplitude infinie. Il est analogique et transcendantal par immanence en tout. Cet acte d'être est exercé par tout être et n'a pas d'abord la signification d'être causé. C'est un acte qui lui est immanent et propre. Etre ne signifie pas de soi exister dans le sens d'être causé. Etre pour la rose, ce n'est ni être *présente* dans mon jardin, ni être *perçue* ou pouvoir être perçue, ni être *actuellement*, ni venir à ma rencontre dans l'apparition pour moi, mais c'est exercer l'activité *d'être* qui la pose pour elle-même hors du néant et d'une manière absolument indépendante de ma connaissance. L'acte d'être rend présent l'étant présent en acte. Etre comme intuition intellectuelle de l'être en fonde la vue, c'est exercer pour soi cette activité fondamentale d'exister comme un acte immanent qui m'est singulier et propre au fondement même de ma substance individuelle. On voit ainsi le progrès que l'intelligence fait quand elle va "par *l'intelligence* même à *l'existence* même." Alors que l'oeil atteint des choses existantes sans *savoir qu'elles sont*, l'intelligence elle *sait* qu'elles sont - c'est pourquoi elle comprend l'être selon les deux aspects d'essence et d'exister-mais sans *voir* et reconnaître l'être lui-même - le *Sein* au coeur des choses - dans le substitut d'être-là.[17] L'exister n'est pas pensé comme tel et l'intelligence ne le *désigne qu'implicitement*. Le *Sein* est caché dans un autre concept, potentiellement contenu dans un autre intelligible ou encore aveuglément contenu et spiritualisé en puissance prochaine seulement[18]. L'intuition de l'être n'est pas l'expérience d'un singulier existant[19], mais la vue intellectuelle d'un acte singulier au fondement d'une réalité concrète, mais aussi universel en ce qu'il enveloppe toutes choses dans leur diversité. Cette intuition de l'être n'est pas non plus une expérience mystique du Soi ou de Dieu qui demeure non conceptuelle en elle-même. Elle n'est pas non plus une intuition poétique qui n'a pas son terme dans un concept comme dans la connaissance intellectuelle, mais "dans l'oeuvre extérieure en laquelle elle s'objective et qu'elle produit."[20]

Je voudrais discuter en terminant de l'opinion de thomistes éminents qui vont à l'encontre des vues de Maritain. Il s'agit, en particulier, de celles de P. Geiger et de Cornelio Fabro. L.-B. Geiger, quant à lui, croit que l'acte constitutif de la métaphysique consiste dans la *separatio* ou jugement négatif par lequel "on ne considère pas seulement des points de vue différents, mais on affirme la relative indépendance dans l'être de certains principes de l'être. Dans la *separatio*, comme en tout jugement, c'est sur la structure de l'être qu'on se prononce. On nie que tel principe de l'être soit ontologiquement solidaire en sa raison formelle de tel monde de l'être où l'expérience nous le présente réalisé en fait. On le dégage ainsi en la pureté

de sa raison formelle tout en le maintenant en relation avec le mode
déterminé où il a été découvert d'abord. La séparation fonde bien l'objet de
la métaphysique."[21] Ainsi dans le jugement l'homme est être, mais il n'est
pas l'être, mais ne sommes pas au niveau d'une simple appréhension
abstractive de l'être qui laisserait échapper l'immanence de l'être au profit
de son universalité alors qu'on ne peut pas considérer l'être à part de quoi
que ce soit. Dans l'acte de séparation au fondement de la métaphysique,
l'être est cette nature qu'on attribue à tout être - l'homme est être -, mais
aussi qu'on sépare de tout être par un jugement négatif - sans être l'être.
L'abstraction analogique ne peut être qu'une appréhension confuse de l'être
et doit faire place à un jugement négatif sur l'être. Quelle réponse Maritain
peut-il fournir à une réflexion aussi stimulante et respectueuse du caractère
unique de l'être? Il répond d'abord qu'un jugement négatif sur l'être qui
doit avoir un plan métaphysique et qui n'en reste pas au niveau de
l'extension de l'être et de son universalité enveloppant tous les autres êtres
doit être précédé d'un jugement positif d'existence où l'intelligence *voit* la
valeur transcendantale et analogique de l'*exister* comme principe au
fondement de l'essence en tant que cette dernière le participe et n'est qu'un
modus essendi. Si l'être "peut être séparé de la matière selon l'opération de
jugement (négatif), c'est qu'il se réfère dans son contenu à l'acte d'exister
signifié par le jugement (positif) et qui déborde la ligne des essences
matérielles, objet connaturel de la simple appréhension."[22] Ensuite,
l'abstraction de l'être en tant qu'être est une abstraction formelle au
troisième degré d'abstraction qui consiste dans une visualisation eidétique de
l'être appréhendé dans le jugement. C'est une intuition "abstractive" non
pas au premier niveau d'abstraction, mais au troisième et qui n'a un sens
métaphysique pleinement éclairant qu'en supposant la vue de l'exister
comme tel et dans sa valeur propre. C'est justement "selon un jugement
déclarant que l'être *n'est pas* nécessairement lié à la matière et se fait le
concept métaphysique de l'être en tant qu'être." L'acte de la *separatio* n'a
pas à se substituer à l'abstraction dite analogique du troisième degré
d'abstraction intensive, "cette "séparation" *est* l'abstraction analogique de
l'être."[23] Une dernière remarque doit être faite. Si les principales thèses du
P. Geiger peuvent être critiquées à juste titre, celles en particulier qui portent
sur la notion d'essence, sur son interprétation de la limitation par
composition d'une essence et d'un acte d'être et sur les degrés de l'être, cela
est dû fondamentalement à son interprétation formaliste de l'être qui, malgré
le vocabulaire employé qui fait souvent illusion, en reste à la compréhension
aristotélicienne de l'être en acte sans parvenir vraiment à l'*esse ut actus*.

C'est le reproche que fait avec raison Fabro à Geiger, mais la surprise
est grande quand on voit cet éminent thomiste n'accorder dans ce débat
qu'une importance minime à Maritain, et, surtout, quand il accuse ce dernier
d'en rester au premier concept d'existence qui concerne la réalité du
composé. Il est difficile d'être plus injuste envers un auteur dont la gloire

même entre autres mérites immenses est d'avoir mis l'*esse* comme acte d'être au coeur de la métaphysique. En effet, dans son grand livre *Participation et Causalité selon S. Thomas d'Aquin*, Fabro ne mentionne le nom de Maritain que deux fois et, encore, par l'intermédiaire d'auteurs qui le citent comme A. Marc et F.- X. Maquart.[24] A aucun moment, il ne discute sérieusement les thèses de Maritain selon une lecture de première main de ses oeuvres. Ce qu'il lui reproche en tout cas, c'est de réduire l'*esse* à l'existence parce qu'il se serait arrêté à la correspondance directe entre l'*esse* du jugement et l'actualité du réel auquel le jugement se conforme. L'auteur a sans doute été trompé par l'emploi du même mot existence dans le cas de l'emploi ordinaire que nous faisons du concept d'existence comme au niveau de l'intuition eidétique de l'exister comme acte. De plus, l'insistance qu'apporte Maritain avec raison à montrer que l'âme du jugement consiste dans l'affirmation de l'existence peut donner à penser à tort qu'il en reste à la valeur existentielle du jugement. Pourtant, le philosophe français s'emploie à effectuer ce passage de l'existence affirmée dans tout jugement à l'exister vu pour lui-même comme *actus essentiae* dans un jugement "*qui est d'un autre type que tous les autres jugements*,"[25] car en pensant vraiment cette affirmation de l'exister, elle le saisit intuitivement, directement et immédiatement (*statim et sine discursu* comme le répète sans cesse saint Thomas). Il y a là le passage de la notion méthodologique de l'être décrit selon les deux aspects d'essence et d'existence à la notion métaphysique de l'exister *ut actus*. En ce qui concerne une certaine "*intuitio abstractiva*" dont quelques auteurs parlent expressément et dont Fabro ne nomme aucun représentant, il souligne sans discuter le fond de la question, qu'il s'agit d'une terminologie inconnue de saint Thomas et "dont la composition même dénonce l'embarras et l'expédient purement verbal."[26] Nous avons dit plus haut que d'autres auteurs ont pourtant reconnu que cette expression qu'on ne trouve pas comme telle chez saint Thomas exprime la pensée profonde de l' Aquinate. Le P. Fabro réserve quant à lui le nom d'intuition à la perception d'une substance singulière ou d'un acte singulier, mais jamais un acte premier ne peut être objet d'une intuition, y compris l'acte premier entitatif qui est l'*esse* comme *actus essendi*.[27] Mais si l'intuition de l'être a lieu dans ce jugement "d'un autre type que tous les autres jugements" il est possible à l'intelligence de percevoir l'acte d'être lui-même comme détenu et non seulement signifié par et dans l'acte même d'affirmer l'exister. Par ailleurs, il faut noter l'embarras du P. Fabro lui-même quand il décrit la méthode de la métaphysique thomiste.

Elle n'est, écrit-il "ni intuitive, ni démonstrative, mais "résolutive"; ce qui veut dire qu'elle procède des déterminations vagues aux déterminations plus propres, d'acte à acte, de puissance à puissance, des actes multiples et superficiels aux actes plus constants et profonds, et ainsi jusqu'au dernier ou premier acte qui est l'*esse*."[28] Il s'agit d'une "fondation" et cette forme de "passage" "ne peut être sans une certaine expérience ou appréhension directe." Mais le procès de fondation pourrait-il avoir un sens, s'il n'impliquait l'émergence de l'acte ultime qui doit être présent au point de départ pour justifier le procès lui-même? Autrement, il n'y aurait qu'un procès logique sans aucun éclairage métaphysique. C'est pourquoi, l'auteur parle d'une "intuition implicite", en entendant par là la "co-présence" de l'*esse* en toute présence ou présentation d'existence....."[29] Cette intuition implicite est pourtant inefficace pour assurer l'émergence dans la conscience à l'acte d'être. Ce n'est là qu'une condition nécessaire mais non suffisante pour rendre compte de l'émergence de l'*esse* en toute clarté. On en revient donc ainsi à la nécessité d'une intuition eidétique de l'être. L'analyse "résolutive" est une analyse rationnelle qui montre la nécessité de l'être en tant qu'être comme objet suprême de la connaissance. On peut, en effet, montrer que c'est en apparence seulement qu'on peut se passer du concept d'être et d'existence puisqu'il est pensé implicitement en tant que ce que nous pensons. Il est aussi facile de montrer que tous nos concepts se résolvent dans le concept d'être comme le fait saint Thomas dans l'article premier du *De Veritate*. On peut montrer ainsi qu'il doit y avoir un acte au fondement de tous les autres actes et selon un ordre à part des déterminations essentielles. Cette analyse rationnelle est nécessaire, et "sans une telle analyse rationnelle, on risquerait d'avoir une intuition non confirmée en raison, dont la nécessité rationnelle ne serait pas rendue manifeste."[30] Si d'autre part, on en restait à la seule analyse rationnelle, on verrait bien la nécessité d'une telle intuition comme semble le reconnaître Fabro, mais à elle toute seule elle ne fournirait pas une telle intuition, et, comme dans le cas des cheminements concrets qui préparent une telle intuition, elle laisserait l'intelligence au seuil de cette intuition sans pouvoir d'elle-même la produire en nous. Il faut donc admettre ce que Maritain affirmait déjà dès 1934 dans les *Sept leçons sur l'être* qu'une analyse rationelle confirmative et l'intuition doivent aller ensemble.[31]

Université de Montréal

NOTES

1. *Sept leçons sur l'être*, Paris, Téqui, 1934, p. 52.

2. *La philosophie bergsonienne*, 3e éd., Paris, Téqui, 1944, p. 127, en note.

3. *Raison et raisons*, Paris, Eglof, 1947, pp. 21-22.

4. *La philosophie bergsonienne*, p. 125.

5. *Ibid.*, p. 125.

6. R. Jolivet, *L'intuition intellectuelle et le problème de la métaphysique, Archives de philosophie*, XI, 2; Péghaire, *"Intellectus et ratio"* chez saint Thomas; R. Verneaux, *Epistémologie générale*.

7. *Epistémologie générale*, pp. 78-79.

8. *La philosophie bergsonienne*, p. XXIX.

9. *In Boeth., de Trin.*, V. 3.

10. J. Maritain, *Court traité de l'existence et de l'existant*, chap. 1, "L'être", pp. 25-26.

11. *Raison et raisons*, p. 22.

12. J. Maritain, *Court traité...*, p. 34.

13. *Ibid.*, p. 35.

14. Marie-Vincent Leroy, "Le Savoir spéculatif" in J. Maritain, *RT*, 1948, p. 284.

15. *Approches sans entrave*, Paris, Fayard, 1973, p. 267, en note.

16. *Ibid.*, p. 266.

17. *Ibid.*, pp. 267ss; *Court traité...*, pp. 49-50, en note.

18. *Ibid.*, pp. 275-176.

19. *Sept leçons...*, p. 68.

20. *Quatre essais sur l'esprit*, Paris, Desclée, 1939, p. 141.

21. *La participation dans la philosophie de S. Thomas d'Aquin*, 2e éd., Paris, Vrin, 1953, p. 318.

22. *Court traité...*, p. 51, en note.

23. *Ibid.*, p. 52, en note.

24. *Participation et causalité*, Louvain et Paris, Beatrice Nauwelearts, 1961, pp. 63 et 289.

25. *Approches sans entraves*, p. 264.

26. *Participation et causalité*, p. 80.

27. *Ibid.*, p. 80.

28. *Ibid.*, p. 80.

29. *Ibid.*, p. 80

30. *Sept leçons...*, pp. 63-64.

31. *Ibid.*, p. 64.

BERGSONIAN RECOLLECTIONS IN MARITAIN

Peter A. Redpath

That Jacques Maritain is one of the greatest, if not the greatest, Catholic intellect of the twentieth century is something which most members of the American and Canadian Maritain Associations would readily admit. Yet it is this very greatness of Maritain which makes him somewhat enigmatic. For, on the one hand, his reputation for greatness is partly built upon his association with the work of St. Thomas; on the other hand, however, his reputation lies in the very original manner in which he utilizes the wisdom of St. Thomas to confront issues of modern and contemporary thought. Indeed, Maritain's originality is, at times, so profound that it is easier to read St. Thomas in order to get some insight into Maritain than it is to read Maritain to get some insight into St. Thomas.

This paper is devoted to Maritain's originality. As such, it is designed to get some awareness of the creative genius of Maritain; it seeks to probe the core of Maritain's thinking so as to uncover how, if in any way, Maritain's thinking departs from the thought of the Angelic Doctor so as to give Maritain's teaching an essence of its own - an essence which makes it Maritainian as opposed to Thomistic or Bergsonian, or anything else.

It seems fitting that such an undertaking begin with an intuition for, as a student of Bergson, and given his way of interpreting St. Thomas, Maritain himself would agree that this is the most appropriate place to begin. Indeed, if, as we contend, Maritain is one of the greatest Catholic intellects of our time, Maritain's own words dictate that we begin with intuition, for he says as much directly in *Bergsonian Philosophy and Thomism*. "It is true," he states, "as Bergson has expressed it,...that each of the great philosophers has spent his whole life developing in every possible direction, a single intuition; in reality the intuition in question has been an intellectual intuition, a living intellectual perception expressible in concepts."[1]

The question which we wish to consider in this paper is, "Is there a single intuition expressible in ideas or concepts which formally distinguishes Maritain's thought as Maritainian, and, if there is, what is it?" What we wish to propose in this paper is that we seek to answer this question by looking at

Maritain's work, *Bergsonian Philosophy and Thomism*, as Maritain's own intellectual autobiography. Within this work, we wish to suggest, is indeed contained the seed of the fruit which blossoms later on in works such as *Existence and the Existent* and *Degrees of Knowledge*. To understand these later works of Maritain, one must, we think, first understand the original intuition which began to take root in Maritain's first book - for just as the whole of any science is contained in its principles so, in a way, the whole of Maritain's thought is contained in *Bergsonian Philosophy and Thomism*.

What, however, is the intuitional seed which lies at the foundation of Maritainianism? We contend that it is the intuition that the Bergsonian critique of the intellect could be rectified within the wisdom of St. Thomas. For Maritain the primary mistake of the Bergsonian doctrine of intuition is that it opposes intuition to the idea, to the concept, to abstract knowledge, and to reasoning. It presumes that an intuitive grasp of the real, true attainment of the real, must occur without a subjective intermediary between the subject and the object. For Bergson, that is, true apprehension of the real must be a lived coincidence which takes place without the intervention of concepts or of the intellect. This is so because concepts for Bergson are wholly practical instruments (they are wholly utilitarian signs), and because for him the human intellect is not made for truth - it is made to fabricate. For Bergson man is not *homo sapiens*; he is *homo faber*.[2]

Having made concepts and the intellect obstacles to knowledge, rather than its specific instruments, having made the function of ideas and of the intellect something practical rather than something speculative, Bergson, Maritain thinks, is forced by logical necessity to seek the specific instrument of philosophy in a non-conceptual and non-intellectual reality. As Maritain sees it, philosophical intuition for Bergson "is sought outside of and above the normal functions of the intellect. It is called *supra-intellectual* intuition."[3] For Bergson the specific instrument of philosophy is neither the concept nor the intellect; it is spirit and intuition. Beyond the concept and abstraction, "intuition bears upon spirit."[4] "In other words, a direct and supra-conceptual grasp of the nature of spirit, an immediate and concrete perception of the metaphysical universe, fugitive as it is said to be and contrary to the natural bent of the intellect, is the sole organ proportionate with philosophical knowledge to the extent that this knowledge rises above matter."[5]

In Maritain's mind the mistakes made by Bergson about the matter of the nature of the intellect, of the concept, and of intuition, were no small errors. They were mistakes which Maritain would recall for the rest of his life, and the intuition of these mistakes was, we believe, the negative first principle of Maritainian thought. We think, however, that these egregious errors of Bergson caused in Maritain a mistake of equally egregious proportions. For, just as Bergson had gone wrong in reducing the concept to a practical tool, and the intellect to a practical device, so Maritain was equally wrong in attempting to counteract Bergson's extremism with an extremism of his own.

The Bergsonian critique of the intellect and of the intuition could be restored, Maritain thought, within the framework of the epistemology of St. Thomas, but the key to this restoration lay in recognizing that the proper order of the intellect, of the concept, and of philosophy, is not the practical order, but the speculative order. "...Bergsonian philosophy," Maritain states, "operates with the intellect not according to its proper and properly speculative mode...."[6] For philosophy properly so-called "approaches things *modo speculativo* only."[7] Indeed even practical philosophy is philosophy for Maritain only because it is speculative in its mode. For him the proper mode of the intellect is not fabrication; it is speculation. Hence the proper mode of philosophy and of philosophy's proper instrument - the concept - is similarly speculation, not fabrication.[8]

The philosophical consequences of this sort of speculative reductionism on Maritain's part are nothing short of enormous. Maritain was convinced that Bergson's practicalistic reductionism had led Bergson to misunderstand the nature of the intellect an to view philosophical intuition as a violent and unnatural act, albeit one which produces metaphysical ecstasy.[9] Maritain thought that if Bergsonian philosophy were rehabilitated according to a properly speculative philosophical mode it would, as he himself put it, "release and order its potencies in the great wisdom of St. Thomas."[10] It is our contention that the doctrine of Jacques Maritain is this rehabilitated Bergsonianism releasing an ordering its potencies in the great wisdom of St. Thomas. What we find in Maritain is an "inverted"[11] Bergsonianism translating into the language of later scholastic Thomism and speculative metaphysics the major principles of Bergsonian thought.

To support this contention let us take a look more closely at some of the criticisms which Maritain levels against Bergsonian philosophy in general and specifically, and let us consider whether or not we find Maritain applying inverted Bergsonianism to his own interpretation of St. Thomas. When we do this we find Maritain faulting Bergson for doing the following: 1) seeking philosophical intuition over and above the normal function of the intellect; 2) denying to the concept its proper role as the specific instrument of philosophy, and incorrectly appropriating this role for spirit (a felt and lived coincidence of the human subject in the process of becoming); 3) attributing to non-conceptual intuition a speculative and metaphysical grasp of the real - a grasp which is said to be contrary to the natural bent of the intellect; 4) making the concept a practical tool; 5) making the proper activity of the intellect practical; 6) identifying the real with becoming rather than with being; 7) presuming that, for intuition to attain the real, intuition cannot occur with any subjective intermediary; and 8) failing to make a real distinction between God and the world.[12]

Having found these faults in Bergson, Maritain was, nonetheless, both indebted to Bergson and convinced that Bergsonian thought could be rectified. He himself put it: "I have several times remarked in my book that, if one were to transfer to intellectual perception properly so called - which takes place by means of abstraction, and whose object is being - certain of the values and privileges that Bergson attributes to 'intuition,' the Bergsonian critique of the intellect would find itself as it were immediately rectified and, instead of ruining our natural power of attaining the true, would be directed only against the wrong use of it."[13] Maritain's problem, however, was how precisely to rehabilitate the Bergsonian intuition by transferring to speculative intellectual abstraction some of its values and privileges.

Obviously this could not be done unless one were to know precisely where Bergson goes wrong in his own doctrine. According to Maritain, the "essential vice" of the Bergsonian doctrine of intuition lies in "undertaking from a wrong angle to deal with the immediate character of intuitive knowledge...." In doing this, "it supposes that all knowledge truly attaining the real must be a lived coincidence, without subjective intermediary of the subject and the object, thus known, it is thought, in all the plentitude of its reality, thus exhausted to the very root; Bergsonism then opposes its intuition to the idea, to the concept, to abstract knowledge - and to reason, to discursive knowledge."[14]

To remedy this situation the key for Maritain is to consider knowledge of the real to be a lived coincidence, not without subjective intermediary but with it. Knowledge of the real does not occur without ideas; it occurs with them. Thus intuition is not opposed to conceptualization, abstraction, reasoning, or discursive knowledge; it is naturally joined to them. In thus considering knowledge, however, two problems occur: 1) what becomes of the genuine intuition of the Bergson of fact; and 2) what justification do we give for claiming that intuition can use subjective intermediaries and still be called "intuition"?

With respect to the first question, the genuine intuition of Bergson is resituated by Maritain in the realm of productive knowledge (*poieton*). "If one brings this 'intuition' back to its true proportions...," Maritain tells us, "one finds oneself facing an effect of the whole being which normally has its place in the creative invention of the artist or in the psychological application to an internal observation. This effort remains intellectual but, because it is a question of penetrating the contingent singular, the intelligence in it is 'pushed out of doors,' into the domain peculiar to sense."[15]

For Bergson metaphysical intuition of real duration ends "in a fusion of the mind in the thing, it transports us into the object and identifies us by an intense and even painful effort of sympathy with what is unique, inexpressible, incommunicable in the thing,...with matter itself - which, united to form, makes the singularity of the thing."[16] Metaphysical intuition thus "projects us into the object and makes us coincide with reality in its very depth. This intuition, according to Bergson, is related to animal instinct much more than to reason and, because Bergsonian intuition has a purely speculative nature, whereas everything in us is ordered to practice, this intuition 'demands of us an effort contrary to nature.'"[17]

Now, is not this description of Bergson's metaphysical intuition an uncanny verisimilitude of Maritain's view of the philosophy of art? For Maritain philosophy *qua* philosophy is speculative. Science is of the universal. It is achieved in intellectual abstraction, and is the proper domain of man-the- rational-animal. Man *qua* man is at home in the speculative realm. His knowledge, strictly speaking, is a speculative apprehension of universals, and his abstractive intuition consists in removing from the object of knowledge whatever is material, contingent, and particular.[18] Hence, at best, man has only an indirect knowledge of the singular by reflection from the senses or by affective connaturality. Man's intellect is projected into the unique, inexpressible, and incommunicable in a thing through affective sympathy, and, thereby, finds itself in a place much more related to instinct than to reason. Since everything in philosophical intuition is ordered to speculation, this intellectual projection, in a way, demands an effort contrary to the nature of the intellect and philosophy. Maritain himself states:

In order to...establish a general theory of art and making we must have recourse to the highest and most universal concepts and principles of human knowledge. Such a theory therefore belongs to the domain of philosophy.

The province of philosophy thus defined is indeed practical, since it is concerned with making, and its object is to order from above the branches of practical instruction. Nevertheless, since it is in the strict sense a science, it cannot be essentially practical, but remains essentially speculative in virtue of its object, method, and procedure; moreover it is extremely remote from actual practice. Indeed not only has it no concern with the application of rules of art to a particular work to be accomplished, but further it formulates rules which are far too general to be capable of such immediate application and to be correctly termed rules of art in the strict sense; it is therefore practical only in an improper sense and very imperfectly.[19]

Having thus placed Bergson's own intuition into the realm of the creative artist, Maritain is still left with the question of how intuition can remain intuition and yet be a lived coincidence with a subjective intermediary. The answer for Maritain lies in rehabilitating the notion of intuition and in relocating both intuition and speculative concepts within the range of intellectual abstraction. Maritain puts it this way:

For Bergson, as for St. Thomas, knowledge, if it attains the absolute, must be a vital act which establishes a sympathy, a communication, a real assimilation between object and subject. But he ascribes this act to an intuition foreign to the intellect, contrary to our nature, an intuition which absorbs the spirit in the materiality of the object. St. Thomas on the contrary teaches that by intellectual perception it is the object itself which, thanks to 'abstraction,' being present in the understanding, makes it produce like a common first fruit of life the mental word (*verbum mentis*) and thus finds itself assimilated to the immateriality of intelligence. The latter then becomes the object in a perfectly vital way.[20]

For Bergson the real signifies time, and intuition is the lived and felt coincidence of the duration of the subject and the duration of the object in the materiality of the thing.[21] For Maritain, on the other hand, the real signifies being, and intuition is the lived and felt coincidence of the being of the subject and the being of the object in an intellectually immaterial super-existence of the subject.[22]

The problem for Maritain, however, is to express as best he can in the epistemological language of St. Thomas how the being of the subject and of the object coincide in intellectual intuition. Maritain accomplishes this goal by doing three things. 1) He extends the meaning of the word 'intuition' to cover both the scholastic and Bergsonian senses. (For him the scholastic sense of intuition is knowledge of a singular, physically present reality, while the Bergsonian sense of intuition is an immediately felt and speculative projection of spirit into the matter of the real.) Maritain's own meaning of intuition is a direct knowledge of a thing which does not result from reasoning. 2) Maritain distinguishes among three Thomistic meanings of intuition as a direct perception: a) sense intuition in which we directly perceive an individual physical being not in its essence but in the action it exerts upon our organs of sensation in its accidents here and now in space and time; b) a directly and immediately felt intuition of the active self connaturally obtained in the apprehension of the intellect's own operations; and c) intellectual abstraction. 3) To correspond to these three meanings of intuition as direct perception he distinguishes three forms of *esse*: a) *esse naturae*; b) *esse cognitum seu objectivum*; and c) *esse intentionale*.[23]

The coincidence of the subject and the object in intellectual intuition requires for Maritain all of the above, that is: 1) extending the meaning of intention; 2) the three meanings of direct perception; and 3) the three forms of *esse*). It especially requires the last of these, which Maritain states is founded upon the use of the real distinction between *esse* and nature in everything which is not God.[24] The reason for needing all these divisions is that, for the subject and the object to coincide in a sympathy of being, a union between the subject and the object must take place in an existence which is neither accidental, subjective, nor objective. He says:

The essence of such an activity [intellectual intuition] is not to produce but to *become* or to *be*, in virtue of oneself, infinitely above and beyond simple existence in one's own nature; so that, becoming thus by intellection that which is not us, knowledge does not only issue complete from the knowing mind; at the same time it issues complete from the object known.

It is so true that what formally constitutes intellection is a certain doubling of existence, or rather, if I may say so, an active *superexistence*, peculiar to spiritual natures...."[25]

The way this superexistential union is achieved is, for Maritain, through an immaterial transformation of knowledge.[26] Knowledge must be made to pass from one essential degree to another through the abstraction of the *intellectus agens.*[27] For Maritain, "there is a rigorous correspondence between knowledge and immateriality. A being is knowledgeable in the measure of its immateriality."[28] The reason for this is that to know is "to become another thing than oneself."[29] To know, that is, for Maritain, consists

> in a degree of existence greater than that of being removed from nothingness: it is an active, immaterial super-existence, by which a subject exists no longer only in an existence limited to what it is as a thing included in a certain kind, as a subject existing in itself, but with an unlimited existence in which it is or becomes so by its own rightful activity and that of others. To know then becomes identical with advancing oneself to an act of existence of super-eminent perfection, which, in itself, does not imply production.[30]

Knowing, in short, for Maritain, is a *vital* speculative identification of knower and known which projects a knower into the known through spirit, in much the same fashion as Bergsonian intuition projects the knower into the real through felt sympathy. The vital identification for Maritain is not achieved through felt sympathy with becoming, but through intellectual sympathy with possible being.[31] Still, Maritain states, "this point, which is of capital importance, must be emphasized. Bergson is perfectly right in demanding that our knowledge, if it is true, if through it we actually conquer the real, be an assimilation of the subject and the object, and much more than a rebirth of the object through the subject, a birth of the subject in the object, and a vital identification with it."[32]

The point of capital importance to realize, that is, is that, for Maritain, as much as for Bergson, knowledge is a vital identification which projects the knower into reality through *spirit*. For Maritain this projection occurs not without a subjective intermediary; it occurs in and through it - it occurs in and through *esse intentionale* (or, as the later scholastics would say, *esse essentiae*[33] formed by the *intellectus agens*. For Maritain the knower cannot be in the known according to the knower's *esse naturae*, nor can the known be in the knower according to the known's *esse naturae*. To avoid absurdity Maritain thinks it is necessary to admit another form of existence - *esse intentionale* or, as he says the scholastics frequently call it, *esse spirituale*.[34]

By means of this *esse* the thing exists in the soul by an *esse* other than the thing's and the soul becomes the thing by an *esse* other than the soul's. The soul and the thing meet in the *esse intentionale* of the *species impressa*, which union is nothing other than the marriage of the knower and the known in the spiritual existence of the concept. Maritain states:

> ...as arising in the soul as a fruit and expression of the intelligence already formed by the *species impressa*, already perfect and under the action of this created participation in the intellectual power of God, of that center of immateriality perpetually in act, the highest point of spiritual tension naturally present in us, which should be called the active intellect (*intellectus agens*) where the intellect which knows derives all its formative energy, this quality, this modification of the soul which is the concept has (like all the objectifying forms) the privilege of transcending the function of entitative information exercised by it, and of being present in the faculty *like a spirit*. It is from the intelligence itself, from the intelligence in living act, that it holds this privilege, as though the intelligence gathered all its own spirituality into this one active point there to bring it to a maximum. Thus the concept is in the intelligence not only entitatively or as formative form, but also as a spiritual form not absorbed in the actuation of a subject in order to constitute with it a *tertium quid*, but on the contrary as terminating the intellect *per modum intentionale* and in the line of knowledge, in the very degree to which it expresses and volatilises the object.[35]

Thus, for Maritain, the objects of intellectual knowledge are objects abstracted from actual existence. In themselves they hold only a possible being. Actual being is consequently not known to the intellect in simple apprehension except as conceived *per modum quidditatis*.[36] For Maritain "this apprehension of being is absolutely primary and is implied in all our other intellectual apprehensions."[37] Nevertheless, this is not enough. The intellect is not content with this sort of apprehension. Hence it projects into existence through *esse spirituale*, and it is only in this projection that, for Maritain, the rightful function of judgment becomes intelligible.[38]

While Maritain's way of speaking might sound to some more Bergsonian or Augustinian than Thomistic, nonetheless, the reality of *esse spirituale* is of such importance to him that he thinks it is because they refuse to grant real being to possible being that modern thinkers such as Descartes become trapped within their own minds.[39] For Maritain the key to avoiding the egocentric predicament of modern philosophy is to recognize that extra-mental existence includes not only the spatially external existence of actual beings but also the rightful necessities inherent in essences independent of actual cognition. He says:

> It is essential to add that in speaking of extra-mental existence I am not only thinking of actual existence but also and first of all of possible existence, for our intellect, in the simple act of apprehension abstracts from existence in act, and in its judgments does not only judge of what exists,but also of what might or might not exist, and of the rightful necessities inherent in essences, so that it is first of all with regard to the *possibly real* that it 'justifies itself' or, better, confirms itself or makes explicit to itself reflexively the value of intellectual knowledge, whence the critique of knowledge must primarily proceed. It is because of their misunderstanding of this fundamental point, because they confound possibly real being with rational being and only recognize the actual as real, that the noetics of so many modern writers go astray from the outset.[40]

That is, it is because they fail to distinguish the *esse* of the known from the *esse* of the *cogitans* that, in Maritain's view, modern noetics are failures. Hence, for Maritain, it is not actual existence which is the point of departure of intellectual knowledge; it is possible existence - possible existence loaded with *esse spirituale*. How Thomistic this view is we will leave for our readers to decide for themselves. As for us, it looks remarkably similar to the spirit of inverted Bergsonianism being scrupulously relocated and corrected within the wisdom of John of St. Thomas. Indeed, this seems to us to be a fitting way to describe the essence of Maritain's thought as a whole.

St. John's University

NOTES

1. Jacques Maritain. *Bergsonian Philosophy and Thomism*, transl. Mabelle L. Andison and J. Gordon Andison (New York, 1955) p. 158.

2. *Ibid.*, pp. 123-124 and pp. 155-156.

3. *Ibid.*, p. 27.

4. *Ibid.*, p. 28.

5. *Ibid.*

6. *Ibid.*, p. 294.

7. *Ibid.*, p. 39, footnote 3.

8. Jacques Maritain, *Existence and the Existent*, transl. Galantiere and Gerald B. Phelan (New York, 1948) p. 47.

9. Maritain, *Bergsonian Philosophy and Thomism*, p. 126.

10. *Ibid*, p. 294.

11. By using "inverted" I imply that Maritainianism is not a simple relocation of Bergson's views into later scholastic Thomism. Maritainianism is a synthesis which takes place in two stages. First, Maritain to some extent disagrees with and negates a view held by Bergson. Second, he relocates the corrected view (the view of the Bergson of intention, had Bergson known better) into its proper place within later scholastic Thomism.

12. Maritain, *Bergsonian Philosophy and Thomism*, pp. 119-203.

13. *Ibid.*, pp.21-22.

14. *Ibid.*, p. 155.

15. *Ibid.*, p. 29, footnote 3.

16. *Ibid.*, pp.108-109.

17. *Ibid.*, p.126.

18. Jacques Maritain, *The Degrees of Knowledge*, transl. Bernard Wall and Margot R. Adamson (New York, 1938) p. 35 and p. 45.

19. Jacques Maritain, *An Introduction to Philosophy* (New York, 1959) p. 199.

20. Maritain, *Bergsonian Philosophy and Thomism*, p. 292.

21. *Ibid.*, p. 72.

22. *Ibid.*

23. Maritain, *The Degrees of Knowledge*, pp. 144-155.

24. *Ibid*, p. 149, footnote 2.

25. Maritain, *Bergsonian Philosophy and Thomism*, p. 32.

26. Maritain, *The Degrees of Knowledge*, p. 157.

27. *Ibid.*, p. 104 and p. 157.

28. *Ibid.*, p. 135.

29. *Ibid.*, p. 136.

30. *Ibid.*, p. 137.

31. *Ibid.*, pp. 117-119. See especially p. 119, footnote 1.

32. Maritain, *Bergsonian Philosophy and Thomism*, pp. 155-156.

33. For an introduction to the doctrine of *esse essentiae* in later scholasticism, see Etienne Gilson's *Being and Some Philosophers* (Toronto, 1952) pp. 74-107.

34. Maritain, *The Degrees of Knowledge*, p. 139. About *esse spirituale* Maritain states: "I hold that a great field of interest lies open for philosophers in the study of the part it plays even in the world of physics, which is doubtless the cause of that form of universal animation by which movement brings to bodies more than they are in themselves, and colours all nature with a semblance of life and feeling." (To us this sounds more like the World Soul of neo-Platonism than the metaphysics of St. Thomas!) On the same page (footnote 1) Maritain adds: "The movement of projectiles, which caused so much difficulty for the ancients, could be perhaps explained by the fact that, at the first instant of movement and because of it, the qualitative state which exists in the agent and is the immediate cause of the movement (speaking in ontological terms; it is by design that I do not use the terms which belong to the vocabulary of mechanics) passes *secundum esse intentionale* into the mobile object." From this standpoint it would be possible to hold the Galilean principle of inertia viable not only from the point of view of physico-mathematical science (at least, according to the mechanics of Einstein, for a space ideally supposed which would be totally devoid of curvature), but also from that of the philosophy of nature."

35. *Ibid.*, pp.152-153.

36. *Ibid.*, pp. 110-111, and p. 119, footnote 1.

37. *Ibid.*, p. 115.

38. *Ibid.*, p. 118.

39. *Ibid.*, p. 111.

40. *Ibid.*, pp. 111-112.

PART TWO

EXISTENCE AND THE EXISTENT

C. Action

Métaphysique et éducation

Michel Legault, s.ss.a.

Summary

For John Dewey, philosophy is "the theory of education in its most general aspects." Throughout history we see a close tie between an author's philosophical thought and his educational principles. Jacques Maritain is quite aware of this, and manifests it in his own writing. In Maritain the educational theorist is Maritain the metaphysician.

His metaphysics of the human person and of human action, of knowledge and free will, treated in *Existence and the Existent*, are at the heart of *Towards a Philosophy of Education*, not only in a general way but even in its practical application, such as the choice of a curriculum and the pedagogical methods used.

***

John Dewey, dans *Démocratie et éducation* ne craint pas d'affirmer que la philosophie est <la théorie de l'éducation dans ses aspects les plus généraux>,[1] dans ce sens il écrit:

> Si nous sommes disposés à concevoir l'éducation comme
> le processus de formation des dispositions fondamentales,
> intellectuelles et affectives, à l'égard de la nature et des
> hommes, nous pouvons même définir la philosophie
> comme la théorie générale de l'éducation.[2]

Il suffit de parcourir l'histoire de l'éducation pour noter le lien intime qui existe entre la conception philosophique d'un auteur et ses positions en matière d'éducation; qu'il s'agisse de Kant, de Locke, de Jean-Jacques Rousseau, nous devons reconnaître ce lien organique entre la pensée philosophique et la pensée éducative des grands auteurs pédagogues. Maritain n'échappe pas à ce fait qui, d'ailleurs, ne fait qu'illustrer l'adage ancien selon lequel on agit comme on pense. Jacques Maritain est pleinement conscient de ce lien entre sa pensée philosophique et sa conception de l'éducation; c'est dans ce sens qu'il écrit: <Il n'y a pas de

philosophie de l'éducation sans une certaine métaphysique et une certaine anthropologie ou philosophie de l'homme> (PE, 19-20).[3]

Ces simples remarques permettent déjà de bien situer la relation qui peut exister entre ces deux ouvrages de Maritain: d'une part, en métaphysique, le *Court traité de l'existence et de l'existant* et, d'autre part, *Pour une philosophie de l'éducation*. C'est le même homme qui est à la fois métaphysicien et éducateur. Aussi n'est-il pas naturel de trouver dans l'oeuvre de l'éducateur les convictions du métaphysicien. C'est ce que nous allons tenter de faire dans les lignes qui suivent.

Le métaphysicien est un philosophe <enivré de l'être> (CT,42)[4] Maritain recourt à

> cette sorte supérieure de savoir qu'est la sagesse métaphysique parce qu'elle s'applique à pénétrer les premières et les plus universelles raisons d'être, et à jouir, comme fruition, de la délectation spirituelle de la vérité et de la saveur de l'être (PE,128).

ainsi qu'il l'écrit dans son ouvrage sur la philosophie de l'éducation. L'intuition de l'être et la recherche de la vérité sont deux voies fondamentales pour la conception de la nature de la personne humaine qu'il faut éduquer. Maritain fait remarquer que déjà la métaphysique, qui est sagesse, répond <sur le plan purement humain, - à la suprême aspiration de la nature intellectuelle et à sa soif de libération> (PE,128). Il croit donc à la capacité de la métaphysique d'éclairer notre connaissance de l'homme; la connaissance de ce qui est <au- dessus du temps> éclaire celle des choses temporelles.

Dans son ouvrage sur l'éducation, Maritain affirme hautement, comme base de toute recherche éducative, la saisie, par la métaphysique, de l'être et de la vérité. Dans son traité sur l'existence, il affirme qu'un authentique existentialisme professe <la primauté de l'existence, mais comme impliquant et sauvant les essences ou natures, et comme manifestant une suprême victoire de l'intelligence et de l'intelligibilité> (CT,13).

Maritain enseigne que le thomisme, qui sous-tend toute sa pensée tant métaphysique qu'éducative, est <un *intellectualisme* existentialiste> (CT,78); en effet, dit- il, les <grandes thèses spécifiquement thomistes n'ont de sens [...] que pour une pensée tournée avant tout vers l'existence> (CT,65). Mais il affirme, en outre, que le thomisme est un existentialisme qui <devient *volontariste*, si l'on considère le rôle essentiel qu'il reconnaît alors à la volonté, par laquelle seule un homme est constitué purement et simplement bon ou mauvais...> (CT,80). <L'existentialisme thomiste, ajoute-t-il, s'ordonne à l'acte que la liberté du sujet fera surgir dans l'existence> (CT,80).

Nous sommes ainsi amenés à considérer les deux points majeurs que l'on retrouve dans les deux ouvrages de Maritain: l'étude de la connaissance et celle de l'agir. Le rôle de l'intelligence et celui de la volonté libre constituent les deux pôles de l'ouvrage éducatif de Maritain et nous les retrouvons au coeur de son traité de métaphysique sur l'existence.

1. LA CONNAISSANCE

1.1 La vérité et l'être

Avant d'entreprendre l'explication métaphysique de la connaissance, Maritain pose le problème fondamental de la vérité et de sa relation avec l'être. Cela est clairement établi dans *Pour une philosophie de l'éducation* ainsi que nous l'avons souligné précédemment: il établit clairement que la métaphysique permet de saisir l'être et la vérité de l'homme parce qu'elle reconnaît et garantit la valeur même de l'être et de la vérité. Maritain réagit contre le subjectivisme idéaliste: <la vérité ne dépend pas de nous, mais de *ce qui est*> (PE,27), écrit-il. La vérité est quelque chose d'objectif que la raison humaine est capable d'atteindre. Maritain professe sa foi en la valeur de la raison humaine comme capacité d'atteindre

> l'univers de l'être intelligible et de la valeur sacrée de la vérité comme telle, [...] un univers de réalités qui rendent votre pensée vraie en vertu de cela même qu'elles sont, et non pas simplement par l'effet d'une action qui réussit. C'est l'univers de l'être intelligible et de la valeur sacrée de la vérité comme telle (PE,117).

On retrouve la même position philosophique dans le traité sur l'existence où il affirme que la <vérité suit l'existence des choses, ou des sujets transobjectifs auxquels s'affronte la pensée> (CT,24). La vérité est présentée comme <l'adéquation de l'immanence en acte de notre pensée à ce qui existe hors de notre pensée> (CT,24).

En éducation, la saisie de la vérité est le but premier de tout travail éducatif (PE,76 et 128). La vérité sera le premier critère pour l'établissement d'un programme d'étude (PE,182). Quant au professeur, il doit être passionné par la vérité et être capable de la manifester avec franchise (PE,125 et 142). Maritain écrit encore que c'est <une obligation sacrée pour une école ou une université chrétiennes de conserver vivant le sens de la vérité dans l'étudiant> (PE,164).

2.1 La théorie de la connaissance

En éducation, il est indispensable d'étudier la théorie de la connaissance car, <sous-jacente à toutes les questions concernant l'orientation fondamentale de l'éducation, se trouve la *philosophie du connaître* à laquelle l'éducateur adhère consciemment ou inconsciemment> (PE,126).

La connaissance est considérée par Maritain comme <une existence spirituelle> (PE,23). Nous retrouvons la même expression dans les deux ouvrages comparés (CT,24 et 69). L'homme est un <microcosme dans lequel le grand univers peut être embrassé par la connaissance> (PE,130). Par l'acte de connaissance, l'homme s'unit le monde, il doit <l'embrasser> en lui-même (PE,130). L'acte de connaître comme <l'action la plus vitale par le moyen de laquelle les choses sont spiritualisées afin de ne plus faire qu'un avec l'esprit> (PE,65). Connaître c'est devenir l'autre en tant qu'autre (CT,24); la connaissance apparaît <comme la surexistence immatérielle dans laquelle le connaissant est ou devient intentionnellement le connu> (CT,69).

Pour analyser la connaissance, Maritain s'intéresse aux opérations de l'esprit. Dans le traité sur l'existence, il étudie systématiquement les deux premières opérations de l'esprit: la simple appréhension (CT,27 et 31) et le jugement (CT,32-37).

2.1.1 La simple appréhension

En faisant l'étude de la simple appréhension, Maritain se penche sur les deux facteurs essentiels à la formation d'un concept; il aborde successivement le rôle des sens et celui de l'intelligence.

2.1.1.1 Le rôle des sens

Les sens jouent un rôle primordial dans la connaissance (CT,39-40). Maritain affirme que <l'existence, - l'existence des réalités matérielles, - nous est donnée d'abord par les sens> (CT,25). Le sens, qui <atteint l'existence en acte [...] la donne à l'intelligence, il donne à l'intelligence un trésor intelligible que lui-même ne connaît pas comme intelligible et que l'intelligence, elle, connaît et nomme par son nom, qui est: l'être> (CT,25). La connaissance sensible est d'une extrême importance pour la saisie de l'être; ainsi Maritain peut affirmer:

> Et son objet lui-même la métaphysique le saisit dans les choses: c'est l'être des choses sensibles et matérielles, l'être du monde de l'expérience qui est son champ d'investigation immédiatement accessible [...]; avant de s'élever aux existants spirituels, c'est l'existence empirique, l'existence des choses matérielles qu'elle tient sous ses prises, - non comme empirique et matérielle, mais comme existence (CT,56).

Dans son ouvrage sur la philosophie de l'éducation, Maritain insiste sur le rôle des sens qui sont les <fenêtres> par lesquelles l'homme est mis en contact avec le monde car <rien n'entre dans l'intellect sinon par les sens> (PE,128). <Assurément, soutient-il encore, l'expérience des sens est l'origine même de toute notre connaissance> (PE,60). Mais à eux seuls, les sens ne peuvent pas produire la pensée abstraite et universelle.

2.1.1.2 Le rôle de l'intelligence

Dans ses deux ouvrages, Maritain étudie l'intelligence dans sa fonction d'abstraction:

> Et l'intelligence, se saisissant des intelligibles, qu'elle dégage par sa propre force de l'expérience des sens, atteint au sein de sa propre vitalité interne ces natures ou essences qu'elle a détachées par l'abstraction de leur existence matérielle en tel point donné de l'espace et du temps (CT,25).

Dans son ouvrage relatif à l'éducation, Maritain décrit l'intelligence comme <le principe vital et actif de la connaissance> à l'intérieur de l'homme; elle a un pouvoir <intérieur de vision>, celui

> de dégager de l'expérience les connexions rationnelles et nécessaires dont celle-ci est prégnante, et qui ne deviennent visibles qu'au moyen de l'abstraction et des concepts universels, et dans la lumière des premiers principes intuitifs de la raison (PE,60).

Maritain étudie la formation de l'idée d'être (CT,49-50) ainsi que l'abstraction et ses degrés (CT,49-54). C'est vraiment par l'intelligence que l'homme peut embrasser l'être, l'intelligible, le monde réel et possible. <L'intelligence tend à saisir et à conquérir l'être> (PE,127), écrit-il.. C'est pourquoi on peut la considérer comme <la faculté première de l'être humain> (PE,42). Maritain consacre plusieurs pages de son traité sur l'existence à étudier <l'intuition de l'être> (CT,37-42). Il reconnaît que <l'existence est la source première de l'intelligibilité> (CT,41 et 60).

2.1.2 Le jugement

Dans son traité sur l'existence, Maritain reconnaît que <la fonction du jugement est une fonction existentielle> (CT,26). C'est <l'acte en lequel s'achève et se consomme l'intellection> (CT,26 et 33). Maritain consacre plusieurs pages de son traité à étudier le jugement dans <sa fonction existentielle> (CT,32- 37):

> La fonction propre du jugement consiste [...] à faire passer l'esprit du plan de la simple essence, ou du simple *objet* présenté à la pensée, au plan de la *chose* ou du sujet détenant l'existence (actuellement ou possiblement), et dont l'objet de pensée prédicat et l'objet de pensée sujet sont des aspects intelligibles [...] (CT.33-34).

Le jugement affirme l'existence (CT,35-36); en effet, l'existence est l'objet du jugement (CT,43-44). <Pour avoir l'idée de l'être, dit Maritain, il faut avoir affirmé et saisi l'acte d'exister dans un jugement> (CT,47-48).

Appliquant sa réflexion au domaine de l'éducation, Maritain insiste sur la formation de l'intelligence: loin de prôner l'érudition ou <une inculcation encyclopédique> (PE,130), il favorise l'éducation du jugement et du raisonnement. C'est ainsi que, lorsqu'il s'agit du choix du contenu des programmes, il soutient que le principe directeur qui doit l'éclairer est celui-ci: <moins de faits à enregistrer et plus de joie intellectuelle à éprouver> (PE,147). Il faut, dit-il encore, donner à l'adolescent l'occasion d'exercer son jugement et le former <peu à peu à la réflexion critique> et <favoriser l'exercice de son raisonnement> (PE,75). Tout cet effort d'éducation de l'intelligence doit amener l'adolescent à la sagesse qui <est de soi la valeur la plus élevée pour l'esprit humain> (PE,61). Cette sagesse déborde la science; elle est aussi une manière d'être et d'agir.

2. L'agir: volonté et liberté

Dans son traité sur l'existence, Maritain étudie les implications de l'intuition de l'être, dont l'amour qui est

> comme la surexistence immatérielle dans laquelle l'aimé est ou devient dans l'aimant le principe d'une pesanteur ou d'une connaturalité intentionnelle par où l'aimant tend intérieurement, comme à son propre être dont il serait séparé, à l'union existentielle avec l'aimé, et s'aliène dans la réalité de l'aimé (CT,69)[5].

Dans son livre sur la philosophie de l'éducation, Maritain affirme que, contrairement aux instincts et aux tendances qui ferment l'homme sur lui-même, la volonté le conduit <à se donner librement à des êtres qui sont pour lui comme d'autres lui-mêmes> (PE,132). La volonté apparaît comme la faculté de l'amour; c'est la puissance de l'amour qui <surabonde en action> (PE,132). L'idée d'amour implique celle de liberté. Parce qu'il est intelligent et doué de volonté, l'homme peut poser des actes libres qui ne lui sont dictés ni par l'instinct, ni par la société. La liberté personnelle <dans laquelle il se détermine lui-même et pour laquelle il est fait> (PE,18) découle du fait que l'homme est capable de connaissance et de réflexion (PE,190).

L'acte de liberté (CT,80) est l'acte de choix moral (CT,84-85). La liberté, selon Maritain, est une <liberté d'autonomie> (CT.110 et PE,26), une <liberté de choix [qui] consiste dans l'indétermination active et dominatrice de la volonté qui rend elle-même efficace le motif de la détermination> (CT.143). Cette liberté est <intérieure et spirituelle>; en conséquence, <le premier but de l'éducation est la conquête de la liberté intérieure et spirituelle à atteindre par la personne individuelle, ou, en

d'autres termes, la libération de celle-ci par la connaissance et la sagesse, la bonne volonté et l'amour> (PE,26).

Reprenant dans le *Court traité de l'existence* l'enseignement de saint Thomas qui affirme que <chacun est tenu de tendre vers la perfection de l'amour> (CT.82), Maritain affirme que la perfection de l'être, pour l'homme, <consiste à aimer, en passant par tout ce qu'il y a d'imprévu et de dangereux, d'obscur, d'exigeant, d'insensé dans l'amour> (CT,83). Cette perfection de l'amour humain

> consiste dans la plénitude et la délicatesse du dialogue et de l'union de personne à personne, jusqu'à la transfiguration qui, comme dira saint Jean de la Croix, fait de l'homme un dieu par participation: <deux natures en un seul esprit et amour>, en une seule surexistence spirituelle d'amour (CT.83).

Maritain consacre dix-sept pages de son *Court traité de l'existence* au <jugement moral> (CT.84-100), rappelant que l'acte moral doit être réglé par la raison (CT,84) et que la liberté s'enracine dans la raison (CT,100). Il étudie le <jugement de conscience> (CT,86) et affirme qu'il n'y a pas de vie morale sans le jugement personnel de la conscience (CT,98). <Il y a des normes objectives de la moralité, écrit-il, il y a des devoirs et des règles, parce que le constitutif formel de la moralité humaine c'est la mesure de la raison> (CT,87). De plus, Maritain fait remarquer que <notre choix n'a pas à s'exercer seulement entre le bien et le mal, mais aussi et le plus souvent entre le bon et le meilleur> (CT,91). C'est ainsi que l'homme tend à la perfection de l'amour aidé par les dons de l'Esprit Saint (CT,91).

Dans *Pour une philosophie de l'éducation*, on retrouve aussi le même point de vue sur l'agir moral. L'obstacle fondamental à la vie morale, c'est l'égoïsme: <l'amour est lui- même assiégé par notre central égoïsme et perpétuellement en danger de s'enchevêtrer avec lui ou d'être recapturé par lui> (PE,107). Le grand problème que souligne Maritain est celui de concilier la liberté et l'observance de la loi (CT,96). Comment concilier liberté et bien commun? Pour Maritain, la liberté <est au coeur de la vie sociale> et <une société humaine est en vérité un ensemble de libertés humaines qui acceptent l'obéissance et le sacrifice et une loi commune pour le bien commun> (PE,30).

Enfin, Maritain se préoccupe de former à la liberté, car, pour lui, éduquer, c'est former à la liberté et l'éducation lui apparaît comme un travail de <libération> (PE,22). Pour cela, il faut faire appel à l'intelligence de l'enfant, en l'éclairant; il faut favoriser l'exercice de sa liberté et son sens des responsabilités (PE,101). Eduquer à la liberté, ce n'est pas laisser l'enfant faire tout ce qu'il désire. En effet, continue Maritain, <la personnalité signifie intériorité à soi-même; ce royaume de l'autonomie

internelle [sic] grandit dans la mesure où la vie de la raison et de la liberté domine sur celle de l'instinct et des désirs des sens> (PE,48). L'éducateur qui veut former la liberté ne doit donc pas nier <la valeur de toute discipline et de toute ascèse> (PE,48 et 18). Maritain propose comme méthode de formation aux responsabilités l'auto- organisation, le système des équipes (PE,144). L'éducation, selon lui, n'est ni <dressage animal>, ni <élevage animal> (PE,24-25), mais appel à la volonté libre: <les maîtres doivent se soucier avant tout d'aider les esprits à devenir articulés, libres et autonomes> (PE,137).

Conclusion

La lecture comparative du *Court traité de l'existence et de l'existant* et de *Pour une philosophie de l'éducation* permet de vérifier l'unité de pensée que l'on retrouve chez Maritain à travers ses oeuvres. Sa pensée métaphysique éclaire sa pensée éducative. L'homme que l'on doit éduquer, c'est le même homme qu'étudie le philosophe. Sa conception philosophique de la connaissance et de l'agir moral se retrouve dans sa conception de l'éducation jusqu'en ses applications pratiques, comme celles de choisir le contenu d'un programme ou d'utiliser telle ou telle méthode pédagogique.

Une étude beaucoup plus poussée aurait pu être faite entre ces deux ouvrages pour vérifier l'hypothèse de départ que résumait Dewey lorsqu'il affirmait que la philosophie est <la théorie générale de l'éducation>. Quiconque lit attentivement *Pour une philosophie de l'éducation* a déjà découvert les lignes fondamentales de la pensée philosophique de Jacques Maritain, pensée qui se trouve explicitement exprimée dans le *Court traité de l'existence et de l'existant*.

Collège St. Jean-Marie Vianney, Montreal

NOTES

1. John Dewey, *Démocratie et éducation*, Paris, Armand Colin, 1975, p.392.

2. *Ibid.*, p.389.

3. Jacques Maritain, *Pour une philosophie de l'éducation.* Nouvelle édition revue et complétée, Paris, Fayard, 1969, pp.19- 20. Ci-après PE.

4. Jacques Maritain, *Court traité de l'existence et de l'existant.* 2e édition, Paris, Paul Hartmann éditeur, 1964, p.42. Ci-après CT.

5. Voir aussi *Les degrés du savoir.* 6e édition. Paris, Desclée de Brouwer, 1959, pp. 734-736.

VOLUNTARISM IN ETHICS

Ralph Nelson

There is a pattern running through Maritain's work from the early writings on Bergson, the reflections on Husserl and phenomenology, and the examination of existentialism and that is a defence of intellectualism in theoretical philosophy or, to be more precise, a defence of metaphysical intellect against those who would deny it, distort it, or attenuate it in some fashion. The rise of existential philosophy to prominence provided a new opportunity for mainstream European preoccupation with metaphysical issues. Indeed, we may now look back at this period with some regret for the present leading lights of European philosophy have little interest in metaphysics at all. The shepherds of being are not to be found.

If Maritain in one section of the "short treatise" affirms the merits of an intellectual existentialism against other forms, notably that of Sartre, the emphasis shifts when he turns from the topic of being to that of action. "We must say that in moving into the domain of ethics this existentialism becomes voluntaristic."[1] He then proceeds to indicate that the focal point of his analysis is on judgment. He accordingly notes that, in addition to a purely theoretical judgment, there are two kinds of judgment relevant to ethics: the theoretico-practical and the practico-practical. Theoretico-practical judgments and theoretical judgments are similar in that their assertions are true or false in the same way, since theretico-practical judgments are theoretical in mode.[2] Where confusion is possible is in regard to practical judgments because the truth or falsity of the two kinds of practical judgment are determined differently. Consequently, it is well to point out that Maritain is not defending a voluntarist thesis as concerns the matter of "intellectual moral knowledge",[3] or moral science. It seems clear that Maritain is making a distinction between two kinds of practical judgment, and the voluntarism refers not to the first, the theoretico-practical, but to the second, the practico-practical. Maritain had previously developed the distinction in *The Degrees of Knowledge.*[4]

"Intellectualism would be a term which applies to any philosophical theory according to which the intellect is prior to or superior to the will."[5] Its opposite, "voluntarism", then, "applies to any philosophical theory according to which the will is prior to or superior to the intellect or reason."[6]

To begin with, let us set out two extreme positions. On one hand, there is the intellectualism of Socrates, Spinoza, or Dewey. On the other hand, there is voluntarism, whether it be that of Scotus, Schopenhauer, or Nietzsche. Intellectualism and voluntarism may be subdivided further by referring to the ontic, noetic and moral levels.[7]

Initially, it might be desirable to select unequivocal cases in which intellectualism seems to preclude any role for appetitive influence whatsoever, and instances of voluntarism which border on irrationalism, for reason in such cases are never causes or original influences, but at best an effect or consequence of the will itself. In either case, the tendency will be to set up an irreconcilable opposition between intellect and will.

Now, when Maritain says that Thomism is voluntaristic in ethics, there is a concern that he overstates the case in order to offset a certain temptation toward intellectualism to which Thomism is not immune. When he examined questions of education, he insisted that both intellectualism and voluntarism were misconceptions to be avoided.[8] When he later tried to situate Thomistic natural law with regard to other theories of natural law, he saw it as occupying a middle position between rationalism and voluntarism.[9] We shall see that there is no question of a voluntarism la Ockham. There is no question of a voluntarism which would make obligation rest on the basis of consent, nor of a Nietzschean voluntarism, creative of values. In the war between the "faculties", Maritain seeks to show the role of the will in judgments in which intellect too has its share.

In *Reflexions sur l'intelligence*, Maritain was concerned with "the proper life of the intellect" (*sa vie propre*).[10] In *Existence and Existent*, it is also "the proper life of the will" which is at stake.[11] Before entering into an analysis of "the proper life of the will", some attention should be paid to philosophical objections against speaking of the intellect and will as having lives of their own. John Locke is notable in the history of philosophical psychology for having raised this issue. Here is the way he stated the problem. Will and understanding are distinguished as two powers of mind or spirit. The first is "what orders the consideration", the other is "perception".[12] They can be reduced to motion and thinking. Attributes belong to agents, not to powers. "Agents that have no thought, no volition at all, are in everything *necessary* agents." So, if there are free agents, there is nothing improper in calling them free, but, Locke goes on to say, "liberty belongs not to the will".[13] Leaving aside the problems connected with Locke's notion of basic categories, and his attempt to subsume qualities under relations, the fundamental issue at stake here is whether it is appropriate to employ metonymy, in the particular sense of taking the part for the whole, when speaking of human psychology. It is apparently unavoidable to do so, but is it always misleading and wrong? I would think that the situation is similar to that concerning abstractions. It is necessary in scientific inquiry to use abstractions. One could not imagine a theoretical enterprise which would succeed without them. Of course, one must avoid the fallacy Whitehead dubbed fittingly "the fallacy of misplaced concreteness," that is, treating abstractions as if they were concrete things. So also the use of metonymy is fitting and meaningful as long as we realize that we are speaking of a part rather than the whole, and when we keep in mind that, indeed, *actiones sunt suppositorum,*[14] as Maritain emphasizes. With these cautionary provisions in mind, there does seem to be some reason, then, to investigate the will's proper life and the intellect's proper life, albeit life is attributed properly only to subjects. I make much of this point because some literal-minded critics tend to frame Lockean-type objections to the kind of discourse one finds in Thomistic psychology. Maritain's starting point in the analysis is to compare theoretical and practical judgment. If, in the former, the will has no intrinsic place, in the latter it is determinant. Consider the difference between Descartes and Maritain on this issue. It is not arbitrary in this context to do so since Descartes is discussed at the beginning of *Existence and the Existent,* and there is a specific reference to his theory of the will. The procedure will be to examine Descartes' position on the interplay between intellect and will, then Sartre's extension of Descartes' theory, and only then Maritain's own position. The dispute centers on judgment. According to Maritain, the "operation of assenting no longer belongs to the understanding" for Descartes, "but to the will. It is a decision of the will, which comes to agree to an idea as a faithful representation of what is or may be".[15] This is the case in regard to theoretical knowledge itself. Hence intellectual error stems from the will for it is the will which leads to "precipitancy of judgment".[16] "Human error", says Maritain, "is explained by Descartes in the same way as theologians explain angelic error", another instance of Cartesian angelism. The point is that assent should be given only to certain types of proposition and it is the will which is responsible when a man goes beyond "what he perceives clearly and distinctly".[17] This is Descartes' psychology of error which seems tantamount to the psychology of fault.

So, in the ethics of thought, there is a rule that one should only assent, or consent, for there appears to be no difference between them, to the clear and distinct. Later, in Malebranche, there is a much more elaborate and refined version of this identification.[18]

In his study *The Dream of Descartes,* Maritain indicates that there is an antimony in Cartesian thought concerning the interaction of intellect and will, for "it maintains at one and same time the freedom of the will" (to the extent of attributing to it all theoretical errors) and the principle that the will always follows the understanding (to the point of seeking in the understanding the means sufficient for moral perfecting--*it is enought to judge well in order to do well*), but it 'suppresses without replacing' the solution by which Scholastic philosophy conciliated these two theses."[19]

Finally, understanding and will are distinct powers, and "the difference between moral freedom and error" is explained "by the difference in extent of these two faculties, and judgment" is attributed "to the will, not to understanding".[20]   Maritain points out, as well, that "this voluntaristic doctrine which is already a pretty monstrosity in philosophy, is accompanied by the gravest consequences for the theory of faith".[21]

Jean-Paul Sartre's essay on Cartesian freedom established a connection between Descartes' concept of freedom and that of existential philosophers like Heidegger and himself.[22]   Concerning the tensions, if not contradictions, in this Cartesian concept, there is some agreement between Maritain and Sartre, but Sartre's extrapolation of Descartes' concept goes far beyond what Maritain would consider authentically Cartesian. Sartre, unlike Maritain, is not primarily critical of Descartes, but rather wants to show some radical implications in the Cartesian notion of freedom which Descartes had not drawn out. Freedom, says Sartre, may be experienced in the realm of action or in the realm of understanding and discovery. It may be an experience of creative freedom through action or an experience of autonomous thinking. In Descartes' case it was the latter. And, indeed, in the French philosophical line from Descartes to Alain, freedom has been identified "with the act of judging".[23]   Descartes' position is contrasted with that of Kant, for truth, for Descartes, is not constituted, but discovered. Sartre then points out certain difficulties in Descartes' account since, in some respects, one is free to suspend judgment while, in others, in the presence of evident truths, one is forced to assent. In the second case, Sartre notices similarities between Descartes and Spinoza and Leibnitz. Even when autonomous, the Cartesian understands "a pre-established order of relationships".[24]   Furthermore, there are "two rather different theories of freedom" in Descartes: a negative and a positive one.[25]   It is Sartre's contention that the negative kind consists in the suspension of judgment and, moreover, in this power of refusal, the thinker "discovers that he is pure nothingness".[26]   At this point, it is clear that Sartre is about to effect a transition from a conventional interpretation of Descartes to an existential or Heideggerian recasting in which it is argued that Descartes "did not push his theory of negativity to the limit".[27]   No doubt this assertion would be correct, if one admits that Descartes indeed had a theory of negativity. What Sartre wants to say is that the negativity assures autonomy but that, when Cartesian freedom is positive, when it adheres to truth, it is no longer autonomous.

The next stage in this interpretation concerns the problem of creative freedom and humanism. After having shown that, in a number of texts, the Cartesian notion of freedom is not one of creative freedom, Sartre now attempts to show that creative freedom is revealed in the rules of method. They provide "very general directives for free and creative judgment".[28]   As long as freedom does not entail the invention of the good and the construction of knowledge, man is free in name only. He is "free for Evil, but not for Good; for Error, but not Truth".[29] The giant step is taken when Descartes recognized that the concept of freedom means absolute autonomy. That there is no difference between the infinity of the human will and the divine will. In short, Descartes has attributed to God what belonged to man.

> It took two centuries of crisis--a crisis of Faith and a crisis of Science--for man to regain the creative freedom that Descartes placed in God, and for anyone finally to suspect the following truth, which is an essential basis of humanism: man is the being as a result of whose appearance a world exists.[30]

Here a juncture is made with Heidegger's conclusion, in *The Essence of Reasons*, that "the sole foundation of being is freedom".[31] Even though such a statement surely appears in Heidegger's early treatise, it is a real question whether Sartre's interpretation of it in terms of an extreme metaphysical voluntarism is justified.[32] However, the accuracy of Sartre's interpretation of Descartes and Heidegger is not at issue here. What is significant is that Sartre defines his own position as coming out of Descartes and encountering Heidegger. And so we have the well-known Sartrean themes of creative freedom, freedom from the Good and the True and, of course, his philosophy of atheistic humanism.

Now, after the presentation of a concept of will which is the ground of being itself, Maritain's account of Thomistic voluntarism is bound to be very mitigated indeed. In what precisely does this voluntarism consist? What is its focus? There are two instances in *Existence and the Existent* in which this voluntarism, or priority of the will over the intellect, is operative. The first concerns the notion of practical truth. The second concerns the role of the will in the commision of evil.

Maritain has tried in several instances to distinguish different kinds of judgment. For instance, in a series of lectures which were given about the same time as the publication of *Existence and the Existent*, he distinguished between "value judgments" and "judgments of simple reality".[33] What one finds in the present treatise is an attempt to distinguish between the notion of truth as it is relevant to theoretical matters, on one hand, and to practical matters, on the other. If truth is in the judgment, one must nevertheless indicate the differences between theoretical and practical judgments, while still showing in what sense there is an analogical unity in the term "truth". In a Thomistic perspective, judgments of truth share the common feature of being judgments of conformity or judgments in conformity. Truth consists in a conformity, but there is a difference concerning the kind of conformity involved in a theoretical judgment and the kind involved in a practical judgment, meaning in this context a practico-practical rather than a theoretico-practical judgment.

Now Maritain, after having criticized the Cartesian and Sartrean positions, is led to take up anew the task of elaborating the interaction of reason and will in judgments. In the first instance, that of theoretical judgment, truth consists in "conformity with extramental being"--in knowing what is. And, to the extent that theoretico-practical judgments are theoretical in mode, no doubt they too consist in conformity with extramental being. But practical judgment in the sense of a moral judgment here and now, particularized, cannot be considered true (or false) in this sense; otherwise it would not be action-oriented, but still knowledge-oriented. It consists in making what is not yet in existence, existent. Now, no doubt we are more accustomed to call such judgments right or wrong rather than true or false, but a right or correct judgment is also a true one, and a wrong or incorrect judgment is a false one. But again, in relation to what standard? Let us note that, up to now, little has been said about the role of the will in theoretical knowledge. Of course the will moves the intellect in inquiry. No doubt there must be a will-to-know. Nevertheless, Maritain denies that theoretical judgment, in the final analysis, is an act of the will.

The situation is quite different with practical (practico- practical) judgment for here one begins with the will's orientation toward (or away from) the good. Since distortion can exist, the orientation of the appetite may be skewed. It may also be right (or straight). The judgment of moral conscience consists in conformity with right appetite, that is, the judgment is a judgment of reason in conformity (or not) with the orientation of the will. This is that state of "dependence" referred to by Maritain concerning practical judgment "in regard to the actual movement of the appetite towards the ends of the subject".[34] Thus, far from treating both forms of judgment as completely homogeneous, Maritain notes that only the general feature of "being in conformity" is shared by these two different kinds of judgment.

That is the first instance illustrating the voluntaristic side of moral philosophy. The second instance concerns the more particular situation in which heeding (or turning away from) a norm is at stake. In this account, I leave aside the larger context in which the analysis occurs, "the free existent and the free eternal purposes", and I concern myself solely with the predicament in which, having knowledge of a moral norm, the subject nevertheless turns his attention away from that norm and opens himself to evil. Let us begin with a statement of Sartre: "If we do not invent *our* Good, if Good has an *a priori*, independent existence, how could we perceive it without doing it?"[35] From the perspective of an intellectualist ethics, perhaps still best examplified by the Socratic dictum that virtue is knowledge, it is utterly inconceivable that a rational being knowing what is good would not act upon that knowledge. The final stage in the Platonic dialogues continues to be a search for the explanation of human value-blindness or ignorance. This state of ignorance may be induced by emotional factors, but there is no warrant for the conclusion that the remote or ultimate cause of wrong-doing is emotion rather than the proximate cause, ignorance.

The problem is how to explain the inroad of evil in the free act. According to the analysis this process occurs in two stages, or in two moments. In the first, the existent through its will "*does not* consider the norm of the *thou shouldst* upon which the ruling of the act depends".[36] Then, "at a second moment the will produces its free act affected by the privation of its due ruling and wounded with the nothingness which results from this lack of consideration".[37] The first moment, that of non-consideration of the rule, does not by itself constitute moral evil, but, if, at the moment of action, one wills with this non- consideration, the decision is a bad one. In any case, Maritain's argument is that the will is the key at both moments, for "the first cause of the non-consideration of the rule, and consequently of the evil of the free act that will come forth from it, is purely and simply the liberty of the created existent".[38]

Through this intricate analysis of the process by which those who know the norm or rule nevertheless do what is wrong, Maritain in effect refutes the notion that wrong-doing is simply a matter of ignorance, or inadequate knowledge, or the failure to employ an appropriate method. Maritain insists, then, that it is not ignorance which is the cause of wrong-doing, but *ignoring*, that is, acting with non-consideration of the rule. And it is on this ground that the break would be made with the venerable tradition of moral intellectualism, initiated by the great Greek philosophers, perpetuated by some of the Rationalists, and enduring still in moral philosophy. For, indeed, is it not the case that Aristotle himself must be considered in this group, according to one of his most acute modern commentators? "In the final analysis, reason remains the sole source of value, and Aristotle's attempt to escape from intellectualism falls short".[39] For the real battleground between moral intellectualism and moral voluntarism is to be located primarily, I believe, in their respective explanation of human wrong-doing. And it is on that terrain that Maritain particularly defends a Thomistic moral voluntarism.

University of Windsor

NOTES

1. Jacques Maritain, *Existence and the Existent*, transl. L. Galantière and Gerald B. Phelan (New York, 1948) p. 47.

2. There are several reasons why I prefer to use theoretico-practical rather than speculativo-practical. First, it is more in line with other contemporary usages; secondly, it avoids the pejorative, or at least ambiguous, connotations of "speculative", often considered by social scientists to be little more than free mind-spinning. When you don't know, you speculate. See *Existence and the Existent*, p. 52, n. 2 where Maritain speaks of two practical syllogisms.

3. See G. Kalinowski, *Le probleme de la vérité en morale at en droit* (Lyon, 1967) p. 129.

4. Jacques Maritain, *Distinguish to Unite, or The Degrees of Knowledge*, transl. supervised by Gerald B. Phelan (London, 1959), Appendix VII, pp. 456-464.

5. Richard Taylor, "Voluntarism", *The Encyclopedia of Philosophy* (New York, 1967) Volume 8, p. 270. For a treatise on moral voluntarism, see Taylor's *Good and Evil* (New York, 1970).

6. *Ibid.*

7. G. Kalinowski, *op. cit*, p. 23, n. 1.

8. Jacques Maritain, *Education at the Crossroads* (New Haven, 1943) pp. 18-22.

9. Jacques Maritain, *Nove lezioni sulla lege naturale* (Milan, 1985) pp. 114-116.

10. Jacques Maritain, *Réflexions sur l'intelligence et sur sa vie propre* (Paris, 1926). See chapter 11.

11. Jacques Maritain, *Existence and the Existent*.

12. John Locke, *An Essay Concerning Human Understanding*, II, XXI, 5.

13. *Ibid.*, II, XXI, 13-14. See Leibnitz's comment: "Ce ne sont pas les facultés ou qualités qui agissent, mais les substances par les facultés," in *Nouveaux essais sur l'entendement humain* (Paris, 1966) p. 147.

14. Jacques Maritain, *Existence and the Existent*, p. 62. The point is also made by Kalinowski: "Nous parlons de la raison, de la volonté, des tendances sensibles, comme si c'étaient des res autonomes. Le langage n'tant jamais pleinement adéquat à la richesse du réel et aux nuances de la pensée, notre manière de nous exprimer peut laisser croire que l'unité de l'homme est mconnue, que celui-ci est dissocié en un faisceau de facultés et que ces dernières sont hypostasiées, voir anthropomorphisées. Afin de détruire cette illusion, il nous faut insister sur l'unité de l'homme. C'est au fond l'homme tout entier qui connaît, qui veut, qui devient bon ou mauvais moyennant tel ou tel usage de ses facultés. *Actiones sunt suppositorum* disaient les anciens." *Op. cit.*, pp. 231-232.

15. Jacques Maritain, *Three Reformers: Luther, Descartes, Rousseau* (London, 1950) p. 57.

16. *Ibid.*, p. 60.

17. *Ibid.*, p. 61.

18. Malebranche in *De la recherche de la vérité* elaborates on Descartes' remarks on the will and judgment by drawing a parallel between the realm of knowledge where judgment is suspended and the realm of ethics where consent is suspended. But for all intents and purposes, there is no real distinction between assent and consent. "Cependant la plupart des philosophes prétendent que ces jugements même que formons sur des choses obscures ne sont pas volontaires, et ils veulent généralement que le consentement à la vérité soit une

action de l'entendement, ce qu'ils appellent acquiescement, *assensus*, à la différence du consentement au bien qu'ils attribuent à la volonté et qu'ils appellent consentement, *consensus*. Mais voice la cause de leur distinction et de leur erreur. *De la recherche de la vérité* (Paris, 1945) I, p. 9. See Henri Gouhier, *Malebranche* (Paris, 1929) pp. 146-151. I do distinguish between assent and consent in this paper, when it concerns the Thomistic position. John Henry Newman said that "an assertion is the expression of an act of assent." *An Essay in aid of A Grammar of Assent* (London, 1939) p. 5.

19. Jacques Maritain, *The Dream of Descartes*, transl. Mabelle L. Adison (New York, 1944) p. 46. I have replaced the word "speculative" by "theoretical". Maritain refers to Gilson's *La liberté chez Descartes et la théologie* (Paris, 1913) p. 441.

20. *Ibid.*, p. 46.

21. *Ibid.*, p. 63.

22. Jean-Paul Sartre, "Cartesian Freedom", *Literary and Philosophical Essays* (London, 1955) pp. 169-184.

23. *Ibid.*, p. 169.

24. *Ibid.*, p. 170.

25. *Ibid.*, p. 171.

26. *Ibid.*, p. 179.

27. *Ibid.*

28. *Ibid.*, p. 174.

29. *Ibid.*, p. 181.

30. *Ibid.*, p. 184.

31. *Ibid.*

32. "Nor does Sartre's use of 'freedom' resemble its development in Heidegger's *On the Essence of Ground*, where it is a central concept. On the contrary, Heidegger has there begun to make more explicit the rooting of human being in Being. In this case, through an identification of freedom and 'ground', a relation which, though already present in *Sein und Zeit*, has come more and more to dominate much of his later work. Such a conception of being Sartre would certainly reject." Marjorie Grene, *Sartre* (New York, 1973) p. 65. To be precise, the statement in Heidegger is: "Die Freiheit ist der Grund des Grundes." *Von Wesen des Grundes* (Frankfurt am Main, 1955) p. 53. So it is an inference to replace "ground" by "being".

33. Jacques Maritain, *Neuf leçons sur les notions premières de la philosophie morale* (Paris, 1951) pp. 41-42.

34. Jacques Maritain, *Existence and the Existent*, p. 48.

35. Jean-Paul Sartre, *op. cit.*, p. 177.

36. Jacques Maritain, *Existence and the Existent*, p. 90.

37. *Ibid.*

38. *Ibid.*, pp. 91-92.

39. R. A. Gauthier, *La morale d'Aristote* (Paris, 1963) p. 29.

THE CHRISTIAN EXISTENTIALIST POLITICAL PHILOSOPHY OF JACQUES MARITAIN

Charles P. O'Donnell

Throughout his life Jacques Maritain had a deep personal concern for human persons, their condition and their political well- being. He saw in *L'Action Franaise* a threat to spiritual life because of its excessive reliance on secular politics. In 1934 he was a signer and part author of the manifesto *Pour le Bien Commun* which deplored political divisiveness in France and urged a common stance for the poor.[1] He criticized the horrors of the Spanish Civil War and worked actively for a peaceful settlement and national reconciliation. He denounced the Nazi menace to civilized life. During World War II he condemned the bombing of open cities.

Integral Humanism, the first full presentation of his political philosophy, delineates its problems and his agenda for a Christian existentialist political ideal. There he summed up his position saying "social and political life takes place in the world of existence and of contingency, not of pure essences . . . It is a mistake to forget that essences act only in existences i.e., in ceasing to be pure essences . . . . It is no less grave an error to forget that existence is the place of essences, and that in the measure in which they are realized there, they develop their own internal energies, and their logic, while at the same time combining with other forms and with the whole historical heritage of the matter which receives them."[2] These fundamentals of his philosophy point to the centrality of the political virtues and to the way they relate to the changing circumstances of political life.

This paper focuses on bringing together texts relevant to his political existentialism and on the implications for political thought of the two principles of action, charity and practical wisdom, that he underlined in *Existence and Existent*.[3] It was in that slender volume he analyzed the metaphysical, moral and spiritual foundations on which his existential political philosophy is based.

Of charity, the first of the principles of action, he wrote: "Each of us is bound to tend toward the perfection of love according to his condition and in so far as it is in his power."[4] The second principle, practical wisdom, "concerns the judgment of the moral conscience and the manner in which, at the heart of concrete existence, the appetite enters into the regulation of the moral act by the reason."[5]

The brief discussion of charity in the text relating to Christian morality and to persons rests on the proposition that the perfection of love is the "most existential thing in the world."[6] As I understand it, the secular analogue of that Christian love is civic friendship, sometimes referred to as civic amity or fraternity in Maritain's political philosophy.

In *Man and the State* Maritain said: "Justice is a primary condition for the existence of the body politic, but Friendship is its very life-giving form. It tends toward a really human and freely achieved communion. It lives in the devotion of human persons and their gift of themselves. They are ready to commit their own existence, their possessions, and their honor for its sake. The civic sense is made up of this sense of devotion and mutual love as well as of the sense of justice and law."[7]

Walter Lippmann, as Maritain, saw civic friendship to be fundamental to democracy. He wrote: "Democracy is a fraternity which holds men together against anything that should divide them. It calms their fevers, subdues their appetites, restrains them from believing, saying and doing those irrevocable, irresponsible things which burst asunder the bonds of affection and truth."[8]

In a widely acclaimed and lengthy account of *The Idea of Fraternity in America*, the American political thinker Wilson Carey McWilliams sketched a political philosophy based on a matter-of-fact ideal of fraternity. He argued that America needs a sense of direction. "The only hope for the direction . . . lies in the 'inner city' in the true sense. Such a fraternal city can exist within an unfraternal city only if men know the dangers that beset it and the possibilities it offers. To build a city around strangers, it is necessary to recognize one's fellow citizens when chance casts them in the way and to find means for affirming a national patriotism, . . ; fraternity is a need because ultimately, beyond human imagining, all men are kinsmen and brothers."[9]

John Courtney Murray, S.J., in *We Hold These Truths*, approached the idea of civic amity from the viewpoint of a Catholic theologian addressing the problem of Catholics and politics in the United States.[10] For Father Murray civic amity is a special kind of virtue barely distinguishable from political wisdom. Civic amity, he held, is characteristic of good argument "among informed and responsible men" and "is a sentiment proper to citizens and the community's shared will to justice, though it engages the heart, and finds its measure as it finds its origin in intelligence, in a clear understanding of what is due to the good citizen from the city and the city from the citizen according to the mode of their capacity. The shared will of the community is the ground of civic amity as it is the ground of that unity which is called peace. This unity qualified by amity is the highest good of the multitude and the perfection of its unity."[11]

Turning to contemporary political action, civic friendship where it exists notwithstanding belligerent modern politics which exalts power and techniques, signals a democratic willingness of the people to realize the values of freedom, justice and human rights. To the extent that nations apply human rights policies fairly abroad and honor them at home they mirror that popular willingness. Furthermore, civic friendship moves democratic nations and opponents of dictatorial rule towards the objectives of social justice and the common good. In pluralist democratic societies it creates a healthy climate for the solidarity that prompts labor, business and other groups to seek their legitimate particular goods.

Civic friendship differs from the bonds and ends of the family and of ethnic, racial, and linguistic communities, from the intellectual associations of scholars and scientists dealing with the problems of their disciplines, and from the fellowship of religious faiths.[12] The primary concern of civic friendship on the other hand is the realization of the common good of political society. The other types of friendship, along with that of social and economic groups serving particular goods, help to sustain popular action and the common good when they act in its spirit.

Maritain was keenly aware of the growing interdependence of nations following World War II and of the countervailing insistence of nations on absolute national sovereignty which spurred international hostilities. Because of this contradictory situation, he spoke to UNESCO in the mid 60's on "The Spiritual Conditions of Progress and Peace."[13] Acknowledging that there is no present likelihood of establishing a world political organization founded by the free agreement and cooperation of governments and peoples, he held it necessary to prepare for that distant prospect. By means of education and action he thought it possible that nations in time would renounce absolute national sovereignty and replace international hostility "by the faithful practice of fraternity." In an earlier commentary on world government he had proposed the establishment of an advisory world council whose only function would be to make judgments of "ethical and political wisdom."[14] I believe this suggestion should be given serious study.

I now propose to discuss the second principle of Maritain's existential philosophy of action, which is the virtue of practical wisdom and its counterpart, political wisdom. *Les Degres du Savoir* described practical wisdom as the most practical level of moral philosophy.[15] By the same token political wisdom is the most practical level of political philosophy. In *Existence and the Existent* Maritain observed that "the end of practical wisdom is not to know that which exists but to cause to exist what is not yet."[16] So, too, political wisdom aims at causing something new to exist.

The analyses of practical wisdom in the same volume, and that of political wisdom embedded in Maritain's political writings and more explicitly in those of Yves Simon make it plain that the two forms of wisdom are distinct but not separate. The end of practical wisdom is "the perfection of persons" whose destiny is beyond time, while political wisdom seeks to realize the common good of political society in which persons share only as long as that society endures.[17]

The metaphysical, epistemological and moral bases of practical wisdom are identical with those of practical wisdom described in *Existence and the Existent*.[18] Both concern practical judgments made by individual persons or by officials and citizens of political society. After due deliberation in given circumstances, each decides freely to adopt means worthy of achieving the ends of individual persons or the common good of political society. The means themselves, guided by norms of reason, are propelled into action by the generous good will of right inclination.

Political action normally takes the form of laws or rules, that is, of constitutions, legislation, policies, and executive, judicial, administrative, or electoral decisions. All of them concern practical judgments about existing problems facing political society. If they are shaped by political wisdom, their value will be measured by the degree to which they contribute to the common good. If, on the contrary, they prove to be unwise, procedures especially in democratic countries provide for their revision and improvements in which political wisdom may be able to prevail. Happily, there are also many wise laws born of past or present wisdom. For example, the two hundred year old Constitution of the United States, its provisions for change and the democratic climate it created, are rightly regarded as a classical model of political wisdom. That wisdom is evident not only because it has endured but essentially because it expressed in the words of its preamble the goals of justice, peace, defense, public welfare, and the security "of the blessings of freedom for ourselves and our posterity."

Political wisdom directs our attention to the practical significance of the common good as the highest ideal of democracy, which is to serve freedom, human rights, and social justice. The historical dynamics of political freedom and human rights vested in citizens by law have enfranchised the people and promise them an increasingly effective role in future governments. Social justice is the driving force that undertakes to distribute the fruits of the common good equitably among persons according to their needs. This distribution already under way in democracies assuages human fears and assures the durability and progress of political life.

Concretely, as Maritain noted, the common good includes more than important public service operations including roads, bridges, schools, and defense and health programs. Beyond them, it encompasses such goods as the rule of law, sound customary practices, effective political institutions, historical memories and the development of moral and political virtues.[19]

If political wisdom is to assist officials and citizens to decide on the good use of means for attaining the common good, they must begin, prior to a final decision, to undertake an exacting intellectual procedure. The first step in the process is the gathering of facts relevant to the specific circumstances in which action is to be taken. Following the sorting out of available means, advice should be sought from experts and other persons of recognized wisdom. They too should be consulted about the likely consequences of several proposed means. Such deliberations protect against governmental inefficiency, arrogance, and excessive secrecy, to produce better judgments.[20]

Political wisdom realistically understands that progress towards justice and the common good produced by the good use of power and technology by democratic governments will take place gradually and over a long time. The reason for this realism, Maritain maintained, is that historically the human condition produces a double movement of good and evil in which the justice of political life has to work its way "through its own causality toward welfare and success in the future."[21] Wise decisions, too, may be delayed because of the variety of valuable means from among which men of good will can rightly choose in order to achieve the common good.[22]

Given the increasing human awareness of the importance of world affairs and of practical truths about the common life of the people of all nations, Maritain held that nations, despite divergent ideological reasons for acknowledging human rights, could agree on a draft list of human rights. He went on to state that other agreements among nations "can be achieved not on common speculative notions . . . but on the affirmation of the same set of convictions concerning action." He added that however little these agreements may produce, they represent a basis for common action.[23]

In fact the United States during the 60's opened the closed door of communist China's society by exchanging table tennis teams and later agreeing to establish diplomatic relations, limited scientific and cultural exchanges, and trade and travel arrangements. In 1987 the United States and the Soviet Union reached an agreement setting up a network of communications designed to reduce the risks of accidental nuclear war. Later this year the ideological rivalry between the two powers may be tentatively set aside in favor of a practical mutual reduction of all short and medium range missiles. Although it will be a small percentage of the total 40,000 nuclear weapons presently in the possession of both nations, if concluded the agreement would be the first nuclear arms reduction ever agreed upon.

For democratic nations the decisive choices of political wisdom must frequently be made between the good and better ways of social, economic, and political life. This situation has arisen as the choice of available technologies for better living multiply, while the number of people failing to share equitably in national and international well-being has steadily increased.

The choices between the good and the better are well illustrated in the letter of the American Catholic Bishops on the U. S. economy. The bishops recognized and applauded the many good elements of America's technological economy including its respect for private property, its ability to provide food and other consumer goods on a large scale, and the generosity of its people. But for the millions of poor and the near-poor here and abroad the nation's prosperity is flawed. Their letter addressed a task of political wisdom when it offered practical judgments on appropriate means of applying moral and theological principles related to economic life. The measures they proposed intended to improve economic life were presented publicly after careful studies and discussions with lay experts. The letter explains the nature of their judgments in the following remarks: "Our judgments and recommendations on specific economic issues . . . do not carry the same moral authority as our statements of universal moral principles and formal church teaching; the former are related to circumstances which can change or which can be interpreted differently by people of good will."[24] In democratic societies recommendations such as those voiced by the bishops contribute to the fund of political society's political wisdom once accepted by officials and the people. Their consensus becomes a precedent on which future generations can build in accordance with their own insights.

Political wisdom speaks to the fundamental problem of ends and means because it obliges political decision-makers freely to choose means of achieving the ends of justice, the common good, and the dignity of the human person. The primary principle of political wisdom for Maritain is that "means must be proportionate and appropriate to the end, since they are the ways to the end and, so to speak, the end itself in the very process of coming into existence."[25]

In his discussion of the moral rationalization of politics he challenged the contemporary tendency to rely upon "non-moral and successful politics: the art of conquering and keeping power by any means whatsoever."[26] On the contrary he said that the application of good means to attain the common good advances that good, but the employment of evil means will fail in the long run to do so.[27]

The contemporary problem of nuclear deterrence as a means of keeping the peace is one of the most crucial and complex issues involving the moral rationalization of international politics. Those who favor a policy that accepts deterrence conditionally as a fact of life insist upon the eventual elimination of all nuclear weapons. They also believe that no good use can be made of such technologies. Clearly this position has yet to persuade the major powers to agree to total nuclear disarmament for all time and to abandon "Star Wars," and chemical and biological weapons.

The general debate on deterrence policy and on war and peace tends to focus on the technological and strategic aspects of their problems and less on the profound moral principles and their practical applications for peace. Public interest would be well served if the pastoral message in Part IV of the American Catholic Bishops' letter, *The Challenge of Peace*, were better known and understood.[28] Maritain's discussion of the moral rationalization of politics and of its spiritual implications, in *Man and the State*, would broaden and deepen popular education in the making of judgments about war and peace and their existential dimensions.[29]

* * * * * *

The virtues of civic friendship and political wisdom have a central place in Maritain's democratic philosophy but they are simply components of his architectonic philosophy of political life. Over 50 years he systematically studied and wrote about the principles, practices, and problems of political society. Thus he analyzed the significance of human nature, natural law, and the person, and his rights and obligations in political society. His treatment of that society, its government, people, and communities, gave a fresh insight into democratic politics as did his invaluable studies of freedom, equality, religion and politics, education and the social and economic aspects of politics.

Maritain's political philosophy is indivisibly united with his metaphysics, epistemology, philosophy of history, and Christian moral philosophy. That political philosophy is a prophetic discernment of a practical Christian democratic ideal of human freedom, of the people's role in political society, and of the existential effects of the virtues on national and international political life.

Evanston, Illinois

NOTES

1. *Pour le Bien Commun (Paris, 1934) a manifesto.*

2. J. Maritain, *Integral Humanism*, transl. by J. Evans (Notre Dame, 1973) pp. 219-220.

3. J. Maritain, *Existence the and Existent*, transl. by L. Galantiere and G. Phelan (New York, 1956) p. 58.

4. *Ibid.*, p. 58.

5. *Ibid.*, p. 59.

6. *Ibid.*, p. 58.

7. J. Maritain, *Man and the State* (Chicago, 1951) p. 10.

8. I have been unable to find the source for this quotation which I had jotted down years ago.

9. W. McWilliams, *The Idea of Fraternity in America* (Berkeley, 1973) pp. 623-624.

10. J. Murray, *We Hold These Truths* (New York, 1960).

11. *Ibid.*, pp. 7-8.

12. J. Maritain, *Ransoming the Time*, transl. by H. Binsse (New York, 1941) pp. 115-140. This essay relates only to the fellowship of religious faiths.

13. J. Maritain, *Approches Sans Entraves* (Paris, 1973) pp. 244-246.

14. *Man and the State*, pp. 214-217.

15. J. Maritain, *Les Dègres du Savoir*, nouvelle edition (Paris, 1942) pp. 884-885.

16. *Existence and the Existent*, p. 58.

17. *Ibid.*, p. 59.

18. *Ibid.*, See also the analysis of pre-philosophical knowledge in J. Maritain, *Challenges and Renewals*, eds. J. Evans and L. Ward (Notre Dame, 1968) pp. 229-238. The two books of Robert Coles, *The Moral Life of Children* and *The Political Life of Children* (Boston, 1986), present case studies of his conversations with 7-12-year-old children living around the world which appear to support Maritain's thesis of pre-philosophical knowledge.

19. J. Maritain, *The Person and the Common Good* (Notre Dame, 1946) pp. 52-54.

20. *Prudence Chrtienne* (Paris, 1948) pp. 208-210. These pages are part of a discussion of political wisdom as a special branch of Christian prudence.

21. *Challenges and Renewals*, pp. 357-362, re the double movement of history. *Man and the State*, p. 57, is the source of the quotation.

22. Y. Simon, *A General Theory of Authority* (Notre Dame, 1980) p. 40, and Y. Simon, "The Study of Practical Wisdom," *New Scholasticism*, XXXV (1961) 29-30.

23. *Man and the State*, pp. 77-78.

24. American Catholic Bishops' Letter, "Justice for all," *Catholic Telegraph* (Cincinnati, November, 1986) par. 135.

25. *Man and the State*, pp. 77-78.

26. *Ibid.*, p. 56.

27. *Ibid.*, 56-60.

28. American Catholic Bishops' Letter, "The Challenge of Peace," *Origins* (Washington, D.C., 1983) 12, no. 20. pp. 322-325.

29. *Man and the State*, pp. 58-71.

NATURAL LAW AND ECONOMIC HUMANISM

John W. Cooper

In his 1948 essay, *Existence and the Existent*, Jacques Maritain responded to the philosophical questions raised by a number of thinkers who, for often diverse reasons, were known as existentialists. Maritain was particularly interested in distinguishing what he considered to be an authentic, Christian existentialism (or "existential existentialism" from a bogus academic existentialism (most prominently represented by "atheistic existentialism").[1] In the concluding chapter he writes:

> Having made up its mind to be the sole supreme knowledge and so to replace theology, philosophy has for three centuries assumed the heritage and the burdens of theology. The great modern metaphysical systems are thus only seemingly liberated from theology. The questions which the latter claimed to answer continue to haunt those systems. Nowhere is this plainer than in the philosophy of Hegel. It is not useless to remark that atheistic existentialism itself remains dependent upon theology, though an inverted theology. For it, as for Marxism, atheism is a *point of departure* accepted in advance. These two antagonistic philosophies, the one rationalist, the other irrationalist, both develop in the light of an *a-theo-logy* of which they are the *ancillae*.[2]

Thus, for Maritain, both Sartre and Marx are involved in a fundamental error which vitiates their entire systems. Their prior commitment to atheism makes it impossible for them adequately to conceptualize being, general existence, or human existence. In the final analysis, says Maritain, atheistic existentialism and Marxism are merely "philosophies of action" divorced from any defensible link to the *telos* of action, namely, Truth or the Good.

> Such philosophies are in reality philosophies of action, either of *praxis* and the transforming action of the world, or of moral creation *a nihilo* and liberty for liberty's sake.

> This is why the very notion of contemplation has become
> unthinkable for them and they have no other resource than,
> in the fine scorn of ignorance, to stigmatise with the name
> of 'quietism' the highest and purest activity of intellect,
> the free activity of fruition of truth.[3]

The burden of Maritain's argument concerning being, existence, and act is borne by *Existence and the Existent*. Even a brief review of his argument is beyond the scope of the present essay, except insofar as the fundamental points of the thesis bear on one particularly thorny problem of the modern era, namely the problem of economic justice. I propose to examine the ways in which Thomism leads to certain fundamental truths about economic life in the modern world and to an economic philosophy that Maritain called "economic humanism" and which is today commonly known as "democratic capitalism."

The entire Christian church--Roman Catholic, liberal Protestant, and, to a lesser extent, evangelical Protestant and Eastern Orthodox--is engaged in the larger debate between "capitalism" and "socialism." In the world of nations this conflict manifests itself, for example, in the superpower tension between the Soviet bloc and its allies, on the one hand, and the United States and its allies, on the other. In political terms the "ideological divide" in our world today seems to be between those "capitalist" countries that are characterized by open systems of liberal democracy and the "socialist" countries that are characterized by closed systems of authoritarianism or totalitarianism (and which, ironically, claim to be truly democratic). In economic terms, the ideological dichotomy separates systems of private property rights and market exchange, on the one hand, from systems of state ownership of the means of production and state control of non-market, command economies, on the other.

While the above summary of the ideological debate ignores for the moment a number of interesting nuances in our contemporary world, it serves adequately to define the larger dimensions of global relationships. Even more fundamental than the democracy-authoritarianism debate, I believe, is this "core" ideological conflict of the twentieth century, the capitalism- socialism debate.

Since the Christian church is itself entangled in this great debate of the present era, how Christians resolve the problem of ideology--and how they resolve the specific issue of economic justice--will determine in large part the future of the world social order.

How, then, should we understand the significance of the Marxist worldview and the socialist or communist society? I am fully aware that certain theorists, wittingly or unwittingly, propagate vast confusions by referring to some countries as "socialist" which, in fact, are organized on the basis of market exchanges. Be that as it may, I believe the basic differences between capitalism and socialism are generally understood. How should we understand the significance of the capitalist systems that are present in the countries of the non-Marxist "free world"? I am also aware that many theorists prefer to give other names than "capitalism" to the system of private property rights and market exchanges--I prefer the term "*democratic capitalism.*"

Maritain believed that the awakening of the self- consciousness of the working classes in the nineteenth and twentieth centuries was a positive and necessary step toward the realization of the just society. But, Maritain argued, what the socialists called "class consciousness" should have contributed to, rather that detracted from, the notions of human dignity and vocation. Said Maritain: "Class consciousness [has] been chained to an historic calamity [and] . . . spoiled by the gospels of despair and of social warfare which are at the bottom of the Marxist idea of class struggle and the dictatorship of the proletariat."[4]

Maritain points to a profound ambiguity in Marxism: a deterministic view of the formation and function of social classes and a utopian wish for a fundamental revolution in the social order that would eliminate social classes. Here is the double bind. First, if the social order presupposes class stratification, Marxists who come to power are, in fact, a new elite which rules over its own oppressed classes. Second, if class stratification is not historically determined, then its elimination may come about through a non-utopian evolution. It is no wonder that Marxist-run societies everywhere suffer under a politically hegemonic "new class" of elites that is forced by its own ideology to deny that it is a class at all. Experience teaches that class stratification may be inevitable in some form, but class warfare is not.

The same problem holds for Marxism when we examine the doctrine of man. Marx's prior commitment to historical materialism creates a second enduring ambiguity within Marxism. Man is, on the one hand, determined by his class location and by the material coordinates of his world and, on the other, he makes a pseudo-spiritual leap of faith into that revolutionary consciousness that overcomes all material limits and issues in an economy of automatic abundance. In *The Person and the Common Good*, Maritain concludes:

> The person which [Marxism] strives to liberate is conceived as purely immanent in the group. Hence the only emancipation which it could, in reality, achieve, would be that of the collective man, not at all that of the individual person.[5]

Marxist philsophy, in other words, denies the fundamental freedom of the individual person that the genuine existentialism of *Existence and the*

Existent so adamantly defends. And, in denying the freedom of the individual person, Marxism also denies the possibility that a society of free persons could create political and economic systems that would approximate justice in a given historical epoch. In a book published in Polish before he became pope, Karol Wojtyla described this fundamental error of Marxism under the rubric of "totalism":

> The dominant trait of totalism may be characterized as the need to find protection *from* the individual, who is seen as the chief enemy of society and of the common good. Since totalism assumes that inherent in the individual there is only the striving for individual good, that any tendency toward participation or fulfillment in acting and living together with others is totally alien to him, it follows that the "common good" can be attained only by limiting the individual. The good thus advocated by totalism can never correspond to the wishes of the individual, to the good he is capable of choosing independently and freely according to principles of participation; it is always a good that is incompatible with and a limitation upon the individual. Consequently, the realization of the common good frequently presupposes the use of coercion.[6]

In passing we might note that these fundamental contradictions in Marxism, none of which have been resolved by the vast array of subsequent Marxist or neo-Marxist interpretations, today infect theology and the Church itself by way of some "liberation theologians" who propound Marxist principles rather than Christian and personalist principles of genuine liberation.[7] Perhaps one example will suffice to illustrate the fundamentally anti-personalist perspective of some liberation theologians. Juan Luis Segundo writes: "We give the name of socialism to a political regime in which the ownership of the means of production is removed from individuals and handed over to higher institutions whose concern is the common good."[8] The idea that individual good and the common good are simple opposites is anathema to personalism.

Another philosophical objection may be raised to the presuppositions of much contemporary social thought, whether it be of the Marxist or of the liberal variety. This objection is to the conflation of history with eschatology. When the *eschaton* no longer represents a transhistorical point of reference from which the Divine judges the temporal, it is merely the climax of history and it becomes a justification for the imposition of a utopian vision upon society. In short, without a genuine revelation of Truth beyond history, history itself becomes a god, and historicism dominates philosophy. Maritain made this point on several occasions. This same objection has been raised recently in a remarkable essay by Oliver O'Donovan, *Resurrection and the Moral Order*:

> [Historicism's] use of eschatological categories is characteristically to *legitimize* the immanent tendencies of history rather than to *criticize* them. If there is no locus of value outside history, then history must provide its own critical movements from within, so that the kingdom of God becomes a form without content, an empty 'end' which will receive its definition from the history which has led up to it. Thus historicism represents a return to totalitarian thinking, in which the whole content of the claim of the good is mediated to man through his developing social culture.[9]

In this passage O'Donovan specifically criticizes both liberalism and Marxism, including the neo-Marxism of the Protestant liberation theologian, Juergen Moltmann.

Not only at the philosophical level, but also at the level of social policy, Marxism has shown itself to be deficient. In the twentieth century, many experiments with socialist economic policy have been carried out. Almost without exception they have created greater poverty and more injustice than the essentially precapitalist, "feudal" systems they have replaced. What are the classical characteristics of socialism? Nationalization of basic industries, an economically dominat public sector, centralized economic planning, equal income distribution, the total welfare state. None can be convincingly defended on the grounds of efficiency or justice.

What we are left with, after the death of Marxism as a philosophy and an economic policy, is the task of re-examining market economies in an effort to discover ways to make them more compatible with personalist social philosophies. How do we define "democratic capitalism"? It is a three-part system of political, economic, and cultural freedoms. In the political sphere, it is that set of institutions (universal suffrage, representative government, redress of grievances, independent judiciary, etc.) and the requisite rights and responsibilities of the citizen that are characteristic of a self-governing democracy. In the economic sphere, it is that set of institutions (open and fair markets in both labor and product exchange, legal protection of private property rights, government regulation of economic activity, mechanisms for the material support of the economically non-productive members of society) and the requisite rights and responsibilities of workers and their families that are characteristic of a generally capitalist- oriented society. In the cultural sphere, it is that set of institutions (churches and other religious bodies independent of state control, a free press, non-ideological schools and colleges, voluntary associations representing a wide variety of interests) and the requisite rights and responsibilities of the person that are characteristic of a pluralist and tolerant society.

This capsule definition of democratic capitalist society provides a context for discussing the specific economic questions that must arise in any complete social theory.

Maritain shared the basic aversion to "bourgeois liberalism" that was common to Catholic intellectuals of his era. He believed that the "Protestant" culture of Northern Europe and North America had fallen into the error of excessive individualism and that this had led to theological and political heresies on a grand scale.

Thus, Maritain had little admiration for capitalism and often criticized it "in the same breath" with socialism. Yet, by the late 1950's, Maritain had experienced life in the United States and Canada and had begun to sharpen his views on economics and the future course of the social order in the Western democracies. Maritain wrote in *Reflections on America*:

> A new social and economic regime is, in actual fact, developing in this country--a phenomenon which gives the lie to the forecasts of Karl Marx and which came about not by virtue of some kind of inner necessity in the evolution of capitalism which Marx and overlooked, but by virtue of the freedom and spirit of man, namely by virtue of the American mind and conscience, and of the American collective effort of imagination and creation.[10]

Maritain began to see that profit is merely the calculus of productive work, and money is merely the medium of exchange of work's value.

> Philosophically speaking, I would say that individual profit still remains, as it ever will, an indispensable human incentive but that it is now definitely losing absolute primacy, and that the principle of the fecundity of money is definitely superseded now by the principle of profit-sharing in a contractual association.[11]

Yet, Maritain believed that the embryonic justice that democratic capitalist countries had achieved would require much fuller development and creative adaptation.

> This new social and economic regime is still in a state of full becoming, but it has already brought history beyond both capitalism and socialism.[12]

"Capitalism," in Maritain's mind, represents a system in which individual profit--"an indispensable human incentive"--had absolute primacy, which contradicted other values. An example of this would be a monopoly enterprise in a "company town." Such an enterprise is protected from competition in either the labor market or the product market. Such a monopoly, whether enforced by private or public writ, would contravene the economic rights and freedoms of the persons in that town.

The historic reforms within capitalist societies that forced all enterprises to operate in an open market also caused profit and productivity to be *optimized* over the long term rather than *maximized* over the short term. And, when the market for capital was opened to the forces of competition, many people who did not previously control wealth could come to do so, either individually or collectively. The most important such collective of persons acting in the economic sphere, according to Maritain, was the labor union. Operating according to the principles of private property rights and market exchanges without monopolies-- and ensuring free access to the capital, labor, and product markets--the capitalist societies have progressed over time toward greater economic justice.

By 1958, Maritain saw emerging in North America a new form of economy which showed great promise for the future. It was a system in embryo that arose from a doctrine of "economic humanism." It paralleled the democratic system based on the doctrine of "political humanism" that Maritain had been defending with great force for more than two decades.[13]

In *Reflections on America*, Maritain told the story of a magazine editor who wrote an article in the 1950's entitled "Wanted: A new Name for Capitalism." The editor invited his readers to send in their suggestions. To his surprise, 15,000 replies came back. The suggestions included "industrial democracy," "economic democracy," "the new capitalism," "democratic capitalism," "distributivism," "mutualism," "productivism," and "managementism." Maritain, too, felt the need for a new phrase to describe the inner transformation of the industrial regime. He suggested "economic humanism" as the term that best conformed to the broader personalist and pluralist society that he envisioned. He advocated an economy in which every agent in the productive process, acting with intelligent self-interest, would receive his due proportion of the material reward. Further, there would be freedom to initiate a business for its possible rewards; there would be equality of opportunity in a relatively classless system, with a high degree of upward (and downward) social mobility, and there would be a bond of civic friendship that generated obligations to honesty and fairness in business dealings.[14]

Democratic capitalism as we know it today has continued down that generally positive path that Maritain described in the 1950's. This is not to say that there has been a steady, unimpeded progress toward justice. Justice is never won easily, and it exists today side by side with many injustices.

There are many problems in the democratic capitalist countries today--there is much to be done for the sake of ensuring economic justice for all, as the American Catholic bishops have reminded us. But the overall system of democratic capitalism--private property rights, markets, material incentives, government regulation of the economy, and a limited welfare system--has been vindicated by historical experience.

Modern democratic society is based on the presupposition that individual persons, given the opportunity to make informed choices at the ballot box, in the marketplace, and in the activities of ordinary daily life, can, under the influence of the Truth itself, gradually create a progressively more just society. The modern era, in spite of its many distortions of the Christian vision, has disclosed the moral basis of freedom and, hence, the approximate compatability of democracy, the market economy, the pluralistic culture with the Christian vision of man and society. Genuine Christian political theology cannot celebrate liberty for its own sake, as merely a *freedom from*; it must be a *freedom for* a life based on Truth and Love.[15]

The *economic* choices, then, which each of us makes in his daily life are a part of that larger drama of human existence and responsible action that Maritain describes in *Existence and the Existent*. When a person chooses freely to take one job rather than another (because it offers a variety of advantages: monetary, emotional, even spiritual), when a person chooses to buy or not to buy a certain product or service (based on a realistic perception of its usefulness and appropriateness), when a person chooses to embark upon a financial enterprise at the risk of monetary loss but with the potential for monetary gain (and usually with a creative urge to organize human and material resources for optimum efficiency), when a person acts in these and a multitude of other ways as a participant in the economic life of society, he or she is fulfilling a natural function of human existence, fulfilling the natural law as it applies to this realm of human activity.

It is the responsibility of able-bodied adults to be economically self-reliant. Exceptions are made for those persons with responsibilities for child-bearing and the care of others. Upon the economic productivity of able-bodied adults depends the fate of children, the elderly, the disabled, and others who are unable, either temporarily or permanently, to participate in economic production. The free society is made possible through the uncounted efforts of the majority to grow food, build homes, heal the sick, manage enterprises, and produce all of the other goods and services necessary to human existence and fulfillment. Democratic capitalism is the fairest and most efficient system yet devised by which these diverse efforts of individual persons are organized. As a system it encompasses all those instances of market exchange whereby goods and services are produced and consumed as well as those activities that transcend the market mechanism, such as philanthropy; the maintenance of the welfare of the poor and disadvantaged through the agencies of the state, the church, or other voluntary associations; and the defense of the public order through law enforcement and military deterrence.

Economic dynamism and productivity are key elements in the pursuit of social justice. A portion of the wealth created in the market economy, a portion of the profits, must always be set aside to provide for those persons and sectors of society that do not themselves produce a profit.

What of those able-bodied adults who consciously reject economically productive vocations? Some persons have been called to a hermetic or contemplative lifestyle that minimizes their involvement in mundane existence, including economic activity. But some persons who are not called to the contemplative life are, nevertheless, profoundly alienated from ordinary daily life, especially in its economic dimensions. Those who have rebelled against the organization of economic life sometimes make a vocation, as it were, of their rebellion, although this can only be a bogus vocation. Such persons have sometimes marshalled powerful intellectual energies to justify a system of totalitarian control based on Marxist principles. In so doing they have denied the very bases of human freedom and responsibility set forth in the doctrine of the natural law. By contrast the ordered freedom of the person in his role as an economic actor is most fully maintained under a system of democratic capitalism--property rights, markets, government regulations, a limited welfare program. Totalitarianism is the logical end of Marxist presuppositions. Democratic capitalism is the logical end of personalist presuppositions. Maritain writes:

> From the old socialistic ideas comes the temptation to grant primacy to the economic set-up, and at the same time the tendency to turn everything over to the authority of the State, administrator of the welfare of all, and to its scientific and bureaucratic machinery; which, like it as we will, moves in the direction of a totalitarianism with a technocratic base. It is not this rationalization of mathematical organization that should inspire the work of reconstruction; rather, it should be a practical and experimental wisdom attentive to human ends and means. The idea of planned economy should thus be replaced by a new idea based on the progressive adjustment, due to the activity and the reciprocal tension of autonomous agencies, which, from the bottom up, would bring producers and consumers together, in which case it would be better to say an adjusted rather than a planned economy. Likewise, the notion of collectivization should be replaced by that of associative ownership of the means of production, or of

joint ownership of the enterprise, . . . substituting, as far as possible, joint ownership for the wage system.[16]

The "progressive adjustment" of the democratic capitalist economy comes about through the market mechanism itself and through the interplay of institutions--corporations, labor unions, governments, the media. "Associative ownership" has also begun to take new forms: publicly-traded stock corporations, pension fund investments, home ownership, and similar property-ownership arrangements. In these and many other ways the practical experience of the democratic capitalist countries has confirmed the basic principles set forth by Jacques Maritain in his writings on man's existence and his social responsibilities.

Democratic capitalism is that social system that most closely conforms in the present era to the demands of the Christian ideal of justice. As such, it requires further development in the light of future experience. It is necessary to examine a wide variety of factors in the economy and in the society at large to arrive at a correlation between the principles of natural law and the achievements of man. The present essay attempts to open this question to further scrutiny. There is much work that remains to be done in this field, especially in the area of economics. Many theologians are turning to the task of developing a theology of economics, many will make valuable contributions in the coming years. But it is imperative that Christian theology clearly delineate its objects to the philosophical presuppositions of Marxism and other false ideologies, including even those which appropriate the name of "capitalism" for social programs that contradict the personalist view of man--his existence and his freedom.

Ethics and Public Policies Center

NOTES

1. Jacques Maritain, *Existence and the Existent*, trans. Lewis Galantiere and Gerald B. Phelan (Lanham, Md.: University Press of America, 1987), p. 123.

2. *Ibid.*, p. 135.

3. *Ibid.*, p. 136.

4. Jacques Maritain, *The Social and Political Philosophy of Jacques Maritain*, eds. Joseph W. Evans and Leo R. Ward (Notre Dame, In.: University of Notre Dame Press, 1976), p. 340.

5. Jacques Maritain, *The Person and the Common Good*, trans. John J. Fitzgerald (Notre Dame, Ind.: University of Notre Dame Press, 1966), p. 93.

6. Karol Wojtyla, *The Acting Person*, trans. Andrzej Potocki (Dordrecht, Holland: D. Reidel Pub., 1979), p. 274.

7. Two lengthy "intructions" on the matter of genuine versus false concepts of liberation have been promulgated by the Congregation for the Doctrine of the Faith under the leadership of Cardinal Joseph Ratzinger and with the endorsement of Pope John Paul II: "Instruction on Certain Aspects of the 'Theology of Liberation,'" *Origins* 14 (September 13, 1984) 193, 195-204; and "Instruction on Christian Freedom and Liberation," *Origins* 15 (April 17, 1986) 713, 715-728.

8. Juan Luis Segundo, "Capitalism-Socialism: A Theological Crux," in Claude Geffre and Gustavo Gutierrez, *The Mystical and Political Dimension of the Christian Faith* (New York: Herder and Herder, 1974), p. 115.

9. Oliver O'Donovan, *Resurrection and Moral Order: An Outline for Evangelical Ethics* (Leicester, England: Inter- Varsity Press, 1986), p. 73.

10. Jacques Maritain, *Reflections on America* (New York: Gordian Press, 1975), pp. 114-115.

11. *Ibid.*, p. 115.

12. *Loc. cit.*

13. The pinnacle of Maritain's political thought, in my estimation, is *Man and the State* (Chicago: University of Chicago Press, 1951).

14. Maritain, *Reflections on America*, pp. 112-13.

15. For a fuller discussion of the moral basis of freedom in the social order, see my *The Theology of Freedom: The Legacy of Jacques Maritain and Reinhold Niebuhr* (Macon, Ga.: Mercer University Press, 1985).

16. Maritain, *The Social and Political Philosophy of Jacques Maritain*, p. 43.

MODERNIZATION AND HUMAN VALUES

Joseph J. Califano

INTRODUCTION

The focus of this paper is the contemporary use of the concept of modernization by many historians and social scientists to reinstate pernicious ideas of the past to explain human nature, history, and politics, in respect to the third world.[1] Any attempt to comprehend the global dynamics of the interaction between modernization and human values involves an attempt to understand at least three realities: 1) the process of modernization; 2) human values; and 3) the endeavor of the art of politics to deal with modernization in the light of human values. How we assess the above realities determines whether we have an optimistic or pessimistic future; for there is a universal consensus among developed[2] and developing nations that modernization has produced many advances as well as many results which are understood to be evil. The potency for good and evil develops equally and side by side in human history, because through time man tends to manifest all the potentialities of his nature.[3] The knowledge and power that development concentrates in the hands of men can produce a progression of goods both material and moral, as well as a progression of evils, the likes of which have no historical antecedent. Thus we find that modernization has created an abundance of material goods and also environmental problems of momentous proportions which might even threaten the survival of the human race.

Also modernization has created a development of the democratic state of mind, that is, a deeper understanding of human rights. But also intense perversions of the understanding of human rights. Modernization has produced both the worse forms of totalitarianism and a very intense crisis in personal morality. Such an assessment causes many to ask: what can we do? or what should we do? or can anything be done? At this point we turn to the juncture of the study of history and moral philosophy, what Maritain properly designated as the philosophy of history.[4] A juncture at which it is discovered that there is a necessary relationship between ethics and politics. If politics is to have a genuinely positive goal, its goal must be derived from authentic ethical principles in conjunction with a purification of the means employed.   Now the philosophy of history that one develops will also determine whether one sees the creativity of man as a moral agent as described in the *Existence and the Existent*[5] as having any potency to deal with the issues related to modernization or whether man is trapped in an historical tidal wave which, irrespective of the actions of men, has the results already determined.

Our common experience in regard to notions such as modernization, human values, and politics is that we feel we have a comfortable grasp of their meaning until we undertake to discover an insightful scientific vision of these realities and how they are interacting to determine our lives. Such undertakings cause all kinds of ambiguities to creep into our thought and our judgments become fraught with ambivalence. This is the case because modernization is a process of the transformation of civilizations or cultures, and processes are subject to real definitions only when we can identify their goal. Thus, if we ask what is the goal of the process of modernization, no clear empirically verifiable answer comes forth and very little agreement is found among scholars of various disciplines. In fact some have questioned whether modernization has a final cause at all; a view that leads one immediately to question whether man through history has a final cause. This has lead many, especially in the social sciences, to fashion nominalistic descriptive definitions which while informative do not satisfy the mind in its natural desire for real definitions that are productive of understanding. These persons also tend to define a part of the process as a definition of the whole.   For example, there are those who consider modernization to be primarily economic, and reduce all other aspects of modern history to a function of economic processes.   This view ultimately eclipses man's creative freedom and his knowledge of himself as a moral being. Those who give credence to this popular myth place man in the world as a helpless victim of economic forces simply to be described by the economic historian.

APRIORI DEDUCTIVE VS INDUCTIVE APOSTERIORI APPROACHES TO MODERNIZATION

There are two fundamentally different approaches to understanding history and the process of modernization. The first is the application of deductive models to history from apriori principles.   The second is an inductive aposteriori approach to history and its processes.

The first approach produces a number of variations which assume one or a combination of the following as their apriori principles: a) something akin to the positivistic epistemology of Auguste Comte; b) the Idealistic metaphysics of Hegel; or c) the reductive materialism of Marx. It is interesting that many contemporary theorists in these schools do not recognize the roots of their viewpoint since they have become the unexamined fabric of the *modus operandi* of their discipline.

Within this framework we find two definitions of modernization prevalent today. Modernization means Capitalization or Marxification; and both are essentially moral philosophies whether or not this is generally recognized. What must be remembered is that Adam Smith was a professor of moral philosophy at Glasgow University. His *Inquiry into the Nature and Causes of the Wealth of Nations (1776)*[6] was a work in moral philosophy. Smith viewed his work as moral advice to the British Crown as to the best way to rule the empire. In Smith's view, power and wealth were the criteria for judging the status of nations; and undirected free enterprise was offered as the best means of fostering the growth of the power and wealth of nations. The invisible hand[7] of competition would produce for the Crown and her subjects the greatest economic development. Since this view is primarily concerned with defining the good and providing priority values as a guide for human decisions, it can only be understood as essentially a moral philosophy. Marx on the other hand replaces the invisible hand of competition with the invisible hand of the necessary dialectical forces of matter which, again offers us a set of values and priorities as a guide for human action.[8] Marxism with its glorification of dialectical praxis again is essentially a moral philosophy. Although Marx rejects contemplative philosophy and moral philosophy vis-a-vis Hegel, he does not hesitate to develop a moral philosophy of his own, with its own set of values and prescriptions for human action. There are necessitating laws determining history and human nature.

What causes both not to want to be identified as moral philosophies is that the first wounds our understanding of human freedom and human nature and therefore corrupts our notion of justice; whereas the second eradicates the need for a concept of justice, along with the notions of human freedom and human nature by rendering man a relativistic monad of dialectical forces. Both these views in their pure forms, Liberalism and Marxism, have their myths. If these myths are given credence, one falls victim to the despair that results from attempts to establish justice on concepts drawn from the material order of things. For a more detailed analysis of my view, see "Democracy of the Human Person or Man as a Moral Agent."[9]

What must be avoided is the ever present danger of the creative forces of history being threatened by a pernicious past, in this case the intellectual corpses of two deterministic economic views of human history that are purported to be ultimate explanations of human nature and modern human history. Those who adhere to these views are men suffering from intellectual and moral necrophilia; they represent an attempt to impose dead moral philosophies on the world in the name of modernization. Both share the myth that government is an evil which either will disappear as the process comes to term with the forces driving it, or that government is to be rendered invisible by giving it only a negative role in protecting economic rights. Thus libertarianism and Marxism are not significantly different.

These deterministic reductionistic models reject the need for genuine moral philosophy because they assume a total immanency of human values in respect to the economic process itself, in that the process is posited with the power to produce progressive values in and of itself, independently of human freedom. Therefore actions which appear to be the product of human choices are merely the product of apriori determining forces. What appear then subjectively to be free choices, objectively are merely the ripe economic forces becoming manifest. These views lay claim to being scientific sociology or scientific social history. Once the complexity of the deterministic process becomes known, human history and human actions become quite predictable. The indeterminacy that appears is a consequence of our ignorance of the process, or something akin to Heisenberg's uncertainty principle in physics. The study of values is contained within economics or is viewed as a discipline subordinate to economics.

The consequence of the above is that the creativity of man as moral agent, and man's self-knowledge through his existential experience of his free moral actions, is forever lost. Man is said to make history not by free choices but by conditions bequeathed by the past and the eternal economic force inherent in the process.

There is however an inductive aposteriori approach to understanding the processes of history, an approach that recognizes the fact that human history is the study of the sequence of singular concrete contingent realities, an approach that sees the uniqueness of entire courses of events as reflecting the dynamics of free choices made by men, free choices that enable men to create new currents in regard to the dynamics of development. This understanding of the process of development reflects a genuine grasp of human nature, and the creativity of man as moral agent. In this understanding of the historical process one recognizes that man lives in a world characterized by adventure. In other words, the course of events is flexible and mutable, filled with contingency and chance, even though the world of essences is filled with necessary laws. Therefore there can not be a genuine apriori explanation of history nor a reconstruction of history according to necessitating laws, even though there can be a deciphering of general aspects or tendencies. The necessity proper to laws does not make the events necessary, because laws refer to universal essences known by abstraction while events take place in existential concrete reality, subject to independent lines of causation.

This is not only a true view of the nature of historical processes but the only one that will enable man to rediscover the vitality of his moral creative freedom in regard to historical processes as described in *Existence and the Existent*. In such a view of the historical process man is recognized to be the kind of being who becomes a person and is revealed to himself in his uniqueness through moral action. Man is an existent who becomes a person when the freedom of spontaneity proper to animals becomes, through knowledge and love, the freedom of autonomy. Man is that being who by a genuine act of love and justice can cast a stone at an impervious universe and shatter it with one blow. Man is *homo sapiena*, capable of recognizing means as means to an end, and therefore capable of recognizing that economic systems exist for the sake of man and should be subject to the needs of justice. Man is also that existent who is capable of rejecting the proposition that man exists for the sake of economic systems and that he should put his faith in invisible forces of history to determine the course of future events. Man is a person who refuses to surrender what is most beautiful about human nature; namely, that man like God is the author of his actions and that he is even capable of creating his own hell by failing to have a genuine vision of his calling. For, where there is no vision, the people perish. For we still live in a world full of false gods and we will remain condemned to enslavement unless we exorcise these false gods from our world.[10]

LEVELS IN DEVELOPING A DEFINITION OF MODERNIZATION AND THE GOALS OF HUMAN HISTORY

There are at least three stages to be noted in order to develop a proper definition of modernization. The first stage is understood in terms of the process by means of which men consume natural resources in order to create great quantities of inanimate energy to replace the animate labor of brute animals and men. Thereby human labor is rendered more efficient, and the productivity of human labor geometrically increased. Technological industrialization and the commercialization of human activity became a necessary means to this end. This is economic modernization. The second stage is understood in considering that skilled labor forces were required in order to keep the process going. However, skills become obsolete even within a generation; thus an ever increasing amount of time and energy has to be invested to provide a well trained, if not well educated, commercially usable work force to feed into the technologically advancing economies. Man thus might erroneously come to view himself as a cybernetic economic unit. In this context, urbanization and geographic mobility appear to become a necessary social reality, and the individual's identification with family and communities become diminished proportionally. This process might be termed social modernization, with many concomitant results such as secularization. These processes have created havoc in respect to the common good of mankind, in regard to the environment in which we live, and in regard to our personal lives. The third level of modernization is political modernization. At this level of the process of modernization, man attempts to develop his moral conscience and to properly conceive justice. He strives to attain a proper understanding of human rights in the light of genuine justice. Only when this last form of modernization is properly achieved will the process of modernization tend towards what is its real final cause. Also only through justice can the evils created by the first two levels of modernization be corrected. It is clear that modernization in the end is primarily a matter of man searching for a genuine moral vision of what he is and what he must do.

The great danger is that we can become preoccupied with only one of the three levels of modernization. For when this happens, one commits oneself, by an act of faith, to one of the apriori deductive models of human history, and the principles of that model become the object of a secular religion with an economic eschatology. The danger here is that the believer sees only one of the three major tendencies of modern history, namely that of subduing nature without understanding the serious need for man to organize his freedoms and direct the forces he himself has created. Only if man develops a proper use of his freedom in light of the progress in man's moral conscience can genuine modernization be accomplished.

For only then will the purification of the means take place that is required for man to give primacy to the development of good over the development of evil. For man must not only subdue nature to attain autonomy and he must subdue the mechanisms he has created in order to subdue nature. Man must tame the industrialized world and all the threats to his existence and human rights that it has created.

THE CRISIS IN PERCEPTION OF MODERNIZATION IN UNDERDEVELOPED COUNTRIES

Unfortunately there is a global crisis in the perception of what the process of modernization entails and what means are available to the Third world countries to develop. If this misperception continues it will cause the world to experience ever more traumatic eruptions in the environment and in the social order. The problem is that the prevailing modes of conceptualizing modernization in the third world and in particularly central and south America are in terms of the apriori deductive models discussed above. Here a global perspective has become contracted into a globalist theory. This theory which begins with a fact, namely, that there is a world economic system, but insists that every event in the system can be properly interpreted only in terms of the apriori deductive models described above. The dynamics of modernization for the majority of globalists is to be understood only in terms of Marxist- Leninist dialectics. Thus we have the contemporary Latin American theorists such as Enzo Faletto,[11] Immanuel Wallerstein,[12] and Patrick McGowan[13] advocating the view that less developed counties are faced with a world- imperialistic capitalistic system which is controlled by the more developed countries. They are critical of the realistic conception of international relations in which the desire to maintain a balance of power and peace are advocated by the developed countries. Most globalists view the realistic approach to international relations as a means whereby the developed countries try to keep the less developed countries dependent upon them.[14] All of the above, they claim, is directed to producing and preserving a situation of trade agreements which preserve the *status quo*. This has led some, like Augustin Cueva,[15] to follow rigidly Rosa Luxemberg[16] in the belief that only the hammer blow of revolution can break the relationship of dependency between the developed and less developed countries.   Therefore in order to find their national identity the less developed countries must revolt to break out of the state of dependency.   The less developed countries must overthrow their own rulers who cooperate in and perpetuate this system for their private interest at the expense of their own nation.   What they fail to see is that these revolutions merely exchange one relationship of dependency for another.

Irrespective of the above, globalists persist in the belief that only through a violent pushing forward of the ripened economic forces, and by introducing a good dose of anarchy into the system, can the national identity of the less developed countries be made manifest.   Thus nationalism and marxism become blended together.   Fortunately there are some who advocate a less rigid view of the process e.g. the Argentine economist Raul Prebisch[17] who recognizes the problem of national identity but rules out the rigid view that large-scale historical processes are immune from the actions of human beings.   Fernando Henrique Cardoso,[18] for example, calls for a transfiguration of the present structures, thereby replacing these socialist structures with others not so predetermined, while Prebisch calls for a state-guided capitalism.   Both men however admit that man can use his freedom in a positive way to provides a viable solution.

As I said in 1975,[19] the modern technological mind-set as we have experienced it is inherently violent but it need not necessarily be that way. This can be avoided if the process of industrialization is made subject to the demands of justice by good men, who will purify the means of modernization in light of a genuine understanding of the various levels of the process of modernization and how they are related to the common good of this and future generations.   Only in this way can the aspirations of mankind become fulfilled and the development of good be given precedence over that of evil.   For the natural goal of history is not only that man subdue nature and that all his potentialities be actualized, but also that man civilize the means whereby he subdues nature, the modern technological industrialized economies he has created. This can be accomplished only by fulfilling the democratic political aspirations of man in terms of social justice properly understood, when economics is made subject to justice. Otherwise developing countries will repeat all the past mistakes of developed countries, a scenario that the world in a genuinely human sense might not survive.

What is needed immediately are treaties to be created where   men of different intellectual persuasions agree on a practical mode of cooperation so as to avoid having developing countries repeat the errors of the past. This is in the interest of all, for the world can ill afford the ecological and political consequences that would otherwise follow. We can not afford to have Brazil continue to destroy the rain forest through a misperception of its agricultural possibilities; nor can the world afford further development of nuclear energy where uncontrollable nuclear accidents like Chernobyl are not only likely but morally certain. The health cost of this to present and future generations is immeasurable. In addition it is becoming clear that nuclear energy is economically unsound. The effect of having developing countries invest in another dead end is simply unacceptable. Lastly, the cost of perpetuating in the political realm the misconceptions about modernization will lead as it has in the past to the enslavement of many. These false gods will pervert man's understanding of human rights and the common good. When the common good is misrepresented all forms of evil pour forth. Developed nations must provide less developed nations with a viable alternative in which they can participate in the benefits of modernization without suffering the consequences of repeating the past. This is possible only if we regain the dynamic view of history, and of man as a moral agent, to be found in Maritain's *Existence and the Existent*.

St. John's University

NOTES

1. H. Elbaki, "Changing Patterns in Research on the Third World," *Annual Review of Sociology* 4 (1978) 239-257.

2. See M. B. Jansen, ed., *Changing Japanese Attitudes Toward Modernization* (Princeton, 1965) and D. H. Shively, ed., *Tradition and Modernization in Japanese Culture* (Princeton, 1976).

3. See J. Maritain, *On the Philosophy of History*, ed. J. W. Evans (New York, 1957) ch. 2 and 4.

4. *Ibid.*, p. 17.

5. See J. Maritian, *Existence and the Existent*, ch. 2-4.

6. Ed. E. Cannan (New York, 1937). It is interesting to compare this with his *Theory of Moral Sentiments* (New York, 1966).

7. *Wealth of Nations*, p. 423.

8. See *Capital* (Chicago, 1906-1909), *A Contribution to the Critique of Political Economy* (Chicago, 1904), *Economic and Philosophiclal Manuscripts of 1844* (New York, 1965), and *the Poverty of Philosophy* (1910).

9. J.-L.Allard, ed., *Jacques Maritain: A Philosopher in the World* (Ottawa, 1985) 303 ff.

10. See E. Gilson, *God and Philosophy* (Clinton, MA, 1955) 136.

11. *Dependence Theory and the Development of Latin America* (Berkeley, 1979).

12. *The Modern World System*, 2 vols. (New York, 1974, 1980).

13. P. J. McGowan and B. Kordan, "Imperialism in World System Perspective," *World System Structure*, ed. Hollist and Rosenau (Beverly Hills, 1981).

14. Theories of international relations fall into three categories: (1) Realism, in which the state is assumed to be the principal rational unitary actor in international relations and and in which national security is the primary final cause influencing foreign policy; (2) Pluralism, in which the foreign policy of the state reflects the interaction of competing individuals, interest groups, multinational corporations, and bureaucracies within the state (a multipurpose foreign policy develops, stressing social and ecological issues as welll as national security issues); (3) Globalism, in which all foreign policy is understood in terms of the history of economic hegemony and the mechanisms of domination that economic hegemony produces. Realism stresses peaceful change by minor adjustments in the balance of power. Pluralism advocates the peaceful transformation of world politics, hoping that international institutions can aid in the process. But Globalism stresses revolutions as the only means of changing international relations. See P. R. Vikotti and M. V. Kauppi, *International Relations Theory* (New York, 1987).

15. "Perspectives of Dependency Theory, *Latin American Perspectives* (1976).

16. *Reform and Revolution* (New York, 1973). The original German text dates from 1889.

17. *Toward a Dynamic Development Policy for Latin America* (New York, 1963).

18. "The Consumption of Dependency Theory in the United States," *Latin American Reach Review* (1977).

19. "Technology and Violence," *Divus Thomas (Piacenza)* 78 (1975).

PART TWO

EXISTENCE AND THE EXISTENT

D. The Existent

THE FOUNDATIONS OF MARITAIN'S NOTION OF THE ARTIST'S "SELF"

John G. Trapani, Jr.

"The difference between the right word
and the almost-right word is the
difference between the lightening and
the lightening-bug."   Mark Twain

Introduction

For disciples of Maritain's aesthetics, his definition of Poetry[1] in the opening of *Intuition in Art and Poetry* is particularly familiar: Poetry, he says, is the "intercommunication between the inner being of things and the inner being of the human Self ...."[2]

Although undoubtedly obscure for philosophers from some philosophical traditions, this definition always appealed to me as a Thomist philosopher, and I felt reasonable confidence about my ability to understand what Maritain was saying. The attempt to explain this definition to a non-Thomist interlocutor presented an unanticipated challenge, however, especially when our discussion about the "intercommunication of the inner being" necessarily led us to the metaphysical principles underlying this idea ... principles like the analogy of being and the Thomistic notion of the human person.

After some preliminary success at understanding each other and the specific jargon of Thomistic vocabulary, my colleague unwittingly went straight for the linguistic jugular when he inquired about Maritain's awkward use of the term "Self." Why had the definition not been written: "... and the inner being of the human *Person*..."? Surely, my friend suggested, that is what Maritain had in mind, and that word-choice would have decreased the text's esoteric tone and increased reader comprehensibility.

My initial inclination was to agree. Interchanging "Person" and "Self" certainly appeared sufficiently appropriate to Maritain's meaning, and I thought at first that the discrepancy could be traced to a translator's preference. Closer investigation, however, revealed two things to the contrary. First, since *Creative Intuition* was initially published in English, the existing word-choice could not be explained away by attributing it to a translator's decision. Secondly, since *Creative Intuition* itself contains no detailed discussion of either of the terms "Person" or "Self," it was safe to assume that Maritain presupposed a certain measure of background-understanding on the part of his readers. Unfortunately, regardless of the truth or falsity of this presupposition, it still leaves the present problem unaffected and unresolved. Are the terms "Person" and "Self" interchangeable, or was there instead serious purpose in Maritain's mind when he selected the term "Self", a choice which he reiterates several pages later:

> I need to designate both the singularity and the infinite
> depths of this flesh-and-blood and spiritual existent, the
> artist; and I have only an abstract word: the Self.[3]

Far from being an exercise in intellectual or philosophical trivia and minutiae, the investigation and subsequent resolution of this problem -- what are the foundations of Maritain's notion of the "Self" such that he would prefer to use this term in reference to the artist's personhood? -- actually provided deepened insight into the "infinite depths" which Maritain undoubtedly desired to convey to his readers through the intentional selection of that solitary and "abstract" word: the "Self."

Maritain's Notion of the "Self"

As mentioned, *Creative Intuition* contains no detailed discussion of either "Person" or "Self." To understand Maritain's mind on this subject, and to appreciate the background or foundation concerning these terms that he presumes of the readers of *Creative Intuition*, we must turn to two earlier works which are especially germane. For a discussion of "Person," the early sections of Maritain's book *The Person and the Common Good* are quite helpful; the most accessible and productive source for understanding the foundations of his notion of "Self" is Maritain's small but seminal work, *Existence and the Existent*.

In his essay entitled simply "The Existent," Maritain not only discusses the terms "Self" and "subjectivity," but correctly initiates his treatment of these ideas within the broader context of the "subject" (or supposit or *suppositum*) and the distinction between existence and subsistence. This latter precision is a metaphysically essential distinction, though it is one that is frequently obscured or over-looked in much modern and contemporary philosophy. "Existence" is a term which refers to anything at all that may be said "to be" -- it encompasses the entire analogical range of the verb "is" and, as such, designates not only material and spiritual beings (i.e., substances, subjects, or supposits) but accidental, imaginary, and purely rational or logical beings as well.

While it is true that all subsisting beings exist, the opposite is not true. Thus, subsistence may be understood to refer to a special class of existing beings, namely those which have their "to be" or existence in and of themselves. The word "substance" is perhaps the most frequent term used to designate these subsisting beings. It is the most common translation for what Aristotle termed *ousia* and Aquinas termed *suppositum*; in *Existence and the Existent*, Maritain employs the term "subject."

Having their being (their "to be") in themselves, these supposits or subjects are substantially composed of essence (*essentia*) and an act of existing (*esse*), according to traditional Thomistic vocabulary. Maritain says:

> Essence is *that which* a thing is; suppositum is *that which* has an essence, *that which* exercises existence and   action -- *actiones sunt suppositorum* -- *that which* subsists.[4]

Esse is traditionally understood as that act of existing by virtue of which a possible or conceivable essence is made actual in the concrete or existential order; *essentia* is traditionally understood as the whatness or the essence of a particular substance -- it is that by virtue of which a thing is *what* it is without accidental qualification. But Maritain does not stop at any reiteration of these traditional metaphysical principles. He goes on to say:

> God does not create essences to which He can be imagined as giving a last rub of the sandpaper of subsistence before sending them forth into existence! God creates existent subjects or supposita which subsist in the individual nature that constitutes them and which receive from the creative influx their nature as well as their subsistence, their existence, and their activity. Each of them possesses an essence and pours itself out in action. Each is, for us, in its individual existing reality, an inexhaustible well of knowability. We shall never know everything there is to know about the tiniest blade of grass or the least ripple in a stream. In the world of existence there are only subjects or supposita, and that which emanates from them into being.[5]

In addition to providing us with a foundation of his notion of "Self," this passage helps us to understand Maritain's notion of "Things." In *Creative Intuition*, Maritain writes:

> I need to designate the secretive depths and implacable
> advance of that infinite host of beings ... of that world, that
> undecipherable Other -- with which Man the artist is
> faced; and I have no word for that except the poorest and
> tritest word of the human language; I shall say: the things
> of the world, the *Things*.[6]

But, unique within this created universe of an unfathomable, "infinite
host of beings" and subjects, the human person stands in a pre-eminent
position. For just as vegatative animate life rises above the inanimate, and
sentient animal life is distinguished from the solely vegetative, in a like
manner the supreme immanence of human intellectual life transcends the
limitations of the non-human animals. Distinquished by the unique kinds of
operations proper to humans (intellectual thought, the exercise of free will
and selfless love), we come to understand why Maritain claims that "the
suppositum becomes *persona*,"[7] why the distinctively human receives its
own name.

From this brief discussion, it is possible to present two contrasting
synopses. The preliminary situation from the perspective of metaphysics
may be expressed as follows: There is a created universe filled with subjects
(and their operations, activities, relations), all of which are infinite sources
of intelligibility, and some of which, by virtue of their unique nature, are in
a potential knowing/loving relationship with that universe. These
knowers/lovers have their own name ... they are persons.

By contrast, the preliminary situation from the perspective of
aesthetics/epistemology, building upon the previous metaphysical
foundation, may be described as follows: These knowing/loving persons,
since they participate in the likeness of the Creator, are also makers or
creators, with one significant difference. The Divine Artist is an "unformed
fashioner" creating out of the unlimited abundance of His own Being, while
the human artist is a "formed fashioner" creating out of the limited resource
of his or her own being. To this point in the aesthetic/epistemological
analysis, the term "Person" is still quite sufficient; no real need for any
preference for the term "Self" is even suggested.

It is only when Maritain grapples with the question of the unique
knowledge proper to the true "Poet," with the way in which the artist's
knowledge is received or "formed" as the knower becomes one with the
known -- the artist "divines" the inexhaustible intelligibility of Things -- that
he finds the traditional logical categories used in the explanation of
conceptual knowledge to be inadequate. It is within this context of the
discussion of knowledge (at first, in general, and then subsequently, of the
artist in particular) that the term "Self" is appropriately introduced. In

speaking of the ordinary knowledge that we have of the created universe, of subjects, Maritain says:

> We know those subjects, we shall never get through knowing them. We do not know them as subjects, we know them by objectivising them, by achieving objective insights of them and making them our objects; for the object is nothing other than something of the subject transferred into the state of immaterial existence of intellection in act. We know subjects not as subjects, but as objects ....[8]

This passage describes the basic nature of our knowing relationship to other subjects by means of conceptual knowledge. But the knowledge that the artist has of the world is different. Certainly the artist knows by means of concepts and developed skill, but when it comes to the discussion of the Poetry of the artist's work, that "secret life of each and all the arts,"[9] the categories that explain our ordinary, conceptual-knowledge relationship to the world break down.

Recognizing that human experience in general and artistic experience in particular admits of a mode of knowing that is non- conceptual and experiential, yet obscure and incapable of giving an account of itself, Maritain develops, over a period of some thirty-three years,[10], his idea of "Poetic Knowledge." And although this mode of knowledge is difficult to explain -- indeed, it is a mode of knowing that is as obscure to the artist as his or her own subjectivity is -- Maritain finds that within this context the language of the duality between subjectivity (or Self) and objectivity (or object) is still eminently useful.

The contrast between the epistemology of philosophy and science, and artistic creativity is clear. In the former, we know the subjects of the world by objectivising them, by knowing them as objects, never as subjects. In artistic or poetic intuition, however, what is grasped is properly speaking not an "object" of knowledge at all since things are objectivised insofar as they are expressed in concepts, and there are no concepts in Poetic Knowledge proper.

> ... poetic intuition is not directed toward essences, for essences are disengaged from concrete reality in a concept, a universal idea, and scrutinized by means of reasoning; they are an object for speculative knowledge, they are not the thing grasped by poetic intuition.[11]

It is in *Existence and The Existent* that we find Maritain expressing those ideas which will reach maturity in *Creative Intuition*. He does this

appropriately within the context of the discussion of the knowledge of
subjectivity as subjectivity. Only in relation to myself do I have an obscure
intuition of my own subjectivity that is not limited or confined by the
objectivising activity of the intellect. "I know myself as subject by
consciousness and reflexivity, but my substance is obscure to me,"[12]
Maritain writes, affirming the intuitive, non-conceptual obscurity that
characterizes this mode of knowledge.

> Subjectivity *as subjectivity* is inconceptualisable; it is an
> unknowable abyss. It is unknowable by the mode of
> notion, concept, or representation, or by any mode of any
> science whatsoever ....[13]

This knowledge of subjectivity as subjectivity can be grasped in either
of three types of connatural knowledge, which Maritain ennumerates as
practical knowledge in moral judgments, poetic knowledge, and mystical
knowledge. In the definition of poetic knowledge below, we can observe
Maritain's forecast of the idea of the "inner being of the human Self,"
despite the fact that the word subjectivity (rather than Self) appears. Poetic
Knowledge is a knowledge

> ... in which subjectivity and the things of this world are
> known together in creative intuition-emotion and are
> revealed and expressed together, not in a word or concept
> but in a created work.[14]

Conclusion

From the foregoing discussion, we may conclude that the term "Person"
is the more suitable metaphysical term designating the nature of a particular
type of being in a universe of other beings or subjects. "Self," on the other
hand, may be said to be the more appropriate epistemological term since it
conveys the epistemic polarity between subjectivity and objectivity,
between the knowing Self and the universe of beings which become objects
for me when they are represented in a philosophical-or
scientific-knowledge-relation by means of concepts. Although it is
instructive to note that the term "Self" is the preferred language for
discussions about knowledge since it conveys the epistemological polarity
just indicated, it is also important to recall that Maritain was particularly
eager to show that this knowledge-by-means-of-concepts is precisely the
type of knowledge that does not operate directly in the poetic knowledge of
the artist. In Poetry, the artist does not know the world by objectivising it.

This reservation, however, does not lessen the sustained preference for
using the term "Self" as desirable for our artistic or aesthetic vocabulary
about Poetry. For just as the knowledge of "Subjectivity as Subjectivity" in

Maritain's discussion transcends the conceptual, though it is still knowledge, so too does Poetic Knowledge retain its claim as a *bona fide* human knowledge which occasions a union of the knower and the known while also transcending the conceptual order. In the creative expression of poetic knowledge that characterizes the artist's work, it is the Self and the Things of the world that are know together -- the "formed" content of the artist's creative knowledge is precisely his or her own subjectivity resounding together with the "inner being of Things." The relation of the artist's Self to the world is one of an infinite openness open to the infinite. To be sure, the penetration of reality's secrets -- that intercommunication of inner being -- is not something assured or necessarily given to all; but to those who have "eyes" and the gift of poetic intuition, all becomes light and brilliance.

> For the content of poetic intuition is both the reality of the things of the world and the subjectivity of the poet, both obscurely conveyed through an intentional or spiritualized emotion. The soul [Self] is known in the experience of the world and the world is known in the experience of the soul [Self], through a knowledge which does not know itself.[15]

Walsh College

Notes

1. Since Maritain assigned "Poetry" a special meaning that goes beyond the art of writing verse, this paper will distinguish these two senses as follows: upper case for Maritain's sense, lower case for the verse-writing sense. The same method will also be employed concerning the term "Self" and "Things."

2. J. Maritain, *Creative Intuition in Art and Poetry* (New York, 1953) p. 3.

3. *Ibid.*, p. 10.

4. J. Maritain, *Existence and The Existent*, trans. L. Galaniere and G. Phelan (New York, 1984) p. 62.

5. *Ibid.*, pp. 65-67.

6. *Creative Intuition*, p. 10.

7. *Existence and The Existent*, p. 68.

8. *Ibid.*, p. 67.

9. Creative Intuition, p. 3.

10. From 1920 and the publication of *Art and Scholasticism* to 1953 and the publication of *Creative Intuition*.

11. *Creative Intuition*, pp. 125-126.

12. *Existence and The Existent*, pp. 68-69.

13. *Ibid.*, p. 69.

14. *Ibid.*, p. 71.

15. *Creative Intuition*, p. 124. The words in brackets have been added for clarity and emphasis.

FREEDOM AND THE UNCONSCIOUS IN MARITAIN'S
EXISTENCE AND THE EXISTENT

Roger Duncan

Maritain's *Existence and the Existent* contributes to the development of Thomist philosophical anthropology. Existentialist thought, with which Maritain's book is concerned, has offered a philosophy of human existence as a deliberate alternative to pictures of man drawn from the tradition of psychoanalysis. Maritain's anthropology mediates between these alternatives, harmonizing truths championed by both sides.

The way we understand the interrelationship between human freedom and the unconscious, or decide what and even whether these exist, is certainly related to metaphysics. Freud taught us to recognize the existence of unconscious personal depths, and to seek the freedom resulting from releasing the hold of buried contents through appropriating them in consciousness. Freud's own philosophical understanding, however, coming out of nineteenth century materialism, tends to lose sight of the higher ranges of human response and, identifying being with essence, tends to reduce free will to a reasonableness still subject to the determinisms of sub-personal reality.

Sartre teaches that we are always choosing, and that our very self-consciousness entails a transcendence of any mechanistic determinisms. But Sartre also reduces being to essence, with the result that "I" must be identified as non- being, a fleeting nothingness who must reject any connection, positive or negative, with supposed unconscious depths of the "self". As a result the Sartrean position comes dangerously close to equating freedom with the naive spontaneity of inadvertence.

Maritain's understanding of essence-existence, applied to the person, can provide the Freudian insight with a more nuanced account of the unconscious and its integration withing the fully personal dimension, accept Sartre's free will while distinguishing it from superficially conscious random behavior, and provide the bais for a positive dialectic of freedom and the unconscious.

FREUD

In the context of the concerns of this paper, Freud must be credited with two great contributions.

First, he struck a most serious blow at Cartesianism by showing empirically that the human individual is so much more than a pure consciousness or a dualistic construction of consciousness plus a body. Levels and levels of motivation, response, and memory mediate between the pinpoint of present consciousness and some purely automatic *res extensa*. And psychosomatic medicine, a direct descendent of psychoanalysis, shows that the lived body is so much more than a Cartesian machine.[1]

Second, Freud showed that psychic wholeness has a lot to do with the subject's ability to be "in touch" with these deeper levels, and that the healing of psychic disorder is related to "knowing" these contents, not just objectively, but in the sense of "working them through" and genuinely experiencing them as one's own, through a knowledge, as Thomists say, "by connaturality." As a philosopher, Freud always remains bound by an inadequate and crudely reductivist conceptual scheme.   Long after abandoning the neurological model of the earlier period, Freud still thinks of the unconscious along mechanistic lines: it is a hidden machine full of strange "parts": repressed memories and subterranean drives. The behaviour of the individual is in principle explainable without remainder by reference to the determinsim of this machine. Thus the mature Freud speaks of "the thoroughgoing meaningfulness and determinism of even the apparently most obscure and arbitrary mental phenomena."[2]

This mechanictic model works, to a point. The idea of a conservation of emotional tension, analogous to the conservation of energy in physics, under which fixed quantities of tension must be redirected when repressed, turns out to be very useful.   The model explains the relief of neurotic symptom following upon the resuscitation of memories or the identification of wishes connected with drives. The memories and the wishes are seen to have been operative all along in the causation of behavior.   In actual practice we see the patient released from this determinism into a capability to respond more freely to Being, though Freud would not put it that way.

That is exactly the problem. The whole battery of Freudian therapeutic concepts--sublimation, the transference, the stages of development, etc.--is oriented toward and productive of psychological wholeness and freedom for individuals.   But when Freud speaks philosophically he offers a model which tends to reduce the person to a play of forces thereby losing the phenomenological unity of the person instead of explaining it. For Freud the person is, we might say, all essence and no existence, meaning that the unity of the act of existing is missing from view; what is left is sheer quiddity, capable of analysis without remainder into smaller "parts". Due to its determinism the model cannot account for the difference between the freedom of the "cured" and the unfreedom of the sick; due to its reductivism the model cannot do full justice to its own insights: sublimation, for example, must be viewed cynically. One suspects that the effectiveness of therepeutic practice is itself blunted where that practice is restrained by a limiting materialism, and that the best practitioners of the method are those who free themselves from that philosophy.

SARTRE

Sartre's philosophy offers one dramatic possibility of dealing with the reductivism of modern positivism and materialism. In one of his bold strokes Sartre rejects the unconscious entirely. Lucid Cartesian consciousness in its self- reflective being-ahead-of-itself becomes the seat of man's ineluctable freedom. Freedom consists in the disavowal of the definite, the flight from determinateness which is the very essence of consciousness. Therefore there is no constitutive individual essence, let alone an unconscious. Consciousness throws itself in any direction it chooses.

Though Sartre does not want to speak of free *will*, we may, following normal usage, call this a doctrine of free will. Everyone possesses it, he says, to an equal degree. Then, if we want to distinguish some doctrine of *freedom* (as distinct from free will) in Sartre's writings, thinking of freedom as something possessed in varying degrees, freedom could be identified as "authenticity," that is, minimal bad faith, the relatively non-self-deceptive use of a free will which is always in operation and which is completely self-determinative.

Of course Sartre must admit the existence of self-deception but he claims that its analysis is not facilitated by the Freudian model. On the one hand, needing analysis are many cases of "bad faith" which do not fit the Freudian model; on the other hand there is no difference in principle between Freudian examples and other types of "bad faith". Sartre quotes with approval a Viennese psychiatrist, Stecke: "every time that I have been able to carry my investigations far enough, I have established that the crux of the psychosis is conscious".[3] To maintain that the patient "really does not know" he is blocking or whatever goes contrary to the precisely what is most interesting about psychoanalysis; why, for example, does the patient resist as the psychoanalyst approaches the sore spot? We keep having to say he both knows and does not know. It is no help to posit a censor standing between the conscious ego and the unconscious depths, for "how could the censor discern the impulses needing to be repressed without being conscious of discerning them?"[4]

Sartre provides an alternative account of the very same phenomena Freud tried to explain, but based on the given non- coincidence with itself of self-reflective consciousness. The For-itself, since it *is* only by being not-itself, may choose to identify itself with what it recognizes in itself (in what it "has been"); this is "sincerity" and "good faith". Or it may choose to identify itself with something else, with what it wishes to be or whatever;

this is bad faith. Of course the first "slides" into the second because in both cases there is the self- deceptive reification of the self. Authenticity, he tells us, is something else again.

We are faced once more with the problem of the unity of the person. For Sartre "I" am nothing more than a flash of consciousness continually fleeing everything static, sluggish and lumpy, and fleeing it by objectifying it. "I" am rooted in nothing long-term, continuous, or given. Insofar as I am conscious I have no self; "The For-itself" he writes, "cannot have a "profound self".[5] It would seem to follow that there is no distinction between a decision that is genuinely in line with who I really am and one that is "off the wall." This picture of the person, if it can be said to be that, is phenomenologically inform.

Sartre is to be praised all the same for his defense of free will: the person makes himself through his actions. The only trouble is that in Sartre's view there isn't any self to which these decisions contribute. (This view also boasts the convenience that there isn't any self to destroy nor any person when we're all finished, except a trajectory of decisions objectified from the outside.

Thus, *if in Freud essence without existence collapsed into atomism, here existence without essence is the existence of nothing. If for Freud freedom dissolved into determinism, here freedom degenerates into flight; if in Freud the "I" disappears from view, in Sartre the "I" is reduced to spasms of Cartesian transparency understood as acts of nihilation.*

MARITAIN

To begin with, Maritain recognizes the unconscious, as we know from *Creative Intuition in Art and Poetry.*

The notion of the psychological unconscious was made into a self-contradictory enigma by Descartes, who defined the soul by the very act of self-consciousness. Thus we must be grateful to Freud and his predecessors for having obliged philosophers to acknowledge the existence of unconscious thought and unconscious psychological activity.

> Before Descartes, the human soul was considered a substantial reality accessible only to metaphysical analysis, a spiritual entelechy informing the living body, and distinct from its own operations; and this, of course, made a completely different picture. The Schoolmen were not interested in working out any theory about unconscious life of the soul, yet their doctrines implied its existence.[6]

It is just the failure to recognize these depths which constitutes the error of so much existentialist thought:

> ... for the unthinkable notion of a subject without a nature
> there is substituted the notion of pure action or pure
> efficiency as the exercise of an option--of pure liberty, in
> short, itself ambiguous and collapsing from within; for
> although it seems to appeal to a sovereign free will, it
> really appeals only to pure spontaneity, which is inevitably
> suspected of being merely the sudden explosion of
> necessities hidden in the depths of that nature which was
> allegedly exorcised.[7]

Maritain cites with approval the existentialists' appreciation of liberty as an "essential transcendence with regard to the specifications and virtualities of essence, though they be those of the 'profound self'."[8] That is to say, Maritain would substitute "Existence transcends essence" for Sartre's "Existence precedes essence".

For Maritain, there is genuine free will which, plunged into action and truly attentive to its exigencies, loosens the hold of lower determinisms and integrates their otherwise blind orginations. The depths of the person, which can never be entirely plumbed by the consciousness of the individual to whom they belong, come into play as supports and guarantees of the truly free act. The free act is always transcending, going beyond the "given" of individual essence.

But Maritain gives the apparent inexplicability of some of the freest, most creative decisions an explanation differing from those of the Boulevard St. Germain's: ". . . the judgment of the subject's conscience is obliged, at the moment when judgment is freely made, *to take account also of the whole of the unknown reality within him*--his secret capacities, his deeply rooted aspirations, the strength or frailty of his moral stuff, his virtues (if he has any), the mysterious call of his destiny".[9]

As we know from his work on aesthetics, Maritain distinguishes between two specifically different unconsciousnesses (a distinction not to be confused with Jung's collective vs. personal unconscious, though it is compatible with it, he tells us). According to Maritain there is a spiritual unconscious distinct from the Freudian "thought in vital intercommunication and interaction with it".[10]

> Reason does not only consist of its conscious logical tools
> and manifestations, nor does the will consist only of its
> deliberate conscious determinations. Far beneath the sunlit
> surface thronged with explicit concepts and judgments,
> words and expressed resolutions or movements of the will,
> are the sources of knowledge and creativity, of love and
> suprasensuous desires, hidden in the primordial translucent

night of the intimate vitality of the soul. Thus it is that we
must recognize the existence of an unconscious or
preconscious which pertains to the spiritual powers of the
human soul and to the inner abyss of personal freedom,
and of the personal thirst and the striving for knowing and
seeing, grasping and expressing: a spiritual or musical
unconscious which is specifically different from the
automatic or dead unconscious.[11]

Thus, for Maritain, a free decision is not a mere nihilation: it is
somehow responsive and responsible to a given nature whose constitution
includes subconscious and unconscious contents.

ONTOLOGY

The difficulty, we have said, is attaining a correct ontological analysis.
Freud is not trying to give us one, in the way that philosophers do, but
Sartre is. Now Sartre sees consciousness as an escape from being, which he
equates with essence, into the openness of non-being, existence. From this
point of view a rock is more self-identical than a person. But from a
Thomistic point of view this is backwards. The Thomist (with the
physicists) would say that beneath the apparent self- identity of the rock is a
Heraclitean flux wherein the stability is really a repetitious present. We
must simplify to speak of essence in this tide of becoming.

Far from being a loss of stability and self-identity, a personal
consciousness is a significant advance along the line of overcoming
diversity, a continual knitting-together, of what would otherwise be lost with
an ever-fresh response, what a more Augustinian tradition would call
memory. It is not, as Sartre would have it, that solid being is now cracked
open irreparably; rather it is that, proceding up the hierarchy of being, we're
at last hitting something with some real density. The human person
represents a higher degree of being, in terms of both existence and essence,
than mere biological life, which in its turn represents a great ontological
ascendency over the inorganic. But here at the human level existence finally
achieves a true transcendence over temporal disintegration; essence takes on
full distinctness.

But human self-identity is never complete. For one thing we are
continually forging our identity through free acts in a process which is
complete only at death. In addition, our materiality means precisely a
continual abandonment of the inner for the outer, a continual stream through
the senses of what cannot be completely digested, and therefore a continual
need to bring the inner, with all its sediments and layers into relation with
the outer. An angel, who has no body, does not have this sort of problem
nor this sort of adventure.

For Maritain a person is the fullest example within the visible world of
an individual substance. A form is individuated such that every bit of matter

in the entire live being shares in the individuation. Conversely, the soul, the rational form extends down to the toes, as it were, and so is a lot more than consciousness. And here there is *essence and existence*, an existence which is always the existence of an essence, and an essence which exists in this free self-determining fashion of human personhood.

We have seen that for Maritain there is a human essence, both specific and individual, and that one important feature of a free decision is that it regards, gives attention to, this "given" which is a part of the self. But these depths of the person are "unknown to him in terms of reason" and grasped through a "dim instinct he possesses of himself." Now Maritain says:

> "Self-knowledge as a mere psychological analysis of phenomena more or less superficial, a wandering through images and memories, is but an egoistic awareness, *however valuable it may be*. . . . The spiritual existence of love is the supreme revelation of existence for the Self.[12]

For Maritain, liberty is found in the choices where I am revealed to myself in the face of the other who draws from me my most hidden eros; my possibilities of attraction and self- determination in commitment are revealed to me simultaneously as I open myself to the love of the other.

This is what is really distinctive about Maritain's vision. The reality of attraction to the good is the key; here I am solicited by that which, genuinely outside myself, beckons to me and challenges me to rise in response with my whole self, to become one with my self in recall and commitment. It is only here that I cease to exist merely as this individual, full of interesting possibilities, and enter the domain of truly personal life.

But the question remains: What place is there for seeking to re-experience (with Freud) or to experience (with Jung) my depths? As regards Maritain's quotation, just how valuable is it, this wanderring through images and memories for the individual on the way to fully personal existence? Does Maritain's scant treatment of these matters reflect a failure to distinguish carefully conceptual knowledge here from the knowledge by connaturality which the psychologist actually aims at for the patient? Karol Wojtyla, within a careful and faithfully Aristotelian description, urges bringing unconscious contents to consciousness.[13]

PSYCHOLOGICAL PRACTICE

Some suggestions for therapeutic practice emerge.

1. The unconscious is not sealed off dualistically from a conscious upper storey. There is a gradation. Certainly there are seriously hidden traumatic memories as well as animal level drives; there is also the permeation of the rational soul, receptive to being and its meanings, into all levels of vegetative, animal, and emotive being. This corresponds with the target of Jungian therapy. 2. The self can never be known completely, either

objectively or subjectively.   Not only can I not know its "contents" completely; I cannot, as Sartre would teach, know my freedom.   It is not in any way a "content" yet it is the most important aspect of my subjectivity.

Two consequences follow:

(1) Therapy must know its limitations.

(2) There must be appeals to freedom.   Approaches like Transactional Analysis are a good supplement here.   T. A. heads for the objective cognizance of an "unconscious" (in the ordinary sense) motive or pattern ("script", etc.) and then appeal to free will: "Change it!"

3.   The Thomist view of the self--the soul is the form of the body--means that the unconscious regions are not located somewhere else. Thus "the body knows."   (T.A. speaks of "cellular memory".)   Classical therapy leaves the body on the couch but, if the body knows, it will know both the twists and the positive potentials.   Therapy must reflect this in its explorations, as well as in attempting to affect the soul through the body (relating to earth, to animals, dance, etc.).

4. Re-experiencing painful memories, knowing my motives, getting in tough with my most creative energies, I-Thou appeals to my freedom--none of these are yet enough.   The psychological level has to give over at some point to the problem of the objective confrontation with the attractive, the valuable, what is *other* than the self.   The role of the properly spiritual, the religious dimension, is to chart a course and provide a living context--both ideational and situational--for the personal Eros.

In short, for Maritain, and perhaps a little beyond Maritain, existence and essence go together; subconscious regions exist together with the lucid spearhead of consciousness in a polar unity; freedom consists in the establishment of inner unity through the habitual option for the good with firmness of commitment, and the attunement of superficial decision with the subject's more hidden propensities awakened and called forth in love.

University of Connecticut

NOTES

1. Karl Stern, *The Third Revolution* (New York: Harcourt Brace & Co., 1954) p. 161.

2. Quoted in A. C. MacIntyre, *The Unconscious* (New York: Humanities Press, 1958) p. 90.

3. Jean-Paul Sartre, *Being and Nothingness* (New York: Philosophical Library, 1956) p. 54.

4. *Ibid.,* p. 52.

5. *Ibid.,* p. 444.

6. Jacques Maritain, *Creative Intuition in Art and Poetry* (Princeton, 1977) pp. 95-96.

7. Jacques Maritain, *Existence and the Existent,* trans. Lewis Galantiere and Gerald B. Pehlan (New York, 1956) p. 17.

8. *Ibid,* p. 59.

9. *Ibid.,* p. 62.

10. *Creative Intuition,* p. 106.

11. *Ibid.,* p. 94.

12. *Existence and the Existent,* pp. 89-90.

13. Karol Wojtyla, *The Acting Person* (Boston, 1979), p. 95.

PART TWO

EXISTENCE AND THE EXISTENT

E. The Free Existent and the Free Eternal Purposes

MAKING SOMETHING OUT OF NIHILATION

John C. Cahalan

Jacques Maritain solved the problem of predestination. He considered the solution to that problem his most important contribution.[1] We should consider it one of the great intellectual achievements of all time. For it is literally true that nothing can solve the problem of predestination. Yet Maritain solved it by recognizing that nothing, or more precisely, nihilation, the making of nothingness, *can* solve it. This study will attempt to enhance our understanding of nihilation by relating it to the following concepts: freedom of exercise, the role of intellectual consideration in choice, the external causes of free acts, the will's determination by the universal idea of goodness, and God's freedom.

For the purposes of this study, I abstract from all aspects of the problem of predestination but the following: how can human evil be the result of our freedom if we are created by an all- powerful God? The causality of the creator must extend to every detail of His creation. If there is anything in our decisions of which God's free choice is not the primary cause, God is not God. That is true of evil decisions as well as good; every detail in an evil human decision is there only as a result of God's causally prior decision. Therefore, why is it not God's will rather than ours that is responsible for evil?

1. Freedom of Exercise

As Maritain shows, the solution to the problem of predestination comes from Aquinas's doctrine of freedom of exercise.[2] Although the term "nihilate" is Maritain's, it expresses Aquinas's doctrine that the will is free not to act as well as to act. The will's act is a response to an attraction offered by a perceived object. If we are unable to refrain from responding to the attraction offered by some object, we are not free with respect to choosing that object. Therefore, to be free with respect to choosing A or choosing B (freedom of specification), we must be able to act or not act (freedom of exercise) with respect to choosing A and act or not act with respect to choosing B. Freedom of specification is freedom of exercise in series. We are not free to choose one from among incompatible possibilities unless we are free to refrain from choosing each of the others.[3]

In *De Malo*, Aquinas traces moral evil to our ability not to act, freedom of exercise.[4] Through not acting, we become the cause of an absence, a lack, in our decision-making process. From that absence comes a morally vitiated decision. To solve the problem of predestination, Maritain simply drew the next logical conclusion from Aquinas's position. God is the primary cause of everything that exists positively in an action. But a decision is not evil because of what exists positively in it. It is evil because of what is absent from it. We cause absence by not acting rather than by acting. Since moral evil derives from our not acting, our ability to cause moral evil neither limits God's causality nor makes Him the cause of moral evil.

Many have discussed freedom of exercise, but only Maritain has seen there the solution to the problem of predestination. Perhaps the reason is that we tend to think of freedom of exercise in terms of sins of omission. But, if the inaction explaining moral evil were confined to sins of omission, no other sins would be possible. Aquinas, however, explicitly includes within freedom of exercise the intellectual non-consideration of the moral rule that vitiates the decision, or the omission of a decision, and the external action, or the omission of an external action, commanded by the decision.[5]

2. Intellectual Consideration and Non-consideration

As Maritain notes, by positing a voluntary absence of intellectual consideration prior to the absence that constitutes moral evil proper, Aquinas brilliantly avoids the vicious circle of explaining moral evil by moral evil.[6] But the theory of consideration and non-consideration is more than a device constructed merely to escape from a dilemma.

As rational beings, we direct our actions by our awareness of their ends and of the relation of means to the ends. Unless I am sleepwalking or hypnotized, when I eat an ice cream cone, I do so because I am seeking a kind of pleasure that I am aware of and because I am aware of the customary relation between the eating of ice cream and the experience of that pleasure. But in addition to being aware of the pleasure that comes from ice cream, I am aware of the calories and cholesterol ice cream contains, and I am aware of the unhealthy consequences calories and cholesterol can have. If I choose to eat the ice cream, I am letting my awareness of its pleasure provide the goal toward which I consciously direct my behavior. Conversely, I do not let my awareness of the healthy effects of avoiding excessive calories and cholesterol provide my goal.

My awareness of the ice cream's pleasure is cognitional; my choice of the ice cream is volitional. But, in producing the choice, I will to use my knowledge of the pleasure to provide the goal at which the choice aims. The will causes the intellect to hold the pleasure in attention so that the decision may have a target. Without an intellectually grasped target, the decision would be blind. Hence, when we choose, the will must cause the intellect to hold an object in consideration; otherwise, the intellect would determine the will, and we would not be free. But willing the existence of consideration of an object is not enough, we must also will the existence of the object. These are the two phases of the will's act found in Aquinas by Maritain.

In order for my behavior to be moral, I must direct my behavior by my awareness of its moral significance. This is what Aquinas means by the consideration or non-consideration of the rule. Good deeds done unconsciously or accidentally do not constitute morally good decisions. If my stepping into the ice cream shop prevents a robbery, I am not morally responsible unless I did it with that end in view. Hence, Aquinas's theory is in complete agreement with human experience. The knowledge that provides the conscious goal of our behavior can be our awareness of what is moral, or, even though we are aware of the demands of morality, the conscious goal of our behavior can be provided by our knowledge of the satisfaction we might get from an immoral act. Everything depends on which part of our knowledge we use to direct ourselves toward a goal. But to the extent that we have rational control of ourselves, we will let some part of our knowledge set the goal of our behavior.

As unfamiliar as "the consideration or non-consideration of the rule" might sound, we express the same idea whenever we describe actions as "thoughtless" or "in-*considerate*," or whenever we use phrases like "All you think about is . . ." or "What is uppermost in your mind is . . .". In accusing someone of being thoughtless, we do not imply that he lacks knowledge of whatever it is he should be thinking of; we imply the opposite. We are criticizing him as a being who consciously directs action by awareness of the objects of action, and we are accusing him of not thinking of what he should be and, hence, could be thinking of, where "thinking of" refers to using awareness of some value to set the goal of action. Likewise, an inconsiderate person is aware of the rights of others but acts without using the consideration of those rights, consideration of the *rule*, to set the goal of his action. He directs his action toward an end by his awareness of something else and in so doing allows that other thing to be what is uppermost in his mind.

Still, mere non-consideration of something does not constitute moral evil. Moral evil is constituted by disordered decisions concerning the existence of the objects of intellectual consideration, decisions disordered because we make them without holding moral values in consideration as their targets.[7]

3. The Cause of the Will's Transition from Potency to Act

The source of moral evil, then, is non-acting with respect to the consideration of what is morally right as we make decisions directing ourselves toward goals. This is what Maritain calls nilhilation. We can learn more about nihilation by using it to solve another problem, just as Maritain used it to solve the problem of predestination.

The problem of predestination concerns the relation between our freedom and divine causality. But there is another more widely known problem of freedom with respect to any kind of efficient causality at all. If a choice is caused, it must be accounted for by the fact that its causes, whether creative or not, are what they are. Causes act because their natures orient them to their actions. If the nature of a cause makes it sufficient to produce an effect, must not the effect be necessitated by the cause's orientation to this action? For, if the cause can be what it is without producing the effect, the cause seems insufficient for the effect, and the cause is not the cause after all. Let us call this the *general* problem of causality and freedom and call the problem of predestination the *special* problem of causality and freedom.

Aquinas's solution to the general problem is that the will is given its specifying object by the universal idea of goodness. Hence, the will would be necessitated by an infinite good and for that very reason is not necessitated by finite goods. When we choose a finite good, it can only be the will itself that bestows efficacious attractiveness on that good.

However, standard presentations of Aquinas's solution to the general problem, while entirely correct as far as they go, do not go far enough. They leave unanswered a question for which nihilation provides the answer. Aquinas says:

> Everything that is at one time an agent actually, and at another time an agent potentially, needs to be moved by another. Now it is evident that the will begins to will something which previously it did not will. Therefore it must, of necessity, be moved by something to will it.[8]

But that puts us right back at the general problem. Whatever moves the will to act must do so by being what it is. What the cause is must therefore be sufficient to move the will to act, but it seems that the cause would not be sufficient if the will's act did not follow necessarily from the cause's being what it is.

The concept of nihilation solves this aspect of the general problem. *Non-acting with respect to some object does not require any new causality.* In the words of Aquinas, "it is not necessary to seek any cause for this not making use of the rule, because the very freedom of the will to act or not act is sufficient for not making use of the rule."[9] To produce a decision, the choice, say, of A, is to cause a new state of affairs to exist. But we are able to prefer the state of affairs already existing when we are not choosing A. Preferring the state of affairs that already exists means letting something that already exists remain as it is without producing a new decision. And since leaving things as they are does not introduce any new reality, no new causality is called for. When we do not choose A, we may choose B. If we produce the choice of B, we do not let something that already exists remain as it is. But we are just as free not to choose B, and thus leave things as they are by not acting, as we are free not to choose A.

When we act rather than not act, on the other hand, causality is called for. What is it that causes the will to go from not acting to acting? Aquinas's answer is that only the will's maker, God, can cause voluntary movement in the will, because the movement of the will is, like a natural movement, from within.[10] But, since this argument also applies to nonfree natural actions, it does not specifically tell us how a free act is caused, nor does it tell us how God may use secondary causes in the process. The only possible answer to these questions is that God produces the will's act by causing the intellect to present the will with an object that, in turn, causes an attraction in the will toward that object. The will's act is a response to the ontological perfection seen in the intellect's object. Therefore, the will's act is caused by an attraction produced by the cognition of that ontological perfection.

This answer is perfectly consistent with Aquinas[11] and with Maritain's description of the "shatterable activations" by which God inclines the will toward good. We should understand the distinction between shatterable and unshatterable activations as we do the distinction between God's intellect and will, His powers and their acts, and all the other distinctions of reason we use in speaking of God. The use of these distinctions does not assert any real multiplicity or potentiality of God's nature. These distinctions derive from the diverse realities that provide the means by which we conceptualize God, not from that which is conceptualized.

To begin with, a divine activation is not some *tertium quid* standing between God and His effects. Nothing stands between God and His effects. The term "activation" simply expresses the causal dependency of effects on the divine agent. Secondly and crucially, calling the causal relation "shatterable" in no way implies that this divine causality fails to produce an effect that is fully actual and existential. Maritain is explicit on this point. In an important passage, in which he corrects a footnote in *Existence and the Existent*, Maritain explains the effects attributable to shatterable activations:

> I am speaking of psychological realities more and more recognized today, and which can depend in us on anything at all, on a truth grasped by the mind, on a prudential consideration, on a natural or supernatural inspiration, on any sort of weighing or tugging on the will, on a love, a desire, on an allurement, nay even on a pressure from the unconscious, or even on some advice received, on an example, on some reading, etc. All these things can elicit under the divine action a movement or a tendency determined toward the good, toward this or that good

> option to be made. And the *movement or tendency in question toward the good* . . . which the action of God causes to be born in us from any one of the above-mentioned occurrences--this is the *effect* produced in the soul by the shatterable motion.[12]

There is nothing mysterious or occult about the operation of shatterable activations. God can cause a tendency to a good act in the will by causing such mundane events as grasping a truth, receiving advice, or observing an example.

If there is anything mysterious about shatterable activations, it might be why they are called "shatterable." As we have seen, the effects of these activations are as actual, as existential, as are any of God's effects. God's causality is not shattered. However, the tendency toward choice that God produces does not necessitate the choice. Since the choice may fail to come into existence, God's causality is describable as shatterable, not in itself or with respect to its immediate effect, but by conceptually relating it to something other than itself which is its final goal. By referring effects of God to something other than themselves, we construct a conceptual distinction enabling us to express two ways in which God's effects are related to this final goal, namely, shatterably and unshatterably. But this distinction in no way asserts a duality of the nature of God, of the actuality of His effects, or of His effects' dependence on Him.

We were asking what causes the will to go from not acting to acting. The answer that intellectual apprehension of a good causes a tendency toward act in the will might appear to be inconsistent with Maritain's analysis of the effects of shatterable activations. Intellectual apprehension covers Maritain's examples such as a prudential consideration or receiving advice, but what about the examples of "a love, a desire, an allurement, nay even a pressure from the unconscious"? The latter pertain to appetite, not knowledge; to the subjective order, not the objective.

The inconsistency is only apparent. The role of subjective dispositions in the production of an appetite's act is to enable the cognition of an object to cause an attraction in the appetite. The subjective dispositions are conditions for the cognition's causing of the attraction, but it is the cognition that is the proximate cause of the attraction.

Aesthetic enjoyment is the most subjectively conditioned of events. If aesthetic enjoyment must be analysed as a response caused by the cognition of an object's intrinsic qualities, a similar analysis is *a fortiori* due acts of the will, the rational appetite. Assume a drug is found that causes us to like a kind of music we would not like otherwise. Does this not show the subjectivity of aesthetic evaluation? That evaluations depend on the abilities and dispositions of the evaluating subject is not in doubt. But what the drug has done is to so modify our dispositions that we estimate a certain cognized set of intrinsic characteristics, those of the music, in a way we did not before. In other words, as a result of the drug, the intrinsic pattern of the sounds now *causes* a different reaction than it did before. But it is that intrinsic pattern that is the proximate cause and object of this reaction. The reaction itself is an esteeming of the sounds for their intrinsic qualities.[13]

Likewise, choices are caused through attractions produced in the will by our awareness of good objects. Not everyone will experience an attraction to the ontological perfection recognized in A or B. If we are to value something for its intrinsic qualities, our faculties may have to be in a certain subjective condition. But, for those whose faculties are in the proper condition, it is the awareness of the perfection in A or B that causes the attraction and hence moves the will to act.

4. The Positively Based Power of Nihilating

We examined shatterable activations to see what the sufficient cause of the will's act is. But can it be possible for us not to act if the cause of an act, namely, our awareness of the perfection at which the act aims, is sufficient to produce the act? If we do not act, it seems that the cause is not sufficient to produce the act. If it is not sufficient and yet we act, the change from not acting to acting does not have an explanation. In other words, it seems that the general problem is still with us. How does nihilation permit an act with sufficient causes to be free?

Why is it necessary that a cause produce a particular effect and no other? Because the cause's orientation to action is its nature, and its nature is concrete and particular, since whatever exists is concrete and particular. As the rational appetite, the will is attracted to goals according to the intellect's awareness of its objects, and the objects of the intellect are universal. By hypothesis, therefore, the will's orientation to behavior is characterized by universality, not particularity. As abstracted from individuals, the universal idea of goodness cannot direct us to prefer this or that individual which instantiates the idea, except for an infinitely good individual, but does direct us to find *some* instantiation to prefer.[14] Confronted with incompatible forms of finite goodness, we must prefer some form of finite goodness, but not necessarily this or that form. Therefore, the will's nature makes us able to respond to finite goodness but, since we are only necessitated to prefer *some* finite goodness, we can also non-act with respect to any finite goodness and prefer the already existing state of affairs instead. When we act, we allow the value perceived in the finite good to draw forth the choice by which we prefer it. Our awareness of the ontological goodness of the finite object is sufficient to cause this response, but only if we do not take the option of not acting.

As an intellectual appetite, the will may sound like a strange bird, a power of the abstract and general, a power of the undefined. On the contrary, since we are determined to seek some form of finite goodness, but not this or that form, when the will is presented with a course of action, we are required to either prefer to undertake that course of action or prefer not to undertake it. The will is so necessitated that we cannot avoid making one or the other our preference.

Confronted with a possible course of action A, how do we go about preferring to undertake A? By exercising our power of choice. How do we go about preferring not to undertake A? By not exercising our power of choice. We are tempted to ask: "How do I go about exercising or not exercising my power of choice? What must I do to succeed in exercising it or not exercising it?" These questions look for some other act preceding the act by which we prefer to undertake A or the refraining from acting by which we prefer not to undertake A. The questions incorrectly assume that some further causal f the refraining from acting by which we prefer not to undertake A. The questions incorrectly assume that some further causal factor is needed to explain the will's action or inaction. But the attraction for A, caused by our awareness of A, is sufficient to cause the exercise of the will's power to act. And the attraction for the situation that already exists, caused by our awareness of that situation, is sufficient to allow us not to exercise the will's power to act. No other cause can be needed by an appetite whose specifying object directs it to select some apprehended good while excluding determination by any particular one.[15]

Seeking some previous act focuses on the will's interior makeup. But the will is a relation to objects other than itself, here course of action A, on the one hand, and the state that already exists without A, on the other. The proper way to examine the will's makeup is to ask about its relation to what is other than itself: how does it bring about our preference for A or our preference for the status quo? The answer is by its action or inaction. That is, the answer describes how the will relates or does not relate to an object other than itself. If there were any other answer, the will would not be a power of relating to objects other than itself. We can learn more about the will's nature, but only by always framing our questions, and their answers, in terms of the will's possible ways of relating to its objects. We must either prefer A or not prefer A. We do so by exercising our power to act or not exercising it. In exercising our power to act, we have preferred to undertake A; in not exercising it, we have preferred not to undertake A.

When we examine that power further, we find that the causal explanation of our preference does not require some preceding act of the will but only our consciousness of the perfection to be aimed at through A and our consciousness of the perfection that already exists before A has been chosen. That consciousness renders our not acting a positive, intentional preference for a state of affairs that does not include A, rather than a mere absence of the preference for A. It is entirely true that, in itself, the non-consideration of the perfection to be accomplished through A is a mere absence. But we are not here looking at that non-consideration just in itself. We are looking at it in relation to (1) the necessity of our either preferring A or not preferring A and (2) the fact that we are aware of what not preferring A means. By consciously not acting under these conditions, we put ourselves in a state of satisfaction with our existing state, at least as compared to the state we would have been in had we chosen A.

Contrast the will's inaction to inaction in the case of determined causes. If my battery is dead, my car does not start. Here, the inaction reflects the absence of sufficient causes. Nihilation, on the other hand, reflects a positively based *power* of not acting. Our power to choose is also the power not to choose. Unlike the car not starting, nihilation requires a positively based power of not acting precisely because there are sufficient causes for the will's act if we do not intentionally non-act.[16] Nihilation in itself is something merely negative. But nihilation can occur because of the supremely positive ontological context in which decisions take place. The context is that of an intelligence aware of a potentially existing good that attracts it, a good whose realization requires a choice. Such an intelligence must also be aware of the good that already exists in the situation, a situation that will cease to exist if a new choice is made. The intelligence's appetite cannot avoid a preference for one of those two situations. But because its nature is determined *ad unum* only by the universal idea of goodness, the intelligence's appetite is not determined to one or the other. To prefer one or the other amounts to acting or not acting. Either acting or not acting is based on the prior positive awareness of the object that is thus made the preference. Freedom derives from the will's roots in the intellect's grasp of being.

5. God's Freedom

The role of nihilation in freedom is by no means confined to cases in which evil, or even a lesser good, is a possibility. In fact, the freedom of God Himself requires a positively based power of the negative. Why was God free in creating us? Because He could have refrained from creating us by not acting. Why would God not have been different had he not decided to create? Because that would have been a non-act adding nothing to the divine reality.[17] Then why did God not change in freely deciding to create? Because the new act resulting from His not non-acting exists entirely outside of Him. If we look for something new in His not non-acting that corresponds to the decision that newly exists in us when we do not non-act, we, God's creatures, are all that is new. From this perspective, we *are* God's decision. That is how close God is to us and we to God.[18]

Methuen, Massachusetts

NOTES

1. See J. Maritain, *God and the Permission of Evil*, transl. J.Evans (Milwaukee, 1966) p. viii.

2. See J. Maritain, *St. Thomas and the Problem of Evil*, transl. Mrs. G. Andison (Milwaukee, 1942) pp. 20-46.

3. For this point, I am indebted to J. Sikora, *Inquiry into Being* (Chicago, 1965) p. 255. Sikora's book has a lengthy discussion of divine and human freedom based on Maritain; see pp. 254-256 and 264-276.

4. *De Malo*, I, 3.

5. In addition to *De Malo*, I, 3, see *Summa Theol.*, I- II, 6, 3, where Aquinas asks whether there can be voluntariness without any act, the kind of voluntariness involved in freedom of exercise. The third objection states that, since knowledge is essential to voluntariness and knowledge requires an act, voluntariness requires an act. Aquinas replies that voluntariness requires the power to consider as it requires the power to will and to act but, just as it is voluntary not to will and not to act, when it is time to do so, it is also voluntary not to consider. This reply does not state whether voluntary inaction with respect to consideration extends to the non- consideration of the moral rule from which moral evil results, but in *De Malo*, I, 3, Aquinas makes that point explicitly.

6. See *St. Thomas and the Problem of Evil*, pp. 20-31; *God and Permission*, pp. 21-25, 34-36, 44-54; J. Maritain, *Existence and the Existent*, transl. L. Galantiere and G. Phelan (New York, 1948) pp. 89-92.

7. On this point, see the places cited in notes 4 and 6 as well as Aquinas, *Sum. cont. Gent.*, III, 10.

8. *Summa Theol.*, I-II, 9, 4; translation, *Basic Writings of St. Thomas Aquinas*, ed. A. Pegis (New York, 1945) II, 254.

9. *De Malo*, I, 3; my translation.

10. *Summa Theol.*, I-II, 9, 6.

11. See, for example, *Summa Theol.*, I-II, 9, 6 ad 2; I, 80, 2.

12. *God and Permission*, pp. 56-57. The footnote corrected in *Existence and the Existent* is note 9 of chapter 4, pp. 94-99.

13. That the intrinsic characteristics may be those of sounds having only phenomenal existence is not at issue here. If the existence of sounds is subjective, this is a different subjective existence from that of the evaluation. For, by hypothesis, the same sounds can be evaluated differently.

14. For a new analysis of the way transcendental ideas abstract from their inferiors, see John C. Cahalan, *Causal Realism: An Essay on Philosophical Method and the Foundations of Knowledge* (Lanham, Maryland, 1985) pp. 421-434. Pp. 477-483 of that work discuss freedom with respect to causality and not acting.

15. Confronted by a bone, a dog cannot avoid either preferring to get the bone or preferring the state it is in without the bone. But if the dog does not prefer to get the bone, the inaction results from the insufficient attractiveness of the bone. The inaction does not result from a power of not responding to a bone whose attractiveness is sufficient to cause the dog to prefer it. On the question of the sufficient reason for our freely choosing one thing rather than another, see Cahalan, *Causal Realism*, p. 483.

16. *Summa Theol.*, I-II, 10, 2 ad 2 implies that the only sufficient cause of the will's act is the infinite good that would necessitate the act. Aquinas is speaking there of an unconditionally sufficient cause. The tendency elicited by cognition of a finite good is a sufficient cause in the conditional sense that it is the tendency that causes us to act, and

hence is sufficient to cause us to act, if we do not intentionally non-act. To act is to allow the tendency to cause the consideration that leads to the choice. Not to act is to allow the attraction for what already exists to prevent that consideration.

17. I owe this point to Sikora, *Inquiry*, p. 255.

18. With reference to the spiritual life, we can say that good acts result from our simply allowing grace to work or from our not doing anything to interfere with grace. This appears to contradict Maritain by making us inactive with respect to good and active with respect to evil. The appearance of contradiction comes from the difference between the speculative vocabulary of Maritain's analysis of freedom and the practical vocabulary of this description of our role in the spiritual life. The practical point of view is the point of view of our first initiative. We act when we do good, but it is grace that causes our act, if we do not take the initiative of not acting. We non- act when we interfere with grace but, in doing so, we take the first initiative of evil. The analysis of the differences between speculative and practical vocabulary is one of the many neglected but essential contributions of Maritain. See J. Maritain, *The Degrees of Knowledge*, transl. G. Phelan (New York, 1959) pp. 311-319, 326-338.

THE SIN OF MAN AND THE LOVE OF GOD

Michael D. Torre

Maritain's views on moral evil in *Existence and the Existent*, and his later articulation of them in *God and the Permission of Evil*, are controversial. Some accuse him of misinterpreting Thomas.[1] My purpose here is to defend him from this charge by presenting the doctrine of Thomas to which he calls our attention. I believe he has performed a great service to Thomists by returning us, in substance if not in every detail, to the teaching of the Common Doctor. I trust this will become evident from what follows.

The most obvious thing one can say about an act of moral evil, as of any other evil act, is that it is in some manner defective. Since there has been some dispute about words here, we should note at the outset that Thomas uses the word "defect" to refer either to a *simple negation* or to a *privation*. He is quite explicit about this: "the word 'defect'," he says, "can be taken either negatively or privatively."[2] This division of defect is from Aristotle[3] and is a constant in Thomas's analysis of evil, from the *Sentences* on. So, too, is his analysis of the difference between a negation and a privation: a simple negation denotes an absence of being, while a privation denotes an absence of being that is *due*, that a being *ought* to have, or "is born to have,"[4] in the words of the *Sentences*. Thus, to give the traditional example from the *Metaphysics*, lack of sight is a simple negation relative to a stone but a privation relative to an animal: for an animal "is naturally fitted to have sight,"[5] and hence a blind animal is deprived of something proper to its nature.

As everyone knows, Thomas holds a privative view of evil. An evil act is one *deprived* of its proper order: an absence of being or order *in* a being by nature ordered otherwise. Moral evil is no exception. The following may be taken as a summation of Thomas's doctrine on its nature:

> *Two* things occur in the nature of sin, namely the *voluntary act*, and its *lack of order*, which consists in departing from God's law. Of these two, one is referred essentially to the sinner, who *intends* such and such an act in such and such a manner; while the other, namely the *lack of order in the act*, is referred accidentally to the

intention of the sinner, for 'no one acts intending evil,' as Dionysius declares.[6]

This is Thomas's doctrine throughout his career. The act of intent is called the *conversion* of the will to the good desired. The lack of order is called the *aversion* of the will from its proper and due end. The aversion is never directly intended, but is rather the accidental yet inevitable consequence of intending the mutable good. He says in the *Summa Theologiae*: "from the fact that man turns unduly ['indebita conversione'] to some mutable good, it follows that he turns from ['aversio'] the immutable good."[7]

Now, while man's aversion from his proper order is the accidental effect of his conversion to a mutable good, this does not lessen its importance for the act. On the contrary, the aversion from God and His rule is what makes the act *sinful*. It is the defect which renders the act *disordered*; it is the formal element of evil in the act. Thus, from *De Malo*: "sin consists in the *aversion* of the created will from its final end."[8] And, from the *Summa Theologiae*: "...two things are to be observed in sin, conversion to the mutable good, and this is the *material* part of sin; and aversion from the immutable good, and this gives sin its *formal* aspect and complement."[9] This position indeed follows from his entire theory of evil, since the *defect in* the act (i.e., something negative) makes a thing evil. On the other hand, the conversion to, or intention of, a mutable good involves activity and order and to that extent is good, not evil.

When Thomas turns to a consideration of sin's cause, he offers two explanations: in terms of its psychology, and in terms of metaphysical principles. Since the second poses the greater difficulty, its full sense is best seen in relation to the concrete psychology to which it is applied.

Thomas here follows and goes beyond Aristotle's analysis as he advances it in Book VII of the *Ethics*. There, Aristotle argues that one can have an habitual knowledge of the true moral good, yet fail to act on it. This failure is to be explained by the influence of passion, which distracts one from the true principle habitually known. Thomas accepts this analysis. A sinful choice is usually based on a faulty judgment caused by the influence of the passions:

> Since the first cause of sin is some apparent good as motive, yet lacking the due motive, viz., the rule of reason or the divine law, this motive is an apparent good and appertains to the apprehension of the sense and to the appetite; while the lack of due rule appertains to the reason, whose nature is to consider the rule; and the completeness of the voluntary sinful act appertains to the

will, so that the *act* of the will, given the *conditions* we
have already mentioned, is a sin.[10]

Thomas keeps to this analysis throughout his discussion of sin in the
Summa Theologiae: inclination of sensitive appetite, judgment of reason,
inclination of the will, is the usual order of human sin.

This position raises the obvious question: are the person's passionate
inclinations and faulty judgment the *sufficient* cause of his will's sinful act,
or, on the contrary, can he avoid sin given these prior conditions? Thomas's
answer is unequivocal: these are insufficient causes of sin, whose avoidance
lies within the power of man's will. His most careful analysis of the
capacity of man's reason and will to resist passion is made in the *Prima
Secundae*. Against the argument that concupiscence impairs reason and
hence causes involuntariness, he responds as follows:

> In those actions which are done from concupiscence,
> knowledge is not completely destroyed, because the power
> of knowing is not taken away entirely, but only the *actual
> consideration* in some particular act. Nevertheless, this is
> voluntary, according as by voluntary we mean that it is
> within the *power* of the will, for example, *not to act* or *not
> to will*, and in like matter *not to consider*, for the will can
> *resist* the passion.[11]

This passage complements our previous one. Passion initially leads our
judgment astray, so that we consider its object good and fail to consider the
moral order that should govern our judgment. Yet it lies within the will's
power to redirect reason to consider that order. It can resist the influence of
passion and the considerations it prompts. Because the will possesses this
power, it is responsible for failing to exercise it and then for choosing a false
good.

Thomas, then, locates the cause of sin in a failure of the will.
Furthermore, he gives this failure a name: it is a *non-use* of reason. The
rule of reason and God's law ought to govern one's final judgment. If it
does not, this is because it is not used: "*not to use* the rule of reason and the
divine law is presupposed in the will *before* an inordinate election."[12] One
should not confuse this use with the act that *follows* election, which Thomas
examines in his treatise on human acts in the *Summa*. Rather, the act of use
here spoken of corresponds to the general ability of the will to move the
rational faculty, as he makes clear in that same treatise: "since the will, in a
way, moves the reason and *uses* it, we may take the *use* of the means as
consisting in the *consideration* of reason according as it refers means to an
end. In this sense, use *precedes* choice."[13] In the language of the

Sentences, "the intellect is able to consider or not consider, according as it is moved by the will."[14]

We are now in a good position to understand Thomas's metaphysical analysis of sin's cause. The groundwork for his mature doctrine is laid in the *Sentences*. Since, however, it reaches its full articulation in the *Summa Contra Gentiles*, we will save time by going directly to that work.

When he there treats of moral evil's cause, he locates it in the will: "...it is necessary," he says, "to presuppose a defect in the will before moral evil."[15] He then poses a dilemma: is this defect natural or voluntary? If it is natural, then the will necessarily sins in willing; if voluntary, however, then it is already an actual sin and will require a cause in its turn.[16] Instead of finding a cause of sin, one will only find another sin, which itself will require a cause.

Thomas solves his dilemma in this way. First, he denies that the voluntary defect is natural, for then the will would always sin in acting; and he adds that the defect is neither casual nor fortuitous, on the ground that this would absolve man's will from responsibility for his sin.[17] It remains that the defect is voluntary. The dilemma does not succeed, however, because this voluntary defect is not itself a sin: "Est igitur voluntarius. Non tamen peccatum morale."[18] Thus Thomas solves his chosen aporia by *distinguishing voluntary defect*. He grants that there is a defect in the will prior to its act of sin. He grants that this makes the will the defective and voluntary cause of sin. But he *denies* that this defect is a moral evil. It is voluntary for the same reason as already noted: because it lies within the *power* of the will to redirect the intellect to overcome its non-consideration.[19] This failure to consider, however, is not itself sinful; for reason can consider any good or no good without being sinful so long as the will does not proceed to election.[20] Although Thomas holds this view throughout the remainder of his work, it is most clearly expressed in *De Malo*: "...this itself, which is actually not to attend to this rule, considered in itself is not evil, neither guilt nor punishment, because the soul is not held to be nor can it always be actually attentive to this rule."[21]

Thus Thomas affirms two sorts of cause of sin. It possesses an *accidental efficient cause*, as already noted: the conversion to or intent of a mutable good. And it also possesses a *deficient cause*: the will itself as not using the intellect to reconsider. He always refers to this cause in his analysis of sin, and he always holds that the will as defective is not yet sinful. This is the view of both the *Prima Pars* and the *Prima Secundae*.[22] It is again in *De Malo* that we have his most explicit testimony of this. For he there gives this defect its proper technical name: it is a simple negation, a "negatio sola" or "negatio pura."[23] This is required by his entire theory. Man's will lacks a being and an order that it *could* possess; yet this order is not due it, is not something it *should* possess, until it actually proceeds to election. Hence it is not a privation but a negation.

Between the two causes of sin, the deficient clearly precedes the accidental efficient. Thomas repeatedly says that the absence of order in the will precedes the evil election. It has to, on pain of making God the cause of sin. For, as mentioned previously, the will's conversion to a mutable good is an activity; as such, then, with all created activity, its source is in God. The reason that God is not the cause of sin, however, is because the formality of sin, the aversion, derives from a creaturely defect. The aversion and privation in sin derive from a voluntary non-use and negation. This is the radical source of man's sin, and it derives from him and not God. God is the cause of all being, but not of all negation. The voluntary negation is the creature's alone.

Although this voluntary defect is primary, it is not sufficient to cause sin. For there will be no sin unless and until the creature chooses a false good. Prior to election, the non-consideration of the rule *can be corrected*, since this lies within the power of the will. Thus, the voluntary defect is only *rendered causative* by the *act* of choice or intention. Each of Thomas's two causes contributes to sin; they are mutually related as causes, in a way analogous to matter and form. *Given* the mutual relation of these latter causes, one must understand the material disposition *as prior* to its individuating effect.[24] Similarly, *given* that the will proceeds to election, one must understand the voluntary defect as prior to the defect it causes in the act. Thus, the defective cause is *really prior* to the accidental efficient cause in relation to the *formality* of sin, but it *supposes* this act in order to be really prior as cause.

It is always tempting to ask, at this point, why does man fail, why is he defective? Thomas cautions us here. He notes that we have located the defectible cause of moral defect: man's will. Thus he says, "...of something of this sort, that is the aforementioned non-use of the rule, it is not necessary to search for a cause, because *the will itself*, by which one can act or not act *suffices* for this."[25] Also, as we have seen, he provides the will with a *motive* for its sin: the mutable good before it. Yet, between motive and act there is a gap, a gap analogous to that between God's motive of creation and His decision to create. In each case, we are dealing with an *absolute first cause*. In the case of man's failure, however, we are confronted with something that makes no sense. Sin is absurd, unintelligible in itself. And this is why Thomas, here following Augustine, cautions us not to look for an *efficient* cause of *deficiency*.[26] We can see that sin *need not be*, but we cannot see *why it is* because *there is no why*. We can only point to the fact.

As we can see, Maritain exposes the central points of Thomas's doctrine. His major effort, both in *Existence and the Existent* and in *God and the Permission of Evil*, is to insist on the voluntary defect that is not itself sin but a mere negation.[27] He brings out this capital point of Thomas's regarding the non-consideration of the rule.[28] He rightly notes that it precedes evil election, and he even corrects his earlier doctrine to affirm that it precedes that election in time as well as in causality.[29] And, perhaps most significantly, he insists that it is a *first* cause.[30] As he says in *Existence and the Existent*, "we are faced here by an *absolute beginning* which is not a beginning but a 'naught,' a fissure, a lacuna introduced into the warp and woof of being."[31] Always inventive in vocabulary, Maritain speaks of this negation as a free nihilation.[32] Certainly, this conveys the radical nature of man's moral failure. Yet this is appropriate to Thomas's position. He himself speaks of free creatures having it within "their power to *withdraw* themselves"[33] from what is ordained by God and "to *fall away* from being."[34] Maritain's expression conveys this doctrine accurately.

Perhaps Maritain's most important contribution, however, is to insist that God is in *no way* responsible for man's sin, not even in His permission of it. He here opposes the doctrine that man sins infallibly given God's permission. This is the basis for the famous (or infamous) doctrine of negative reprobation: God allows a good but defectible creature to fall into sin, and, as a consequence, he inevitably does so. Against this position, Maritain insists that there are *two different meanings* to the affirmation that God permits sin, as there are likewise two different consequences of His permission. If a creature is merely *defectible*, then to say that God permits him to sin is to say no more than that God makes sin *possible*: God does not protect the defectible creature from possible defect. If, on the other hand, the creature is actually *defective*, if he is not merely *able* to sin but a sinner already or *committed* to sin, then to say that God permits him to sin is to say that He leaves him to his sin or does not turn him from sin. Given this second permission, it is indeed true that the creature infallibly continues in sin. This is true, however, because this permission *supposes* a determination for sin on the creature's part. If this determination is *not supposed*, then *sin does not infallibly follow* God's permission; on the contrary, supposing the creature to be merely defectible, but not defective, then he may or may not sin.

In making this distinction, Maritain here presents us with the doctrine of Thomas. Once again, it is clearly before us in his text. The first sort of permission, one which makes sin possible but not infallible, is most thoroughly analyzed in his commentary on the *Sentences*. There Thomas notes that one can act outside God's operation (by sinning); but he also says that one can never act outside His permission.[35] The reason for this is that God's permission makes it possible for a creature to fail, but it also makes it possible for a creature *not to fail*. Thus, even if one does not do the sin that is permitted, one still acts within God's permission:

> It is nevertheless possible to do the opposite of what is
> permitted; but this is still according to the permission
> because permission respects the *power of a cause for*

opposites; and neither of the opposites is against permission but both are according to it.[36]

Clearly, Thomas here envisions God's permission as making sin possible but neither infallible nor actual. This is the meaning of "permission" in the only place where Thomas examines it systematically.

This concept of God's permission is the common one of Thomas's early writing.[37] It can also be found, however, in his later work. Thus he interprets 1 Corinthians 10:13 to mean that "God does not permit one to be tempted without the aid of divine grace."[38] Obverting this double negative, we see that God permits us to sin, but with the aid of divine grace to avoid the sin. Hence one need not sin, given God's permission of temptation. Similarly, in his commentary on *The Divine Names* of Pseudo-Dionysius, he affirms that God "permits some to be attacked, but He gives to them the fortitude to resist this attack."[39] Thus, when man is a friend of God and no longer in a defective, sinful state, God's permission of sin is accompanied by aid that allows man to resist temptation, so that sin is only possible, but not infallibly certain.

It is also possible to find the other sort of permission, the one that supposes sin and leaves man to it, in Thomas's early writings. He usually identifies this permission with a subtraction of God's grace, a subtraction merited by a previous sin. Thus:

> God, however, is the cause of the penalty that is the *subtraction of grace*, which is the *effect* of one sin and the *cause* of another, by *not acting*....and in this way He is the cause of a penalty that is itself a deformed act of sin; not because He Himself causes it, but because He *permits* it, by not impeding it.[40]

As can be seen from the passage, God's permission here infallibly leads to sin, but by not impeding man's sinful orientation.

The same understanding of permission is found throughout Thomas's later writings. Take, for example, this passage from the *Summa*:

> ...one sin is the cause of another, by *removing the impediment* thereto.... For...divine grace...is *withdrawn on account of sin*.... [Yet] even when God *punishes men by permitting them to fall into sin* this is directed to the good of virtue.[41]

Note that the same understanding applies in the later as in the earlier work. God's permission is identified with the removal of God's grace, from which sin infallibly follows; yet *this* permission or withdrawal supposes a previous sin, for which it is a punishment. As he says in his commentary on Romans, God "permits some to rush into sin on account of preceding iniquities."[42]

It is now possible to see where the position Maritain opposes makes its fatal error. It *conflates* Thomas's two meanings of permission without realizing that the two meanings involve *different suppositions*. It takes the supposition of a defectible creature from the first permission; it takes the infallible entailment of sin from the second. It thus gets a negative reprobation that supposes no sin. This is a conceptual monster, the progeny of two concepts not meant to be joined. Maritain's opposed interpretation of Thomas's view is the correct one. Thankfully, it exorcises from contemporary Thomism[43] this awful concept of a negative reprobation that supposes no sin.

Finally, by recalling us to the great truth that the origin of moral evil is in our will and not in God's, Maritain makes us renew and deepen our appreciation of the transcendent mystery of God and of His love for creatures. He thus calls us to reflect on our understanding of the divine impassibility and happiness and to purge it of any false simplifications. And he does this not with a new esoteric theory but by faithfully recalling us to the authentic doctrine of Aquinas.

Consider some of the truths that Maritain places before us regarding our eternal God. Had God not chosen to create us, He never would have seen the ugliness of our sin. He never would have had to witness the everlasting spectacle of His most beloved creatures turning from Him. Again, in sinning, the creature falls from one order of God's providence to another, as Thomas frequently says.[44] The creature is the first cause of that first order being impeded--even though God can remove the impediment. Man is the first cause of not receiving all the glorious goods that God is prepared to give him. And, most significantly, man's sin resists and rejects the solicitations of God's love. In wounding ourselves, we wound that love, placing obstacles to all that it desires for us. We set ourselves against the antecedent will of God that desires eternal glory for all men; we don't let it caress us, lavish us with its deathless and profound love. We impede its joyful fruition.

What, then, does sin mean for God? This is the meditation towards which all Maritain's work here tends. Perhaps this was really Maritain's central spiritual preoccupation throughout his life, from his encounter with Léon Bloy and his devotion to Our Lady of La Salette to one of his final reflections on theological wisdom. What does it mean for God's truth that it is forever faced with the false and unintelligible, for His love that it is forever faced with resistance and rejection, for His being that it is forever faced with nothingness, for His happiness that it is forever confronted with the misery of the creatures brought into and kept in existence by His love? Is there not work to be done here to speak better of these matters than many

Thomists have in the past? Is not the suffering and resurrection of the Lord of glory revealing something to us about the divine joy? Are not the marks of the crucifixion in the glorified body of Christ a sign to us here, a sign that sin is not taken up into some false dialectical synthesis?[45] For my part, I agree with Maritain when he says that sin remains something "inadmissable"[46] to God, which He tolerates in His wisdom only because He can bring greater good from it. Perhaps there is here a need to speak of a divine suffering that is not entirely metaphorical. So much of our instinctive language points in this direction: God is patient with us, He is long-suffering with our sins, He has com-passion for the misery wrought by them. Maritain, for his part, believed that something should be said about this and I think he is right. Let us let him have the last word:

> That which sin 'does' to God is something that touches the depths of God.... ...this mysterious perfection, which is in God the unnamed exemplar of suffering in us, is an integral part of the divine beatitude, perfect peace but exalted infinitely above the humanly conceivable and burning in its flames that which is apparently irreconciliable for us.[47]

University of San Francisco

NOTES

1. See J.-H. Nicolas, "La permission du péché," *Revue Thomiste* 60 (1960) 5-37, 185-206, and 509-46, and H. R. Smith, *Man's 'Conquest of Liberty' and the Problem of Evil: A Study of the Meaning of Salvation in the Writings of Jacques Maritain*, (Washington D.C., 1979).

2. Aquinas, *Scriptum Super Libros Sententiarum Magistri Petri Lombardi* (Paris, 1929-47) II, 31, 1, 2. All Latin references given hereafter are to works of St. Thomas Aquinas and will be cited by title alone. My translation of his commentary on *The Sentences* is used here and throughout.

3. See Aristotle, *Metaphysics*, transl. H. G. Apostle (Bloomington, Indiana, 1966) G, 2, 1004a 9-16, and Aquinas, *Commentary on the Metaphysics of Aristotle*, transl. J. P. Rowan (Chicago, 1961) 3, #565.

4. *In II Sent.*, 30, 1, 2.

5. *In IV Meta.*, 3, #565.

6. *Summa Theologiae*, transl. The English Dominicans (London, 1912-36) I-II, 72, 1, emphasis added.

7. *Ibid.*, I-II, 73, 2 ad 2.

8. *Questiones Disputatae De Malo* (Turin, 1965) 3, 1, emphasis added. My translation of *De Malo* is used, here and throughout.

9. *Summa Theol.*, II-II, 152, 6, emphasis added.

10. *Ibid.*, I-II, 75, 2, emphasis added.

11. *Ibid.*, I-II, 6, 7 ad 3, emphasis added. For reason resisting passion, see *ibid.*, I-II, 80, 3; II-II, 53, 5; II-II, 155, 4; and II-II, 156, 1. For the will resisting passion, see *ibid.*, I-II, 6, 7 ad 3 and II-II, 175, 2 ad 2.

12. *De Malo*, 1, 3, emphasis added.

13. *Summa Theol.*, I-II, 16, 4, emphasis added.

14. *In II Sent.*, 35, 1, 4.

15. *Summa Contra Gentiles*, transl. The English Dominicans (London, 1928) III, 10.

16. *Loc. cit.*

17. *Loc. cit.*

18. *Loc. cit.*

19. *Loc. cit.*

20. *Loc. cit.*

21. *De Malo*, 1, 3.

22. See *Summa Theol.*, I, 49, 1, ad 3 and I-II, 75, 1, ad 1.

23. *De Malo*, 1, 3 and ad 13.

24. See *Summa Theol.*, I, 76, 7 ad 1. For further examples of the presupposition of material disposition to form, see *In II Sent.*, 31, and *Summa Theol.*, I, 76, 6. For Thomas's use of the word "praeintelligitur" related to voluntary defect and act, see *Sum. cont. Gent.*, III, 10, and *De Malo*, I, 3.

25. *Ibid.*, 1, 3, emphasis added.

26. *Loc. cit.*, emphasis added.

27. See J. Maritain, *Existence and the Existent*, transl. L. Galantière and G. Phelan (New York, 1948) p. 90, and *God and the Permission of Evil*, transl. J. Evans (Milwaukee, 1966) p. 21 and throughout. Hereafter these works are cited as *Existent* and *Permission.*

28. *Existent*, p. 90.

29. *Permission*, pp. 51-54.

30. *Existent*, pp. 91-92 and particularly *Permission*, p. 6 and throughout.

31. *Existent*, p. 91.

32. *Ibid.*, p. 92.

33. *Summa Theol.*, I, 17, 1, emphasis added.

34. *Ibid.*, I, 20, 2 ad 4, emphasis added.

35. *In I Sent.*, 45, 1, 4.

36. *Loc. cit.*

37. See also *In I Sent.*, 46, 4; *In II Sent.*, 23, 2, 1; and *Disputed Questions on Truth*, transl. R. W. Mulligan, S. J. (Chicago, 1952) 23, 3, ad 2 and ad 4.

38. *Epistola II Ad Corinthios* (Rome, 1953) II, 5. My translation.

39. *Expositio Super Dionysius De Divinis Nominibus* (Turin, 1950) 8, 5. My translation.

40. *In II Sent.*, 36, 1, 3 ad 1.

41. *Summa Theol.*, I-II, 87, 2 and ad 1.

42. *Epistola Ad Romanos* (Rome, 1953) 9, 3. My translation.

43. That witness was not without effect. I have collected over thirty supporters of this distinction and its correlative concept of a sufficient grace that is impedible (by man's sin). Many of these philosophers and theologians were openly influenced by Maritain. See the third appendix of my dissertation, "God's Permission of Sin: Negative or Conditioned Decree? A Defense of the Doctrine of F. Marin-Sola, O. P., based on the Principles of Thomas Aquinas" (Ann Arbor, University Microfilms International, 1983), pp. 850-894.

44. For examples see *In I Sent.*, 40, 1, 2; *In I Sent.*, 47, 1, 3; *De Ver.*, 5, 7; and *Summa Theol.*, I, 19, 6.

45. See J. Maritain, "Reflexions sur le savoir théologique," *Revue Thomiste* 69 (1969), 22.

46. *Ibid.*, 18.

47. *Ibid.*, 21-22. My translation.

EXISTENTIAL REALISM AND FREEDOM OF CHOICE

Vukan Kuic

Contrary to what Sartre and some other contemporary existentialists want to believe, Maritain insists that while only natures can have being, having a nature does not deprive man of his freedom. Sartre reminds Maritain of Descartes who held that God could have created mountains without valleys, square circles, and contradictions both of which were equally true. In Sartre's version, this sort of "freedom of choice," in the absence of God, belongs to man. Thus we may say that while Descrates endows God with the most radical kind of Sartrean existentialist freedom, what Sartre wishes for is god-like power, *à la* Descartes, for man. And why do they do this? Most likely because along with many other philosophers, both ancient and modern, they want desperately to make sure that Being is not imprisoned in Necessity. Thus Descartes is afraid that, if God's creation and rule of the world were in any way rationally determined, He would not be "free." And Sartre fears the same for man just in case there was a God. In *Existence and the Existent*, Maritain claims that Thomist existential realism has a sound philosophical as well as a theological solution to this age-old problem, and anyone who has studied this slim but rich volume cannot but be impressed by both its scope and its intensity.

Condensed in those relatively few pages, we not only find a solid exposition of a realist existential metaphysics, epistemology, and theory of ethics, including an ontological definition of the person; despite his disclaimers, Maritain's discussion also reaches deeply into the mysteries of the Christian faith, among which the problem of evil in the world is certainly not the least puzzling. This short treatise is thus but another brilliant example of Maritain's passion and talent for "distinguishing in order to unite," and in fact we find in it repeated references to at least ten of his other major works, from *Science et sagesse* and *Frontières de la poésie* to *La Personne et* le bien commun and *De la Philosophie chrétienne*, as well as his majestic *Les Degrés du savoir*.

Add to this the inimitable Maritain style--which contrasts "the treasures of the intelligibility of being" in Thomist philosophy with "transcendental embezzlement" perpetrated by contemporary existentialism, and notes further that "Herr Heidegger is not lacking in the gift of opportunism," that it is far more comfortable "to excogitate anguish than to suffer it," and that there would be no saints if the Kantian moral imperative, to act so that the maxim of one's act could be a law for all humanity, were valid--add the style to the content, and you have here a work that for the serious students of Maritain is a joy to read and an inexhaustible source of insight and inspiration. Yet this may not be so for the uninitiated casual readers, for whom Maritain's brilliance and passion may actually prove obstacles to the understanding of his theses. And while this is not fatal to Maritain's genius, it does not always help his cause, which in this case is the philosophical defense of one particular principle of Christian existentialism, namely, the reality of human freedom under divine Providence. Thus even as I assume that Maritain interprets St. Thomas correctly on all the topics treated in *Existence and the Existent*, I find his exposition too involved for an audience of non-specialists. But rather than to try to simplify Maritain, which would be a shame even if it were possible, what I propose in this paper is to take a look at what two other contemporary Thomists, Josef Pieper and Yves R. Simon, have to say about the reality and intelligibility of our existence in which, while remaining entirely under divine control, we retain freedom of choice. In my view, their contributions may help even those who know Maritain to understand him better.

I

Only a few years after the publication of Maritain's *Existence and the Existent*, Josef Pieper wrote an article on "The Negative Element in the Philosophy of St. Thomas Aquinas" in which, without ever mentioning Maritain, he in effect presented his own version of existential realism. While in substantial agreement with Maritain's exposition, this brief essay still sheds new light on it by its wonderfully clear treatment of the concept of creation.

According to Pieper, underlying the whole of the philosophy of St. Thomas Aquinas is the assumption that nothing exists which is not *creatura*, except the Creator Himself, and that this createdness is what determines the inner structure of things.[1] This is what Aquinas takes for granted when he says that "all that exists is good," or that "all that exists is true." Philosophers who conceive of existence as composed of a neutral world of objects fail to understand that rather than in some sort of secondary qualities, things are good and true in their very existence, precisely because they are created, because they come from the "eye of God," as, Pieper recalls, the ancient Egyptians used to say.[2] The idea of creation, in other words, makes a decisive difference in how we look at the world. In fact, only creation makes the world both real, "good," and intelligible, "true," even as it remains itself wrapped in mystery. And no one has explained all this better than Aquinas.

Pieper holds that Aquinas would readily agree with modern philosophers from Bacon to Kant that in the strict and proper sense truth can be predicated not of what exists but only of what is thought. But he would then quickly remind them also that real things *are* something thought. Things exist precisely *because* they are *creatively* thought by God and, because they thus have the "character of the word" (as Romano Guardini put it), they may legitimately be called true.[3] The essence of things is that they are creatively thought, and nothing exists therefore that does not have a "nature." Here Pieper finds that Aquinas would agree even with Sartre, since they both hold that things can have an essential nature only insofar as they are fashioned by thought. For instance, Sartre concedes that a letter opener has a "nature," because it was invented by man; but he denies that man has a nature, because "there exists no God to think it creatively."[4] For Aquinas, on the contrary, the very fact that "a creature has its special and finite substance shows that it comes from a principle."[5] This is why the existentialism of St. Thomas is called "realist." As Maritain never tires of pointing out, existential realism is nothing if not grounded in "the intellectual intuition of being."[6]

"*Res naturalis*," Pieper quotes Aquinas, "*inter duos intellectus constituta [est]*," that is, "a natural thing is placed between two knowing subjects."[7] As Pieper explains it, by thus placing things between "the absolutely creative knowledge of God and the non-creative, reality-conformed knowledge of man," and using the qualitative sense of *mensura* as something on the one hand given and on the other received, Aquinas is able to set up the whole structure of reality as follows. *Mensurans non mensuratum* is God's creative knowledge which gives measure but receives none. *Mensuratum et mensurans* is the created, natural reality, which is both measured and gives measure--to human knowledge, which is, in this context, *mensuratum non mensurans*, that is, strictly determined by the object of knowledge.[8] And what all this really means is, simply, that we can indeed know "the truth of things," but only if we recognize them as *creatura*, as creatively thought by God.

Being created, or fashioned by divine thought, however, things have reality and truth not only for us but also for themselves.[9] St. Augustine put this well, when he said that we see things because they exist, but that they exist because God sees them. And while we thus know that "things are true," we do not and cannot know them exhaustively. The mystery of creation remains and must remain for us a mystery, not only because our intellect is far from perfect but also because, as creatively thought by God, the nature of things is inexhaustible. Pieper makes this point effectively by saying that we fall short in our knowledge of reality precisely because in itself that reality is *all too knowable*. Thus according to St. Thomas, while there is obscurity in things, because they come from nothing--*creatura est tenebra inquantum est ex nihilo*,[10]--their reality is light itself--*ipsa* actualitas rei est quoddam lumen ipsius.[11] In short, there is a single reason why things not only exist but are also both knowable and unfathomable, and that reason is their createdness.[12]

Turning now to our main topic, let us ask how this structure of created reality underlying existential realism can accommodate the privileged position of Maritain's "free existent." In the Thomist scheme, human nature, like all things created, is placed between two intellects, God's and our own, which means--*mensuratum et measurans*--that what we know about it is for real. Thus regardless of how it is explained, the constant need to decide what to do, whether accompanied by levity or agony, is the primary human existential reality. This sense of necessary self-involvement and, indeed, creative power is comparable to what we experience when we make things, say, a letter opener. Even though both these kinds of activities are subject to laws, moral in one case, physical in the other, they are free in the sense that they are our own. Honest people attest to this truth every time they accept blame for failures which all too often attend efforts in both the practical and the productive order.[13]

But acting as free existents and knowing ourselves, as Maritain explains, both as objects and subjects, does not necessarily entail that we know ourselves, or our capacity for freedom, exactly the way God does Who created us. The intuition of subjectivity, Maritain writes, surrenders no essence to us: "We know *that which* we are by our phenomena, our operations, our flow of consciousness," but precisely the more we thus know ourselves, "the more, also, we feel that it leaves us ignorant of the essence of our self."[14] But if subjectivity *as subjectivity*, in Maritain's terms, is "inconceptualisable," is not the same necessarily true of our freedom of choice as such, *as freedom of choice*, as it is creatively thought by God? Created "free existents," we are able, in contrast with the rest of nature, to do something about our existence by measuring it out, so to speak, in actions (and in a different sense, in productions) of our own. But that does not mean that this clearly perceived ability of ours to do so is in itself any less unfathomable, because all too knowable, as Aquinas held, than the rest of God's creation. Our freedom, in other words, is in the last analysis a mystery, and we miss something of its objective nature if we do not recognize it as such.

Because this last remark may sound agnostic, I turn again to Pieper who has a convincing explanation of how what he calls "the negative element" in the philosophy of Aquinas in no way undermines its existential realism grounded in the intelligibility, or the "truth," of things. St. Thomas insists not only that we do not know God (we know Him only as *unknown*, *tamquam ignotum*) but also that we do not even know things in their essence.[15] Indeed, Pieper adds, Lao-Tse's saying that "That name which can be pronounced is not the Eternal Name" applies not only to God but to things as well. But Pieper also reminds us that Aquinas insisted with equal firmness that the mind does make its way to the essence of things--*intellectus . . . penetrat ad usque rei essentiam,*[16] and that these statements are not necessarily contradictory. For Pieper, the positive and the "negative" elements in the philosophy of St. Thomas are perfectly reconciled in his account of creation. In so far as they are creatively thought by God, he writes, things "possess these two properties: on the one hand their ontological clarity and self-revelation and, on the other hand, their inexhaustibleness; their knowability as well as their 'unknowability.'"[17]

Mystery thus remains, but we know it for what it is. And Pieper concludes with a message that is quite similar to what I believe Maritain wanted to convey in the poetical and mystical flourishes of his last chapter, "Ecce in Pace." Maritain contends there that even though philosophy is and should always be an autonomous intellectual discipline, all honest philosophy "tends to go beyond itself in order to attain to the silence of unity, where it will harvest all that it knows in a purer and more transparent light."[18] For his part, Pieper too presents the knowing subject as a *viator*, as someone "on the way," and reflects faithfully Maritain's sentiments in his concluding section, which he entitles "Hope as the Structure of Creaturely Knowledge."[19] Aristotle had compared human intelligence to the eyesight of bats dazzled by sunlight. St. Thomas, while not disagreeing, offered however another possibility: though the eyes of the bat do not avail to behold the sun, he commented, it is clearly seen by the eye of the eagle.[20]

II

While few would associate the general philosophy of Pierre-Joseph Proudhon with that of Jean-Paul Sartre, when it comes to thinking about God and man's freedom of choice, their positions are not so different. For even though Proudhon equivocates about the existence of God, he is as convinced as Sartre that human liberty is incompatible with the idea of a transcendent Providence. This leaves Proudhon no other alternative except to reject submission to any Supreme Being in the name of true morality. Indeed, topping anything that Sartre has written on the subject, Proudhon, stung by a casual slur on his personal integrity, expounds his views in no less than 1,700 closely argued as well as highly emotional pages. "It is a doctrine held by saints," he writes, "that damnation should be preferred to sin if, supposing the impossible, God should impose such an option . . . . Religion and morality made siblings by popular consent are in fact heterogenous and incompatible. Today one has to choose between the fear of god and the fear of evil, between the risk of damnation and the risk of improbity--such is my thesis."[21] In terms current before the advent of existentialism, the battle line is here drawn between transcendence and immanence, as these notions are applied to human destiny. As Proudhon saw it, if this destiny is found in something that transcends the human person, religion is the answer. But if its meaning lies in the human person, any transcendent religion is plainly immoral.

Even today this is not an uncommon view, and some believe that choosing between these alternatives is ultimately an act of faith. But Yves R. Simon holds not only that there is a third choice but also that the way out of Proudhon's dilemma may be opened by a philosophical as distinguished from a theological argument.[22] What give Proudhon's thesis a certain plausibility, according to Simon, are various interpretations of divine transcendence found in Cartesianism, Jansenism, fideism, and sometimes even in statements by the spokesman for the Church. For instance, in the famous dictionary of Bergier, a high prelate remarks that "no purely human reason can establish the distinction between good and evil; if it had not been God's good pleasure to let us know of his intention, a son could kill his father without culpability." When an archbishop says things like that, Simon comments, one cannot expect a mere printer to correct it.[23] But Proudhon remains nevertheless at fault, because he does not bother to consider a different doctrine of transcendence in which God's work is not at odds either with our moral sense or with our freedom of choice.

Simon admits that interpreting transcendence is a task that belongs ultimately to theology. But he believes that philosophy can help, and that the open-minded philosopher's first care is to establish a valid idea of *nature*. Whether things exist or not may be entirely up to God, but if they exist, shouldn't they be true to themselves? If it is God's creative idea that gives them being, what He bestows upon each thing as he draws it from nothingness is precisely the power *to be itself*. In other words, a *nature* is above all a principle of autonomy which is placed so deep in things that it cannot be distinguished from their realization. Nature is thus present in every created being, and it enables even the humblest thing to be itself and to act out the its divine idea on its own.[24]

Moreover, while to some privileged beings God has given not only nature but also freedom, their case is not substantially different. As created beings they depend on God, but through their nature they depend on Him precisely to be free. By reason of their identity with themselves, free natures no less that other natures are linked to certain determined ends. But in contrast with other natures, free natures are themselves responsible for attaining those ends and are even able to choose other ends that do not lead to their fulfillment. But as Simon has written elsewhere, we must not confuse freedom with our ability to choose between right *and* wrong, good *and* evil. For human beings are truly free only when they are able consistently to choose the true good over the apparent good, as befits rational agents.[25] Thus again we see that free natures are not so different from other natures for, as Simon explains, "God remains the total cause of all their activity, even as their freedom--which after all is their nature--enjoys the fulness of reality."[26]

What Proudhon, and he is not alone, fails to understand is that moral decisions depend no less on the existential circumstances of individual cases, including personalities, than on general principles of ethics. For him, and others, Cicero's formal statement that natural law is the same in Athens and in Rome is proof enough that any idea of transcendental morality rules out freedom of choice.[27] But the true notion of transcendence, as just explained, far from excluding freedom of choice, clearly calls for it and is alone capable of giving it meaning. For if man were a law unto himself, or without nature as Sartre would have it, which amounts to the same thing, man would be like a caricature of the god of Descartes, totally indifferent to all contradictions. That Proudhon does not end with such a divinization of man, is due, according to Simon, to what amounts to an accident, namely, his exclusive commitment to the notion of justice as equality, not only among men but apparently among all things.[28]

Nevertheless, Simon acknowledges that the idea of a limited autonomy is rather obscure and that not everyone may be equally willing to accept the interpretation of the human condition on the basis of doctrines of creation, fall, and redeeming Incarnation. And to accommodate all who would approach this problem with an open mind, he goes back to Aristotle who actually has a theory that shows how unqualified dependence does not necessarily destroy and may actually promote autonomy.

In contrast to the reaction of ordinary physical things when they are acted upon, our senses, Aristotle points out, respond by being themselves. When acted upon, a physical thing undergoes either transformation, replacement, or destruction. "If the ontological condition of matter could be translated into feelings," Simon writes, "one could say that its joys are never without a cloud, nor its sadness without consolation."[29] But there are no substitutions and no losses in sense perception. "It is a case of simple becoming, where our senses do their own thing, so to speak, without having to give up anything in return. In other words, 'being acted upon' in no way affects their autonomy."[30] And what goes for sense perception goes *a fortiori* for intellectual perception. The object of knowledge acts upon the knower both as an efficient and as a formal cause-- *mensurans qua mensuratum*, as Aquinas might put it. The knower faced with this object cannot not know it, or know it as something else than it is. And yet, being so determinately acted upon, far from changing the knower in his being or nature, actually enhances his autonomy and makes him be more of what he is, namely, a knower. As an object under the influence of other objects, the soul moves toward its own finalities and completes or perfects itself according to its own law.[31]

For anyone who has problems with transcendence and immanence, this Aristotelian version of what amounts to a realist existentialist epistemology, without the benefit of the notion of creation, should be quite helpful. For here is a case of infinitely strong influence that nevertheless safeguards fully the autonomy of those exposed to it, and the interpretation leaves God out of it. But in direct reply to Proudhon's doubts, and as a suggestion to those who might share them, Simon submits that the action of the known object on the knowing soul is the best analogy for the influence of God on things. Things are what they are, because God has given them their everything. And in the case of rational natures, this includes their freedom and moral responsibility.

But finally, Simon suggests also another way of thinking about divine transcedence respecting the autonomy of creatures that I find effectively complements Maritain's suggestion that we should think of eternity not as time stretched in opposite directions but rather as an everlasting instant, an enduring "divine today."[32] We must not, Simon warns, think of God as a kind of superman busily and jealously controlling everything. Such a despotic model conveys the idea of an absolute power exercised over things, as well as people reduced to mere automatons, without a law, nature, or will of their own. God's power is far greater than that. Every single thing He creates acts by itself and for itself precisely by the power given it with its nature. And what is true of the humblest creature, is true in a distinguished way of creatures who have been given freedom as well as a nature. They may have their freedom in God, but in God *they have it.*[33]

III

The concepts of creation and of nature, as explained above by Pieper and Simon respectively, make it easier, in my opinion, to understand the relation between existential realism and freedom of choice. Reduced to its simplest terms, that relation may be stated as follows: what is is real and true, including human nature which puts us in charge of our own human, that is, moral existence. This position may be said to take care not only of the absurdities of Sartrean naked existence but also of the Kantian gap between the starry skies above and the moral law within. It represents a unified, realistic, and eminently practical view of the world and the human condition. And it is, of course, also exactly the position that Maritain has consistently expounded in all his works.

In *Existence and the Existent*, however, Maritain, irresistibly drawn as usual to questions of faith, investigates more than just the basic philosophical problems that need to be solved to show that our freedom of choice is not an illusion. To put it crudely, while treating of the problem of evil in the world, he takes it upon himself also to defend God, so to speak, from any complicity in our sins and, in doing so, manages, in my view, to obscure the issues. I have no doubts whatsover that Maritain fully subscribes to the proposition that while we have our freedom *in* God, in God *we have it.* But virtually the only concrete example of freedom of choice he offers in this book is our ability to "nihilate" what we may call God's true wishes, namely, the tendency to do good that He has built into our nature.[34]

In fact, while Maritain helps us think about God's eternal plan by suggesting that we think of it not as a scenario prepared in advance but rather as a play forever "improvised under the eternal and immutable direction of the almighty Stage Manager," he again confuses the reader when he adds that while man cannot alter this eternal plan, "he enters into its very composition and its eternal fixity by his power of saying, No!"[35] Consequently, according to Maritain, in the order of nature "the whole world is seated in wickedness", and "the terrible, the incorruptible, divine fair play leaves us to flounder in the mire." And while he balances this conclusion on the very next page by saying that, fortunately, there is also the order of grace, and that for those who serve God there is the certainty that "in spite of everything, they participate in guiding history towards its accomplishment,"[36] this is hardly enough, in my view, to convey the idea that acting deliberately "in the line of good," that is, doing God's will rather than nihilating it, is the real proof of our freedom of choice.

Remote ages, Yves R. Simon has written, may find it relevant to know that Maritain was "the philosopher who, in case of conflict, never hesitated to fulfill his calling rather than follow his choice."[37] In *Existence and the Existent*, Maritain himself distinguishes between two fundamental postures which he calls *cause-seeking* (essentially philosophical) and *saving my all* (basically religious), even as he refrains from admitting that, fulfilling his calling, he inclines toward the latter.[38] Thus as in so many of his other writings, in this "essay in Christian existentialism" he does battle not only with Sartre's atheism but with all sorts of heresies, philosophical as well as religious, and he does get sometimes carried away with polemical zeal. Reacting against the replacement of "moral tragedy by sophisticated metaphysics,"[39] Maritain is anxious to establish that evil is "man's invention"[40] and to alert us against "the swoon of liberty"--which is what sin is.[41] I believe his message comes across, even if we cannot all follow the subtle theological arguments he obviously loved so much.[42] This is why I thought a little help from some fellow-Thomists may be in order. And if one still does not understand how man can be free under divine Providence, let him be consoled by the "negative element" in Aquinas' thought recalled by Pieper. Yes, our minds are rather imperfect; but the real reason why we know so poorly is that the existent as well as existence are genuinely inexhaustible, super-intelligible divine mysteries.

University of South Carolina

NOTES

1. J. Pieper, *The Silence of St. Thomas*, transl. J. Murray and D. O'Connor (New York, 1957), p. 47.

2. *Ibid.*, p. 55.

3. *Ibid.*, p. 51.

4. *Ibid.*, p. 53; J-P. Sartre, *L'Existentialisme est un humanisme* (Paris, 1946), p. 22.

5. *Summa Theol.*, I, 93, 6.

6. J. Maritain, *Existence and the Existent* (Garden City, NY, 1956), p. 135.

7. *The Silence*, p. 53.

8. *Ibid.*, p. 54.

9. *Ibid.*, p. 55.

10. *Ibid.*, p. 67; *De Ver.*, V, 2, ad 11.

11. *The Silence*, p. 56; *Liber de Causis*, I, 6.

12. Cf. *Existence*, pp. 43-44: "The very notion of *essentia* signifies a relation to esse, which is why we have good grounds for saying that existence is the primary source of intelligibility. But, not being an essence or an intelligible, this primary source of intelligibility has to be a super- intelligible."

13. On the distinction of "practical" from what he calls the "speculative," i. e., theoretical order, see J. Maritain, *The Degrees of Knowledge* (New York, 1959), Appendix VII; for a general explanation of what is called above "productive order," see J. Maritain, *Creative Intuition in Art and Poetry* (New York, 1953).

14. *Existence*, p. 76.

15. *The Silence*, pp. 64-65; *Summa Theol.*, I, 2, ad 1; I, 3, prologue.

16. *The Silence*, p. 68; *Summa Theol.*, I, II, 31, 5.

17. *The Silence*, p. 69.

18. *Existence*, p. 152.

19. *The Silence*, p. 68.

20. *Ibid.*, p. 71; *Apologia doctae ignorantiae*, 2, 2 off.

21. *De la Justice dans la Révolution et dans l'Église* (Paris, 1858), p. 3.

22. Y. Simon, "Le Problème de la transcendance et le défi de Proudhon", *Nova et Vetera*, IX (1934), pp. 225-238; transl. C. O'Donnell and V. Kuic, "The Problem of Transcendence and Proudhon's Challenge," *Thought*, LIV (1979), pp. 176-185.

23. "Proudhon's Challenge," p. 183.

24. *Ibid.*, 181.

25. See Y. Simon, *Freedom of Choice*, ed. Peter Wolff (New York, 1969, 1987).

26. "Proudhon's Challenge," p. 182.

27. *Ibid.*, p. 183.

28. *Ibid.*, 179. Simon offers following illustrations from Proudhon's *Correspondence*: "In brief, I reject not only the absolute God of the priests but also the idea of Man- God." "The truly universal principle of philosophy, the principle which concerns equally mathematics, mechanics, logic, aesthetics, is the principle of justice, equity, equality, equilibrium, harmony."

29. "Proudhon's Challenge," p. 184; *De Anima*, 417b2.

30. "Proudhon's Challenge," p. 184.

31. *Ibid.*

32. *Existence*, p. 93.

33. "Proudhon's Challenge," p. 182.

34. For example, *Existence*, p. 99: "It follows from this that whereas the created existent is never alone when it exercises its liberty in the line of good, and has need of the first cause of all that it produces in the way of being and of good, contrariwise, it has no need of God, it is truly alone, for the purpose of freely nihilating, of taking the free first initiative of this absence (or 'nothingness') of consideration, which is the matrix of the evil in the free action--I mean to say, the matrix of the *privation* itself by which the free act (in which there is metaphysical good in so far as there is being) is morally deformed or purely and simply evil."

35. *Ibid.*, p. 125.

36. *Ibid.*, pp. 127-28.

37. Y. Simon, "Jacques Maritain: The Growth of a Christian Philosopher," in *Jacques Maritain: The Man and His Achievement*, ed. J. Evans (New York, 1963), p. 21.

38. *Existence*, p. 130.

39. *Ibid.*, p. 134.

40. *Ibid.*, p. 120.

41. *Ibid.*, p. 129.

42. For example, *ibid.*, p. 106fn: "From the moment we understand that if the shatterable impetus is not shattered by the free nihilating of the creature, then it reaches of itself its proximate term, in order to give way to an unshatterable impetus specifically distinct from itself, in which it fructifies of itself and by which the moral good *to-act* is given; from the moment we understand that the *non-nihilating*, which conditions the fructification of the shatterable impetus in unshatterable impetus, does absolutely not imply the slightest contribution made by the creature to the divine motion--from this moment we have beyond question exorcised every shadow of Molinism."

WITHOUT ME YOU CAN DO NOTHING

Desmond J. FitzGerald

When I was a beginning teacher many years ago one of my colleagues remarked to me that the problem of divine concurrence was the most difficult problem in metaphysics. He meant, of course, the problem of preserving the freedom of human choice given that God is the first cause of the movement of our will as it makes its decision, and all this in accord with God's providential plan for history.

My colleague was largely but not entirely correct. For it seems to me the mystery of divine concurrence in the human act is escalated when one takes into account that the free act we are considering is sometimes a sinful act.

For here one must balance the insight that God is the first cause of all that exists, and some things that exist are sinful acts, and therefore, in some sense God is the cause of them, with the other insight that God who is Goodness Itself cannot be the cause of evil. And so the question becomes: how can God be the cause of our choices and not be the cause of our evil choices?

In his *Summa Theologiae*, I, 49, 1, ad 3, reflecting on whether or not God can be the cause of evil, St. Thomas simply says

> ...But in voluntary beings the defect of the action comes
> from an actually deficient will in as much as it does not
> actually subject itself to its proper rule. This defect,
> however, is not a fault; but fault follows upon it from the
> fact that the will acts with this defect.

In 1942, in giving the Marquette University Aquinas Lecture, Jacques Maritain turned his attention to this problem in giving his analysis of the Thomistic explanation. He returned to this subject just a few years later in his work *Court Traité de l'Existence et de l' Existant*, translated into English by Lewis Galantière and Gerald B. Phelan and published in 1948 with the title *Existence and the Existent*. In presenting my comments on Maritain's analysis I shall begin with the Marquette lecture and move to the somewhat later work, though in my judgment in the later version there is only a more succinct expression of what Maritain had noted in the *St. Thomas and the Problem of Evil*. In both works he is following his guide, St. Thomas Aquinas, but presenting an elaboration not in the mentor's texts.

To return to the problem itself: how can God not be the cause of sin when He is the cause of everything which exists? As is well understood the solution lies in the nature of evil. Evil is not a being, it is the lack of being, the privation of a due good. Thus a sinful act, an evil choice, will be a mixture of good and evil. The evil will be a defect, a disorder in the being of a choice which, to the extent that it has the actuality of a human choice, will be good.

Let Maritain speak for himself as he outlines the conditions for the consideration of the problem:

> The general principle I mentioned a while ago remains the same: evil of action or of operation always derives from a certain presupposed defect in the being or the active powers of the agent, that is to say, in this case, in the will. But this time the defect itself, that failure in the being which is the root of evil of action, must be a *voluntary and free* defect, since it is the evil of a free action or a free choice which results from it. And furthermore, contrary to what happens in the world of nature, this defect itself must *not be an evil* or a privation, for if it were an evil of the will in the very nature or in the physical being of the latter we should not be dealing with a voluntary and free defect: the cause of this defect must be the will itself, not nature; but on the other hand, if this defect were *an evil of the will in its free activity*, then the defect itself would already be an evil-free action, and we should be explaining the evil of a free action by the evil of a free action, which would be a vicious circle.
>
> What then is this defect--what is that failure in being which is the metaphysical root of evil of action and which is itself free without, however, being already an evil?[1]

Now I have quoted Maritain at some length here and, where my quotation ends, Maritain's quotation from St. Thomas' *Disputed Question on Evil* begins (*De Malo*,I,3).

The issue again is how the creature, who can do nothing positive without God's help, introduces the disorder which warps or twists a good action into the deflected action which is the sinful act.

Maritain quotes St. Thomas:

"Suppose we take a craftsman who must cut wood in a
straight line according to a certain ruler: if he does not cut
it in a straight line, that is, if he makes a bad cutting, that
bad cutting will be caused by the fact that the craftsman
did not hold the ruler in his hand. Similarly, delectation
and everything that happens in human affairs should be
measured and ruled according to the rule of reason and of
divine law. That the will does not use [let us take careful
note of the simple negation expressed there] - that the will
does not make use of the rule of reason and of divine
law," that is, does not have the deficiency: which must be
considered in the will before the faulty choice in which
alone moral evil consists. And for that very absence or
that lack which consists in not making use of the rule, "not
taking the rule in hand, *there is no need to seek a cause,
for the very freedom of will, whereby it can act or not act,
is enough.*"[2]

As Maritain then comments in his expansion of the solution, man's
freedom to consider or not consider the moral principle in question is
sufficient to account for the introduction of the defect which is the privation
of due order giving rise to the sinful choice.

Here we are at the very beginning; impossible to go any
further back: a free defect, a defect of which freedom
itself is the negative and deficient primary cause--and it is
the will thus in default, which in acting with this defect, is
the cause--*in quantum deficiens*--of moral evil.[3]

The simple non-consideration of the rule is not itself the sinful choice; it
is the logically prior, not temporally prior, condition of the choice. For it is
in that movement of choosing a particular act that the act issues forth from
us in its disorder. God is the first cause of the being of the act, but the
disorder of the act is due to our failure at the crucial moment to guide our
act by the applicable moral principle.

My act is the telling of a lie; the act of speaking is a good, but the
deception involved proceeds from my non- consideration of the moral
principle of our obligation to tell the truth.

Again, Maritain says:

What is required of the soul is not that it should always
look to the rule or have the rule constantly in hand, but
that it should produce its act while looking at the rule.

Now in the metaphysical moment we are examining here
there is as yet no act produced, there is merely an absence
of consideration of the rule, and it is only in the act which
will be produced, in terms of that absence, that evil will
exist. Therein lies an extremely subtle point of doctrine,
one of capital importance. Before the moral act, before
the *bonum debitum*, the *due good* which makes up the
quality of this act and whose absence is a privation and an
evil, there is a metaphysical condition of the moral act,
which, taken in itself, is not a due good, and the absence
of which consequently will be neither a privation nor an
evil but a pure and simple *negation* (an absence of a good
that is *not* due), and that metaphysical condition is a *free*
condition.[4]

Then, returning to Maritain's quoting of St. Thomas' *De Malo*, we have
the original statement:

That which formally constitutes the fault or moral evil,
writes St. Thomas, comes into being in this--that, without
the concurrent consideration of the rule, the will proceeds
to the act of choice. Thus the craftsman does not err in
not always having his ruler in hand but in proceeding to
cut the wood without his ruler. The faultiness of will does
not consist in not paying attention in act to the rule of
reason or of divine law, but in this: -- that without taking
heed of the rule it proceeds to the act of choice.[5]

And Maritain adds: "Its fault lies in the fact that, without considering
the rule--an *absence* of attention of which freedom alone is the cause--*it
proceeds to the act of choice*, which is consequently *deprived* of the
rectitude it should have."[6]

While I indicated before that the analysis of the causality of the sinful
act in *Existence and the Existent* did not differ in doctrinal content from the
analysis in the Aquinas Lecture of 1942, there is a difference in style.
Maritain was appointed by Charles de Gaulle to be the French Ambassador
to the Vatican in 1945. At the end of the latter work is the date "Rome,
January-April, 1947." It would seem that Maritain in those few months of
intensive composition came to express himself with a polish and fluidity that
sharpened his understanding of St. Thomas' text.

Here is the later version:

In one of his most difficult and most original theses, Thomas Aquinas explains on this point that the emergence of a free and evil act resolves into two moments--distinct, not according to the priority of time, but according to ontological priority. At a first moment, there is in the will, by the fact of its very liberty, an absence or a nihilation which is not yet a *privation* or an evil, but a mere lacuna; the existent does not consider the norm of the *thou shouldst* upon which the ruling of the act depends. At a second moment the will produces its free act affected by the privation of its due ruling and wounded with the nothingness which results from this lack of consideration.

It is at this second moment that there is moral evil or sin. At the first moment there had not yet been moral fault or sin, but only the fissure through which evil introduces itself into the free decision about to come forth from the person, the vacuum or lacuna through which sin will take form in the free will before being launched into the arteries of the subject and of the world. This vacuum or lacuna, which St. Thomas calls non- consideration of the rule, is not an evil or a privation, but a mere lack, a mere nothingness of consideration. For, of itself, it is not a duty for the will to consider the rule; that duty arises only at the moment of action, or production of being, at which time the will begets the free decision in which it *makes* its choice. Non-consideration of the rule becomes an evil, or becomes the privation of a good that is due, only at the second of the two moments we have distinguished - at the moment when the will produces some act or some being, at the moment when it causes the choice to irrupt; at the moment when the free act it posited, with the wound or deformity of that non- consideration.[7]

Here Maritain's elaboration of Aquinas' answer re-states the presentation given in the Marquette lecture. It is a delicate balance preserving God's causality of the actuality of the act (the giving being to the effect) and the failure to follow through with the ruling of the act by the applicable moral principle. It is not easy to express the negativity of the failure to follow through except as Maritain expresses it with variations of the expression "do a nothingness." As he says, "we are faced here by an absolute beginning which is not a beginning but a 'naught,' a fissure, a lacuna introduced into the warp and woof of being."[8]

Maritain continues to explain that this failure to act has no need of God's causality as the will is truly alone, and only its freedom not to do something at a crucial moment is required.

> It follows from this that whereas the created existent is never alone when it exercises its liberty in the line of good, and has need of the first cause for all that it produces in the way of being and of good, contrariwise, it has no need of God, it is truly alone, for the purpose of freely nihilating, of taking the free first initiative of this absence (or 'nothingness') of consideration, which is the matrix of evil in the free act - I mean to say, the matrix of the privation itself by which the free act (in which there is metaphysical good in so far as there is being) is morally deformed or purely and simply evil. 'For without Me, you can nothing;' which is to say, 'Without Me you can make that thing which is nothing.'[9]

So far this paper has been a simple exposition in which I have quoted the reflection of Maritain, who is often quoting or paraphrasing the text of St. Thomas. When all is said and done the question remains: how satisfactory is the analysis, brilliant though it may be in its notion of *doing a nothingness*, letting the ball drop, as it were, instead of bringing the hands together to catch it?

The difficulty that has always bothered me (and the students with whom I regularly discuss the problem in our philosophical theology courses) is that this theory implies that you cannot psychologically consider the moral rule you are breaking while you are choosing to break it. The defect or sin arises from the non-consideration of the rule at the moment of choosing to do something immoral. But common experience confirms our ability to look a moral principle in the face and defy it. To put it in more innocent terms, as my students are inclined to do in classroom discussions: "I can very well know I should be sticking to my diet while I can choose to help myself to a dish of ice cream." Granted that eating a dish of ice cream is trivial enough, substitute fornication for eating ice cream and the psychological insight is the same. The mortality of a mortal sin consists in our "don't-give-a-damn defiance"of the *thou shouldst*, as Maritain might say.

[Here the paper as presented in Montreal ended; as I put it, it came to a stop but not a conclusion. In the discussion that followed a conclusion of a sort developed. Members of the audience enlarged the problem to the classic question related to the Socratic theme that virtue is knowledge. Can one who has had a vision of the Good knowingly do what is evil? Even Plato recognized the conflict we experience when knowing full well what we should do: our desire overpowers our judgment and we do the shameful thing against our conscience.

> ...One day Leontius, the son of Aglaion, was coming up from the Piraeus alongside the north wall when he saw some dead bodies fallen at the hand of the executioner. He felt the urge to look at them; at the same time he was disgusted with himself and his morbid curiosity, and he turned away. For a while he was in inner turmoil, resisting his craving to look and covering his eyes. But finally he was overcome by his desire to see. He opened his eyes wide and ran up to the corpses, cursing his own vision: "Now have your way, damn you. Go ahead and feast at this banquet for sordid appetites."[10]

This observation was supplemented by reference to Aristotle's discussion of *akrasia* in Book VII, chapter 2, of the *Nicomachean Ethics*, wherein he pondered how someone who knows better can misbehave. He reports Socrates as holding that no one acts against what he judges best; that is, people act wrongly only by reason of ignorance.[11] To which Aristotle replies: "Now this view contradicts the observed facts."[12] Thus Aristotle, always the realistic psychologist, recognizes how in some situations, while knowing better with one part of our mind, we can still focus on the immediate pleasure another course of action will bring us. And consequently we can choose to go ahead and do the sinful act.

That would seem to be some form of dropping the rule and, without God's help, doing nothing.]

University of San Francisco

NOTES

1. *St. Thomas and the Problem of Evil* (Milwaukee, 1942) pp. 23-24.

2. *Ibid.,* p. 25.

3. *Ibid.,* p. 26.

4. *Ibid.,* p. 27.

5. *Ibid.,* pp. 27-28. Cf. *De Malo,* I, 3.

6. *Ibid.,* p. 28.

7. *Existence and the Existent* (Garden City, N.Y., 1956) pp. 97-98.

8. *Ibid.,* p. 98.

9. *Ibid.,* p. 99.

10. *Republic,* Bk. IV, 439-440. The text used is the Sterling/Scott translation (New York, 1985).

11. *Protagoras,* 352.

12. *Ethica Nichomachea,* VII, 2 (1145b28). Cf. W. K. C. Guthrie: *A History of Greek Philosophy,* Vol. VI (Cambridge, 1981) 364-368.

EVIL IN MARITAIN AND LONERGAN THE EMERGING PROBABILITY OF A SYNTHESIS

David J. Higgins

The most recalcitrant and recurring of human problems is that of evil. This paper attempts a synthesis of two prominent Thomists in their tackling of this vexing question. The main themes relate: (1) Maritain's inverted intuition with Lonergan's inverse insights; (2) Maritain's detailed and diagrammed analysis of the part of God and creature in the act of choice to do evil with Lonergan's notion of basic sin; (3) the directive power of Maritain's initial intuition of being, with Lonergan's transcendental precepts; (4) the Name of God referring to either the first cause or the ultimate solution.

That further work is needed is indicated by Maritain's *non- inclusion* of Rachel[1] mourning her children and Jacob wrestling with the angel--emblems for existential situations which do not easily lend themselves to philosophy as such--as in distinguishing between "the *sapiential* mien" and "the *imprecatory* mien,"[2] and by Lonergan's appeal that one set aside the logical principle of excluded middle when evil is discussed.[3] Since Rachel and Jacob are beings, their exclusion seems improper to a philosophy which begins with the intuition of being and develops through essence and *esse*. And if "Be reasonable" is a transcendental precept[4] governing a person's internal processes, it seems improper to allow a single violation at the single most vexing question a person brings to philosophy. That the work of again examining evil might be successful is a hope expressed by Lonergan: "Evil is, not a mere fact, but a problem, only if one attempts to reconcile it with the goodness of God, and if God is good, then there is not only a problem of evil, but also a solution."[5]

Maritain begins philosophizing with an intuition into being; within being the first distinction is between that which is, or essence, and the act of existing. The act of existing is properly known only in the judgment, but by careful use of analogy it can be conceptualized and take its place in discourse. This distinction appears throughout the range of being as we directly know it, that is of ourselves and all other created beings. In God, essence is identical with the act of existing; God is good, and creates all things, including free creatures, who, while depending on God for their being, can in a way introduce a nihilation into being. This nihilation is moral evil. Physical evil is part of the structure of things; the divine action causes it *per accidens.* That is, granted that the being of carnivores is good, they need to eat; being eaten will appear evil to the prey.[6]

Lonergan takes as primary datum the understanding of what it is to understand.[7] Intelligibility is "immanent in world process. Emergent probability is the successive realization of the possibilities of concrete situations in accord with their probabilities."[8] This theme pervades all world order.[9] Physical evil is simply the result of the fact that the unordered manifold is prior to the more highly ordered and developed. There are false starts and breakdowns. Moral evil is described as what could and ought to be, but is not.[10]

Both Lonergan and Maritain share the Thomistic tradition, appeal to a world view influenced by faith in God revealing, and use the language of essence, existence, matter, form, act, potency, and substance. There is no great difficulty in understanding either from the point of view of the other. Since synthesis is derived from understanding, it might be inferred to be relatively easy, once ambiguities focusing on possibility-potency are specified. I do not intend to do this here. The greater difficulty in synthesis occurs because of the way evil is discussed. If the discussion of evil cannot be understood, it cannot be part of a synthesis.

Synthesis is important because dialogue within the human community is important. Synthesis is not a marshaling of concepts but derives from understanding. Mutual understanding will occur when contradictions are exposed and resolved, and when the distinctions are made which result in unity.[11] Importance "attaches to the probabilities of the occurrence of insight, communication, agreement, decision."[12]

My thesis then is quite simple: I do nothing much more than suggest a stop to further analysis at the point of explaining moral evil. The stop is required by allegiance to Maritain's intuition of being as the beginning of philosophy, and to Lonergan's "Be reasonable" as a transcendental precept. I delineate two areas where understanding, and therefore synthesis, is impossible in Maritain, and one area in Lonergan. My suggestion is that the analysis and the direction they take on this question simply stop lest, in Lonergan's terms, the counter- positions prevail.

Just as evil appears at the very beginning of the accounts of creation which we have inherited, so too the distress its analysis causes to a philosophic system attacks the very beginning. In Maritain it is intuition which suffers; in Lonergan it is insight. The bulb from which all else grows is inverted. In *God and the Permission of Evil* Maritain intends to elaborate on the positions of *Existence and the Existent.* In order to understand the role of the creature in introducing evil into the world an inverted intuition is necessary. "Now the paths of non-being--once one has, by a kind of inverted intuition, become conscious of it and of its formidable role in reality--are as difficult as those of being."[13]   Almost the same phrasing is used by Lonergan as he accounts for human ignorance, malice, and lack of control. "Then to understand his concrete situation, man has to invoke not only the direct insights that grasp intelligibility but also the inverse insights that acknowledge the absence of intelligibility."[14]

The characteristic feature of moral evil, of sin, is that it is a privation. Privation differs from simple non-being in that it is a form of non-being which in some way ought to be. It is a lack of what is due. For Maritain, to sin is to act while the will is not adhering to the rule of reason or divine law. Were there no act, there would be no moral evil. This doctrine is derived from Aquinas: "Now the fact of not applying the rule of reason or of the Divine law, has not in itself the nature of evil, whether of punishment or of guilt, before it is applied to the act."[15]   In a passage from *De Malo* which is more suggestive of the approach Lonergan was to take, Aquinas asserts that error is regarded as sinful insofar as it is not only simple ignorance, but acting while ignorant.[16]   The key to sin in Lonergan is to act without reflecting: "The reign of sin...is the priority of living to learning how to live...." On each occasion, man "could reflect and through reflection avoid sinning; but he cannot bear the burden of perpetual reflection; and long before that burden has mounted to the limit of physical impossibility, he chooses the easy way out."[17]   Basic sin is a "contraction of consciousness," not an event, not something that occurs; is a failure of occurrence, the absence in the will of a reasonable response to an obligatory motive. Hence it cannot have a cause, and God cannot be its cause.[18]

Nowhere in metaphysics does the influence of faith seem to condition the philosopher's discourse more than in this question of evil. Whereas evil confronts us daily, the notion that God is good, in fact, anything concerning God, is the last thing known by mere philosophy. Nevertheless, since faith has identified God as good, as being, as creator, the faith-filled philosopher can in no way allow God to be cause of sin, a moral evil which consists in aversion from God by a creature.

Lonergan's approach to the problem is to allow an exception to his transcendental precepts. In this case it is the precept to be reasonable as exemplified by the principle of excluded middle. When it is first posited the principle has no exception: "terms of possible meaning are subject to the principle of excluded middle as long as the terms are regarded as acceptable; for if one is to employ the terms, one has no third alternative to affirming or denying them."[19]   But later there are special rules necessitated by the irrationality of basic sin:

> For the familiar disjunction of the principle of excluded
> middle (Either A or not A) must be replaced by a
> trichotomy. Besides what is positively and what simply is

> not, there is the irrational constituted by what could and
> ought to be but is not. Besides the being that God causes,
> and the non-being that God does not cause, there is the
> irrational that God neither causes nor does not cause but
> permits others to perpetrate. Besides the actual good that
> God wills and the unrealized good that God does not will,
> there are the basic sins that he neither wills nor does not
> will but forbids.[20]

In contradiction to this approach, it should be remembered that God is one and simple and there cannot be several wills, nor a split will, nor consequent and permissive decrees. Forbid and permit are each an act of will. Either the unity of God or the permit/forbid type analysis needs to be eschewed.

To the extent that synthesis is a result of understanding it will not come about as long as a firmly established transcendental precept can be violated at the one point where the experiencing human most needs the consolations of philosophy. Problems of method, and of physics and math, were not solved by violating the principle--why should the single problem of evil be so solved? This cannot be understood.

There is a second barrier to understanding. Neither Maritain nor Lonergan is providing a direct insight or intuition into either evil or God. Rather each is elaborating an ideal explanation, submitting hypotheses to the community as it were. Both are elaborating mental constructs.

> And you see also what we must think of the *moments of
> reason* which we introduce into the establishment of the
> eternal plan when we try to picture it to ourselves in our
> fashion. All these moments of reason are absolutely
> nothing in God and in the establishment of the divine plan.
> They are mere beings of reasoning reason, which have
> foundation only in our manner of conceiving when we
> wish to picture to ourselves in terms of time that which,
> dependent on the divine eternity, is of itself exclusive of
> time.[21]

Maritain admits that this is anthropomorphic thinking and sets its limits. All of it "has no reality in God and in the eternal Instant of God; it is a world of clouds which is swept away as soon as we pass to the reality of the eternal Sun and of the divine purposes...."[22]

Lonergan characterizes the probable as the ideal;[23] the essence of probability is that it sets an ideal norm from which actual frequencies can diverge but not systematically.[24] To translate into terms relevant to the present discussion: a synthesis of the philosophies of Aquinas, Maritain,

Lonergan, and ourselves is ideally more probable to the extent that my critique and our disagreements are not systematic. Should we systematically, and with mutual understanding, accept some of what they say and then take a different direction on the question of evil, that different direction would be more probable.

Maritain calls the activity of devising explanations which are not direct insights or intuitions into being, logical watch-making.[25] And so it is. What is achieved is an "auxiliary entity of reason" which enables us to know the lack of being that is evil, which "is in nowise a being of reason; it is indeed very real in things."[26]

There is a third barrier to understanding. A philosophy which begins with the intuition of being cannot leave out any being. Nor can it philosophically appeal to an order outside of being for a solution, as in Maritain's quite authentic claim that "we do not save our souls in the posture of theoretical universality and detachment from self for the purpose of knowing."[27] However, that other order is either being, and so already part of the problem and its connections with other issues, or it is not being and thus not available within a philosophy of being. The tools of analogy, of the *via negativa*, may be suggestive pointers; they cannot be a shibboleth. Again, no understanding occurs. Maritain is certainly aware of the existential significance of the other way--Kierkegaard and the mystics are within his purview. Within a philosophy of being they cannot be considered as "other." Maritain is right, more-over, in asserting that the kind of inclusion within philosophy cannot be the embrace of an Hegelian-type reason. As so included they provide merely a theme for academic philosophy, thereby losing their existential significance.[28] From my point of view, it is more authentic for a person to adopt the *imprecatory* mien, leaving the *sapiential* mien aside, than it is for the philosopher, adopting the *sapiential* mien, to leave the praying person's experience and convictions aside. Beginning with being, the philosopher is to include everything. Beginning with existence as he confronts it, the prayerful person copes as best he can. To sharpen the point of view: it is one thing to say, "I can't handle this philosophically." It is quite another to say, "My philosophy includes all being as being, but this matter in hand is something other, being of another order, or something of an order other than nature." Or to say, as it were, "My principles range wherever reason operates, except when I reason about evil."

There are truths from a source higher than moral philosophy; but moral philosophy cannot be unaware of that beyond, because it is to have concrete and existential significance and is to be existential and genuinely practical. There is the regime of morality in contact with the First Cause via the intermediary of law, and there is the regime of supra-morality in contact with God as a friend in connivance with law, springing from a higher source, a trans-natural aspiration. And the fact remains that if moral philosophy is really concerned with concrete human conduct and possesses the least existential and genuinely practical value, some men live under the regime of supra-morality, delivered from all servitude, even that of reason and moral law--not beyond the distinction of good and evil, but doing good without the will being curbed by the law.[29] In a parallel way, since morals depend on freedom, the analysis of the free act which deals with the moral and spiritual relations of created persons to one another and with God, presupposes the world of nature, but is quite distinct from it, "for the free act is not a part of this world, but of an original universe of its own, the universe of freedom"[30]

There is an analogy advancing from the distinction between act and potency in every created being, from the distinction between essence and existence, towards the claim that they are really distinct in all but God, in whom essence is identical with existence. This advance is the *via negativa*. But there is nothing leading in such a way from creature to God as concerns antecedent and consequent permissive decrees, as concerns resistible and irresistible impulses. This is the place to stop, it would seem. As above, these moments of reason are absolutely nothing in God. Why need Maritain pursue the analysis, the logical watch-making, to the point where the one God now appears to have antecedent and consequent, resistible and irresistible, characteristics? Are these straw men, imaginary objections, to Maritain's Christian presuppositions? If they were real challenges, it could be said that neither do the objectors see into the essence of God to know whether God permits, or is resistible.

Similarly, in Lonergan: what leads to the positing of the trichotomy? In his own language he weakens the position needlessly, leaves the field open to the counter-position. Thus it would be more strategic to simply stop the construct of ideas. This is simply to expect Lonergan to adhere to his own directives concerning the principle of excluded middle: "with respect to each proposition, rational consciousness is presented with the three alternatives of affirmation, of negation, and of seeking a better understanding and so a more adequate formulation of the issue."[31] The evidence is simply not all in on evil; no one sees, in essence, what God is doing in this area. Should the Christian think that faith needs justification by philosophy--evil, as described by Pope John Paul II, is the mystery before which all humans shudder. The analyses of Maritain and Lonergan are too complex, as either admits, to be commonly grasped. Further, they seem to be at variance with their own more significant principles. Thus they are outside the more probable line of emergence towards the understanding of all, by all.

Maritain's friend, Charles Journet, regarded God and evil as polar opposites, both mysterious.[32] The oscillation which the mind makes between the two poles carries one forward; although there are partial insights and schemas of explanation, a final intuition or insight is yet to occur. Let the principle of excluded middle remain part of the transcendental principle of "Be reasonable."   And let the range of the philosophy of being include Rachel and her consolation; although she would not be consoled, when that consolation does come, it too will be being. Lonergan's transcendental precepts can carry the mind a long way; so also can Maritain's intuition into being, and his distinguishing in order to unite. These powerful elaborations are too important to abandon when confronted with evil.   A synthesis were more highly probable were nothing yielded to violation of initial intuition for the sake of logical watch-making, nothing yielded to violation of the transcendental precept "Be reasonable" for the sake of all-inclusiveness.

West Georgia College

NOTES

1. J. Maritain, *Saint Thomas and the Problem of Evil* (Milwaukee, 1942) pp. 9-10.

2. J. Maritain, *Existence and the Existent*, transl. L. Galantiere and G. Phelan (New York, 1948) pp. 124-125.

3. B. Lonergan, *Insight* (San Francisco, 1978) pp. 667-668.

4. B. Lonergan, *Method in Theology* (Minneapolis, 1972) p. 53.

5. *Insight*, p. 694.

6. Existence, pp. 19-26.

7. *Insight*, p. xxviii.

8. *Insight*, p. 171.

9. *Insight*, p. 668.

10. *Insight*, pp. 666-667.

11. The sub-title of Maritain's *Degrees of Knowledge.*

12. *Insight*, p. 210.

13. J. Maritain, *God and the Permission of Evil*, transl. J. Evans (Milwaukee, 1966) p. 32. This explains and corrects *Existence and the Existent.*

14. *Insight*, p. 689.

15. *St. Thomas and the Problem of Evil*, pp. 40-41. This is Maritain's Latin note as translated by English Dominicans. *Summa Theologica* (New York, 1947) I-II, 75, 1, ad 3.

16. St. Thomas Aquinas, *De Malo* (Turin, 1953) III, 7, Resp. This is the author's translation.

17. *Insight*, p. 693.

18. *Insight*, pp. 666-667.

19. *Insight*, p. 576.

20. *Insight*, pp. 666-667.

21. *God and the Permission of Evil*, p. 91.

22. *God and the Permission of Evil*, p. 93.

23. *Insight*, p. 119.

24. *Insight*, p. 102.

25. *God and the Permission of Evil*, p. 84.

26. *God and the Permission of Evil*, pp. 11-12.

27. *Existence*, p. 125.

28. *Existence*, pp. 125-126.

29. J. Maritain, *Moral Philosophy* (New York, 1964) pp. 439-440.

30. *God and the Permission of Evil*, p. 10.

31. *Insight*, p. 381.

32. C. Journet, *The Meaning of Evil*, transl. M. Barry (New York, 1963) pp. 21-23.

FREEDOM, EXISTENCE AND EXISTENTIALISM

Laura Westra

We learn about freedom in Jacques Maritain in two ways: from what he says specifically about it and from what he says about the "wrong" meaning of freedom others entertain. I will discuss the former in the first part of this paper, the latter in the second. I will start by outlining the notion of "freedom" in Maritain through the text of *Existence and the Existent* primarily, but also through a brief examination of related works, such as *St. Thomas and the Problem of Evil*, "The Immanent Dialectic of the First Act of Freedom," in *The Range of Reason*, and a "Philosophy of Freedom," in *Freedom in the Modern World*.[1] I will then turn to Maritain's discussion of "existentialism" in Sartre mainly, but also in Heidegger. In this section I will look at the connection between freedom and existentialism as Maritain sees it, but I will also present Plotinus' understanding of "freedom," the main concept in his philosophy, in order to show how this might help pull together various strands of "existentialist" freedom into one coherent whole, somewhat broader than the one Maritain envisions, perhaps, yet still in line with his thought.

Freedom and Existence in Jacques Maritain

The first point to note is that Maritain starts by linking human and divine freedom, and citing St. Thomas in connection with his doctrine of freedom: our freedom is grounded in our reason, it is inescapably our nature.[2] Maritain sharply distinguishes Kant's doctrine of freedom, which he characterizes as "opposing the order of Freedom to the order of Nature or of Being," from the philosophy of St. Thomas which "unites without confusing them, and grounds the former in the latter."[3] For all his references to our nature and even to nature in general, Maritain sees as a "most awesome mystery" "the problem of the relation between the liberty of the created existent and the eternal purposes of uncreated liberty."[4] This should not be surprising in a thinker who states categorically that metaphysics precedes ethics, and who discusses the question of freedom against the background of good and evil and the moral life.

Maritain approaches the problem of evil in the traditional way, drawing
upon the difference between the human dimension of time and God's
eternal, unitary and timeless way of knowing all that concerns human
existence. I will not belabour this point as our main concern is with the
relation between evil and freedom in the human context. As we saw
freedom is both natural and rational, and therefore a human good. "The
created existent" -- he says -- "possesses the *whole* initiative of the good,"
yet he does so only in a secondary sense, leaving the primary role to
"creative liberty."[5] How is our natural rational liberty reconciled with the
possibility and the reality of an evil act? Maritain locates the problem is the
will in a variation of the Aristotelian "acratic." Evil arises in the action but,
prior to acting, man does not consider the "appropriate rule" governing the
action he considers performing, that is, he ignores the input of right reason.
Consideration of the rule, Maritain says, is not a duty, although "making the
choice" through the right action is. It is our "freedom of the will" which is
to blame.[6]

Now the problem of choice and the failure of the will was originally
posed by Aristotle. Yet, in that doctrine, the acratic *knows* but cannot
overcome, and the question remains one of choice, rather than of freedom.[7]
There is no question of being mistaken or of incapacity, on the part of the
acratic person, either to know the truth about the universal norms governing
his action or about the particular action in the context of a specific situation.
For Aristotle then, it is not a question of lack of consideration of any rule: it
is rather "the impulse that is contrary to right reason (which) bears the
guilt,"[8] so that the failure that permits the man who knows and understands
what is right but acts wrongly instead cannot be blamed on knowledge as
such. It is instead a failure of the will, which brings the problem back to a
question of freedom. How can someone, who knows better, be somehow
coerced by a wrong passion he sees for what it is? Why is even knowledge,
the highest of human capacities and activities, not sufficient? Fr. Owens
suggests:

> But the particular moral knowledge that the act is wrong,
> if it is actually present, is there as detached from its moral
> roots.[9]

Yet it is worth keeping in mind that, while "free choice is discussed at
length by Aristotle, the problem of free will is not."[10] Maritain cites St.
Thomas: "freedom of the will sufficiently accounts for the fact that the will
has not looked at the rule...."[11] He further speaks of the "vacuum" or
"lacuna which St. Thomas calls non-consideration of the rule," and then
adds:

> For of itself it is not a duty for the will to consider the
> rule; that duty arises only at the moment of action, of
> production of being, at which time the will begets the "free
> decision" in which it makes its choice.[12]

I have cited this passage verbatim for two reasons: first, I don't think it reflects fairly the thought of Aquinas, and second, I think it brings Maritain quite close to the very "existentialist" approach he decries.

St. Thomas clearly points the finger of blame at free will for the wrong choices which sin represents: "Defectus iste non reducitur in Deum sicut in causam sed in liberum arbitrium" (S.T., I-II, resp.; ad 2). Now, Maritain bases his interpretation upon *De Malo* (1.3). In that work, St. Thomas discusses whether the case of evil is the good. His argument compares evil in natural things to evil in things which are willed. In both it happens "per accidens" and as a deficiency of the good. The will plays the pivotal role: the adulterer perceives his action as desirable and good, yet he does not see the unavoidable conjunction between that "good" and evil. It is the second aspect, that is, the privation of good, which prompts Aquinas to discuss free will. "Rule and measure are necessary in all things." The craftsman needs to take them into consideration before working his craft, without them he will not draw a correct line or cut right. Similarly, the agent has choice through his free will. Maritain claims it is not required to always consider "the rule"; so does Aquinas, but he adds that man *is* required to do so before choosing, *not*, as Maritain states, only "at the moment of the production of being" (i.e., the moment of action). If rational reflection were not required, we would have obedience to an impulse, rather than a *freely chosen* decision.

Maritain discusses the same problem once again, in *St. Thomas and the Problem of Evil*. Evil lies in acting without reference to the "rule," he states, and then proceeds to outline two "ontological moments": "first moment, not considering the rule, which is a negation, an absence, the lack of a good which is not yet due; and second moment, acting on that negation...."[13] It is a small point of difference between St. Thomas and Maritain, but I think it is important: the high status of freedom, which Maritain wants to extol, is diminished if there is no good or evil in the free choice of non-consideration, but only in the action that ensues.

At any rate, our main concern at this time is the meaning of freedom, and perhaps a consideration of Plotinus' understanding of the concept, might help the task of exegesis. Freedom is at the very apex of his philosophy: it is what the One is, and what our upper sour strives to acquire in its ascending return. Yet it cannot be "freedom" of impulse or--he says--"infants, maniacs and the distraught would be primary examples of free agency. We are free, for him, when we are not constrained by "what is outside us," which encompasses not only circumstances and individuals external to us but also those aspects of our soul which are not truly "us," that is, the upper soul, and are therefore deemed to be "external" to us. In the light of this argument, perhaps Maritain's expressions "freely non-acting" and "non-willing" can be spoken of in a way which might better express their true meaning as "non-freely acting" and "non- willing." If both truly "free action" and truly "free will" have no real meaning aside from the right reason that makes them correspond to Being and Truth, and thus to Uncreated, Creative Freedom, then it is hard to see how Maritain can speak of "creative Freedom," and yet allow the same expression, that is, "freedom" to characterize an action which is a privation of that Being which alone exists in total Freedom. Maritain himself says that "nothingness" has entered into the free initiative of the existent, and then cites Scripture: "For, without Me, you can do nothing" (John XV.5).[14] I would like to add "You can do nothing *free*" as well: not truly free, that is, if ruled by impulse or even ignorance. In the case of the latter, not only would it not be a free action, but not even the action of a moral agent: and therefore it would be incompatible with a consideration of evil.

The reference to Plotinus as a source (albeit an indirect one, may be through Augustine and Aquinas himself) can be extended to Maritain's discussion of the will of God, which--he says--is a "true and active will which projects into the universality of existents the being and goodness that penetrates them...."[15] In his treatment of "Free Will and the Will of the One," Plotinus says:

> Now assuredly an Activity not subjected to Essence is inherently free; God's selfhood, then, is its own Act.[16]

And Maritain says: "The will of God is not, like ours, a 'power' or faculty which produces acts: it is pure act." Freedom, for Maritain, therefore, is primarily Creative Freedom, it "activates" the existents "according to the mode of their fallible freedom, that is to say, according to shatterable motions or activations."[17] These activations arise out of Creative Freedom, and thus should give rise to free action when they are not "shattered." When they are, and to the extent that they are, the actions will be negated in being, goodness and-- ultimately--freedom.

Therefore it seems to me that, whether Maritain says it explicitly or not, at least some measure of "negated freedom" or "un-freedom" should accrue to evil actions so that it might be self-contradictory to term these actions "free evil acts," as Maritain does,[18] and "voluntary evil acts" might represent a more accurate description. Speaking of the first moment in the "ontological order" which, as we saw, Maritain discusses in *St. Thomas and the Problem of Evil, he says: "...the first moment is voluntary, it is free, and it is not yet sin but the root of sin...."*[19] Now "voluntary" and "free" are not identical concepts, so that--given Maritain's own emphasis on Uncreated Freedom as primary, we might want to accept Plotinus' division of the two. After all, Aquinas places the "ratio nem culpae" not in "freedom" as such, but in unconsidered choice:

> ...sed ex hoc accipit primo rationem culpae quot sine actuali consideratione regulae procedit ad huiusmodi electionem (*De Malo*, q.l, a.3, resp.).

Maritain also talks of freedom in chapter six of the *Range of Reason*.[20] He starts with the introspective quest for the first time freedom truly affected his own life in a non-trivial way; the "first act of freedom" refers therefore to "a deep seated determination - a root act" which "impresses a definite direction upon his life as a person." Once again "the first act of freedom" is linked to God, through the good and free choice. The example Maritain offers is that of a child who freely decides to abstain from a moral wrong, choosing a moral good not because of fear or even love, but because "it would not be good". It is a choice for the "moral good," an all-important first choice, which "transcends the whole order of empirical convenience and desire."[21]

What are the implications of this "act of freedom"? It represents a pre-cognitive awareness of a "law of human acts transcending all facts." Yet it is not an abstract law in opposition to myself that I am aware of as a child; rather, I am aware in some way of the coincidence of "*the* good and *my* good." In effect, while the child's act of freedom is not the manifestation of cognitive reflection, it is the precognitive awareness of God:

> ...the child does not think explicitly of God, or of his ultimate end. He thinks of what is good and of what is evil. But by the same token he knows God, without being aware of it.[22]

Therefore the first exercise of individual freedom coincides with the unimpeded unfolding of the child's true nature, a manifestation of his "inclination" towards God, which exists independently of conscious, discursive knowledge of God. Clearly, it is not an ultimate choice for all time, but it is the seed which can "bear fruit," Maritain adds, only through grace.[23] Without God, the first act of freedom could only be "a sin which turns him away from his ultimate end."[24]

The ambiguity I pointed out earlier in Maritain's doctrine of freedom surfaces again: if the paradigm "first act of freedom" entails choosing the good through a pre-cognitive, non-conceptual awareness of God, then it does not seem right to use precisely the same term to describe the choice of evil, as the same description would in fact describe two totally different realities. Therefore, either one or the other action cannot be a "first act of freedom." Given the identification Maritain suggests, of Freedom with Creative Freedom, the choice of evil would seem--as Plotinus would put it in a non-Christian context-- eminently unfree.

In this apparent tension in Maritain's teaching resolved by the examination of other texts such as "A Philosophy of Freedom"? He returns to the interrelation between Nature (or Being) and Freedom in St. Thomas under three headings: 1) How the order of Freedom necessarily presupposes the order of Nature; 2) How it is yet distinct from the order of Nature and constitutes a world apart; 3) In what the dynamism of Freedom consists and what the essential law of its movement is.   The primacy of Nature is obvious, as freedom is natural, "the essence of every intellectual being."[25] But Aquinas himself says that "the whole root of freedom lies in reason" (*De Ver.* 24.2). And, since he specifies in the *Summa* that this is so in two senses, this is where the textual base for Maritain's discussion of the "rule" can be found:

> Regula autem voluntatis humanae est duplex; una propinqua et homogenea, scilicet ipsa humana ratio; alia vero est prima regula, scilicet lex aeterna, quae est quasi ratio Dei." (S.T. I- IIae, 76.1.resp.)

Although Maritain states that consulting the rule is not a requirement, it seems to me that in either of the two senses Aquinas ascribes to it, consulting reason is required of all human beings as a natural requirement of their own nature.

Maritain and Existentialism

One can sympathize with Maritain's worries about existentialism in relation to moral action. Most of the exponents of the movement see freedom as cardinally important, what is essentially human, although they don't accept a metaphysical understanding of either the Universe or of man's nature. "They have an authentic feeling for it and for its essential transcendence," Maritain says, speaking of freedom. Further, existentialism "has a feeling for the creative importance of the moral act," coupled with the "uniqueness of the instant."[26] He sees the real possibility of a "moral philosophy of liberty," but is discouraged by the problematic of "absurdity," and the lack of a "nature" of "Causality and finality."[27] Apparently he alludes to the existentialism of Sartre, yet by tarring all existentialism with the same brush he does injustice to the thought of Heidegger, for instance, which may be deemed "guilty" only in a very limited sense of the "sins" Maritain ascribes to the whole movement.

The only good or "authentic" existentialism for Maritain is that of St. Thomas, characterized by the "primacy of existence," while not denying either "natures" or transcendental finality and still standing by the "supreme victory" of intelligibility and intellect. The "wrong" existentialism, on the other hand, degenerates into a "pure Efficiency or Liberty...positioning itself without reason."[28]   Therefore it is not freedom itself that Maritain condemns, but a freedom which is allied to neither reason nor a transcendental end, that is, existentialism, which is not in the Aristotelian-Thomistic tradition and which therefore "misconceives liberty." It is clear that a liberty which is not modelled upon the "world of Freedom" and man's spiritual nature is not really freedom, though Maritain does not say so in so many words. He refers, for instance, to "the supreme rule or norm of Freedom. In this wise the world of Nature and the world of Freedom have the same head." If God is Uncreated Freedom, any thinker who will not admit His existence will be working within a truncated, incomplete sense of freedom. To this extent at least, Maritain is right about his general assessment of "existentialism": both Sartre and Heidegger, the two main thinkers he cites in this respect, do not admit to a divine sense of freedom, let alone to Uncreated Freedom as the primary meaning of the concept.

On the other hand, the indiscriminate understanding of freedom as "anything goes," which would allow man to make himself as he goes along with no guidance, through an infinity of choices, does not do justice to Heidegger's thought on the topic. What is freedom for Heidegger? It is truth, as the "unconcealedness" of beings:

> Freedom understood as letting beings be, is the fulfillment
> and consummation of the essence of truth in the sense of
> disclosure of beings.[29]

How can one understand freedom as "letting beings be"? Freedom, as we normally think of it, is related primarily to us, to the subjects, who want to be free from impediments and free to pursue our own choices. Heidegger immediately moves the emphasis to the other: I am free when I let other beings be. This letting be is not an attitude of laissez faire, in the sense of lack of concern or interest. If I say "let me be," I usually mean "leave me alone" or "don't concern yourself with me." Heidegger instead wants to understand freedom as letting things be, in the sense of manifesting care (*Sorge*),[30] interest, concern, in order to understand what they truly are, and to allow them to be just that. Such understanding and caring are connected with and represent "the fulfillment and consummation of the essence of truth." If we understand a man as a man, we know truthfully what he is and know the truth of their being. In this "freeing" type of understanding truth comes forth only when beings are approached and viewed in their situatedness.

Yet, one may well ask, is there any moral "substance" to the identification of freedom and truth, any lead to what would constitute a moral choice in his thought? Heidegger does not write specifically on ethical questions, but he does not appear to deem all possibilities equally viable: the notion of "possibilities worth preserving and handing down" expressed by Heidegger through his notion of the "hero" can enable us to differentiate between an infinite range of choices, and the somewhat more limited variety of beings we can "love, favour, and embrace in their essence." The method of choice arises through a consideration of each thing in the light of both its situatedness in Being, as mediated through our context and horizon (or all that is with us now), and the tradition that has formed us and through which we decide what to appropriate and preserve. Thus, the "hero" encompasses at the same time past traditions, the present horizon, and future projections: this understanding is imperative if we are to consider and decide upon the possibilities authentically worth repeating.[31] Thus each instant, if authentically lived, should share in and contain past and future, thus turning the unfolding of time and tradition, with its myriad varied aspects, into one infinitely rich and fruitful totality.

Can we claim that this understanding of freedom, truth, and choice involves God? It clearly does not, as such, but neither does it exclude the possibility of choosing and freely appropriating any aspect of the great traditions that inform us. The strong feeling for the "uniqueness of the instant" which Maritain saw as a great merit of existentialism is therefore, at least in Heideggerian terms, the uniqueness of an enriched instant, in which past, present, and future are uniquely and intrinsically interwoven. In such an instant, truth and freedom are actually and truly present. Schmitz says, speaking of metaphysics:

> Its last word is not that a certain thing is or will be or even that it merely is, but that all being, including what was and what is yet to be, must manifest a presence. This converts past, future, and present into being qua being.[32]

Conclusion

We have discussed two main, related questions in this paper: the meaning of freedom as such in Jacques Maritain, in its relation to existence, and freedom in its relation to existentialism. On the first question we saw that Maritain speaks of Uncreated Freedom, thus linking freedom to the *Ipsum Esse Subsistens* of Aquinas. The identification of Freedom and Existence in the Thomistic sense is thus clear, though a possible difference between Maritain and Aquinas can be traced on the question of evil and free choice. Maritain places evil in wrong action (i.e., action not chosen after due consideration of the rule of right reason) whereas St. Thomas clearly places the first instance of evil in the unconsidered choice itself. The

Aristotelian background of both doctrines in free choice is evident in Aquinas' doctrine and language. I suggested that discriminating between "voluntary" and "free," as Plotinus--for instance--does, would serve Maritain's own understanding of freedom better, although I am not sure that it would help bridge the gap between himself and Aquinas. the Plotinian separation of free from voluntary, I think, would also help to clarify the differences between Maritain's "true existentialism" and "existentialism" as such. The former is described as a philosophy where a) existence is viewed as primary, and b) where man's freedom is seen to be at the same time part of his nature and transcendent, and thus identifiable with Divine Freedom. Non-thomistic existentialism is deemed to be necessarily misleading because of the lack of these components. On the other hand, as we saw, in Heidegger's existentialism there are elements which at least come close to the standards Maritain outlines for "true existentialism." It is clear that there is not much point in seeking a theistic existentialism in either Sartre or Heidegger. That represents a definite lack, particularly in Maritain's view. Yet even a non-Christian doctrine of freedom, such as that of Plotinus for instance, can treat it as a) transcendent, b) man's true nature, and c) tied to truth and the First Principle. Now Heidegger's thought also shows freedom to be more than having an unlimited number of choices. Through his understanding of temporality, the import of historicity, and the real meaning of truth, Heidegger's "freedom" is a much richer concept than the one Maritain ascribes to non-Thomistic existentialism, as we have seen. Further, although Heidegger does not discuss the question or any point of ethics, it seems as though freedom as truthful disclosure of beings is not just any choice, so that for him too one might be able to separate the voluntary from the truly free, at least to some extent.

A close examination of Maritain's understanding of freedom, particularly his view of the possibility of evil being found only in improperly chosen *action*, tends to align Maritain with existentialism, particularly that of Heidegger, although his undoubted Thomism adds dimensions Heidegger did not even wish to explore.

The University of Toledo

NOTES

1. Maritain, J. *Existence and the Existent*, English tr. L. Galantiere and Gerald Phelan (Westport, 1975) *St. Thomas and the Problem of Evil*, Aquinas Lecture, 1942, (Milwaukee, 1942); *The Range of Reason*, Geoffrey Bles, London, 1953; *Freedom in the Modern World*, (New York, 1971).

2. Aquinas, Thomas. *De Veritate*, Q. 24, A. 2.

3. Maritain, J. "A Philosophy of Freedom," in *Freedom in the Modern World* (FMW), *op. cit.*, p. 4.

4. Maritain, J. *Existence and the Existent* (EE), ch. 4, p. 85.

5. Maritain, J. *ibid.*, p. 88.

6. Maritain, J. *ibid.*, p. 91; cp. St. Thomas, *De Malo*, Q. 1, a. 3.

7. Owens, J. "The Acratic's Ultimate Premise In Aristotle," in *Aristoteles Work* (Aristoteles und Seine Schule; Berlin 1985; Walter de Gruyter, pp. 376-392).

8. Owens, J. *ibid.*, p. 385.

9. Owens, J. *ibid.*, p. 390.

10. Owens, J. *ibid.*; cp. Aristotle, *Nichomachean Ethics*.

11. Maritain, J. EE, p. 91.

12. Maritain, J. *ibid.*, pp. 90-91.

13. Maritain, J. *St. Thomas and the Problem of Evil* (S PE), p. 31.

14. Maritain, J. EE, p. 92.

15. Maritain, J. *ibid.*, p. 102.

16. Plotinus *Enneads*, 6.8.20, McKenna tr.; Faber and Faber, London, 1969. On the usage of the word God/divine, Plotinus makes his point in ch. 18 of the same Treatise. The One cannot be defined; he adds: "Thus we must speak of God since we cannot tell him as we would." Maritain's parallel quotation is at EE, ft. 23. p. 115.

17. Maritain, J. EE, p. 103.

18. Maritain, J. *ibid.*, p. 93.

19. Maritain, J. STPE, p. 31.

20. Maritain, J. *The Range of Reason* (RR), p. 66. ft

21. Maritain, J. *ibid.*, p. 68.

22. Maritain, J. *ibid*, p. 69.

23. Maritain, J. *ibid.*, p. 71.

24. Maritain, J. *ibid.*, p. 74.

25. Maritain, J. "A Philosophy of Freedom: (FMW), p. 6.

26. Maritain, J. EE, pp. 48-49.

27. Maritain, J. *ibid.*, p. 49.

28. Maritain, J. EE, p. 4.

29. Heidegger, M. *Basic Writings*, "On the Essence of Truth," (New York, 1977) p. 29.

30. Heidegger, M. *Being and Time*, trans, McQuarrie and Robinson, (New York, 1962) p. 227; cf. also pp. 235-241.

31. Heidegger, M. *ibid.*, p. 437.

32. Schmitz, K. "A Moment of Truth," *The Review of Metaphysics*, 33 (1980) pp. 686-87.

PART TWO

EXISTENCE AND THE EXISTENT

F. *Ecce in Pace*

CAN 'HAPPINESS' BE SAVED?

Deal W. Hudson

My title implies that happiness is in danger. The evidence of its predicament has been mounting for many years. But a serious impasse has now been reached: prophetic voices have warned us to abandon abandon the pursuit of happiness, claiming that it trivializes and even threatens us, while at the same time the popular marketplace of ideas is swarming with pulp paperbacks and videos promoting the "Happiness Business." In our age happiness is being hawked by West Coast channelers, positive thinkers bearing their message of the mind cure, aerobic priestesses, and dietary metaphysicians. They speak of happiness in unison, promising a happy life without moral reform, a life of lasting pleasure and satisfaction resting contentedly in its own thought of itself.

Once found at its very heart, happiness no longer belongs to the discourse of humane learning but to feel-good, look-good, and buy-good hucksters. Ironically, they did not have to steal happiness, it was given to them. Philosophers have considered happiness as dead currency for some time. For example, over seventy-five years ago, Miguel de Unamuno passionately argued that we should choose love rather than happiness; the happy man, he said, was "without substance"; by choosing happiness rather than suffering love he passed through life "without any inner meaning."[1] In our own generation Aleksandr Solzhenitsyn has called happiness "an idol of the market," which should never be pursued since even "a beast gnawing at its prey can be happy."[2] For Solzhenitsyn, as for Unamuno, happiness is the natural enemy of love.

Add to these the voices of the leading moral philosopher Alasdair MacIntyre, who calls happiness a "polymorphous" and "morally dangerous" concept,[3] and the sociologist Robert Bellah who finds in the American pursuit of happiness nothing less than an excuse for national self-absorption.[4] And one does not have to read very far among contemporary poets to realize how far we have come since Pope's *Essay on Man*: commenting upon the legacy of Epicurus, C.H. Sisson concludes gloomily, "It may be that happiness is a sign of evil",[5] while Roy Fuller casts his complaint into a form with which we can all sympathize: "Now that . . . all the new music is written in the twelve-tone scale, . . . anyone happy is this age and place is daft or corrupt."[6]

These represent only several among the latest warnings, grown louder since the initial alarms of Voltaire, Samuel Johnson, and Immanuel Kant, and earlier of Pascal, that the idea of happiness may be, to invert the classical tradition, fundamentally at odds with what is most praiseworthy in human life.

So happiness needs to be saved--but from whom? From the prophetic thinkers who deny its relation to love and moral purpose, or from the frivolous, self-indulgent hucksters who manipulate human eros for popularity and material gain?

Perhaps nowhere is Jacques Maritain's warning about the Cartesian substitution of technique and technology for character and virtue better illustrated than in these popular conceptions of happiness. Maritain would have known firsthand one of the well-intentioned popular writers who between the wars tilled the ground for our present crop of husksters. The philosopher Emile Chartier, known under the psuedonym of Alain, published in 1928 ninety three of his brilliant aphoristic sketches under the title *Propos sur le bonheur*. As memorable and insightful as his writings are, the substance of his thoughts on happiness is not very far from those of the postive thinking movement which begin to thrive in America during the thirties under Norman Vincent Peale. For Alain, as for Peale, happiness was a product of the will applied to the mind; happiness can be created despite all circumstances by technique--smiling, straightening one's posture, not dwelling on sad thoughts, resisting troubling passions, and delving into the work at hand. Although one cannot help but be taken in by by a writer who can persuade you in four hundred words that "learning to drink a cup of tea can civilize a man,"[7] taken as a whole Alain's treatment of happiness is hopelessly middlebrow, giving the impression of profundity while promoting entirely the cultivation of bourgeois pleasures and, most importantly (opposimg Unamuno), the avoidance of all suffering. Perhaps we can see more clearly now why there exists such an impressive chorus of voices opposed to the ancient suggestion that happiness is the greatest of all human ends. Our century has witnessed something far worse than the eighteenth-century reduction of happiness to pleasure and satisfaction. At the very least, the philosophers from Locke to Rousseau who placed happiness at the heart of their ethical and political reflection never allowed it to stray too far from the acquisition of virtue. Popular writers such as Alain and Peale, as well as Bertrand Russell and the novelist John Cowper Powys, who each wrote happiness books in the thirties, convinced multitudes of readers that happiness was little more than a trick of the mind, something akin to conjuring.[8] In *The Art of Happiness* Powys insists that we can be happy in spite of any circumstance by taking advantage of the "magic of the mind."[9]

The recourse to magic is nothing new. What is new is that an entire age seems to have succumbed to it. The protests of Solzenitsyn and Unamuno are far from eccentric when it is recognized that the pursuit of happiness has become a technique of avoidance, not only of pain but also of that part of us that is deepest, most enduring, and most praiseworthy. Maritain described work of the surrealists as a "magical preaching," words and images in obedience to only an internal rule and not the principle of non-contradiction.[10] Thus, happiness has become private and inscrutable; the hucksters buy and sell a product that cannot be tested for its quality; nothing can measure it or refute it except, perhaps, the consciousness of suffering, whose arrival is quickly met with a technique of incantation and auto-suggestion. We see firmly erected in these happiness advocates what Maritain called the "shibboleth of sincerity."[11]

Can 'happiness' be saved from all of this? Surely Maritain would advise us not to be averted from the attempt by the overwhelming odds. In his lectures on *Moral Philosophy* Maritain wrote: "We are starving for happiness, we make the *pursuit of happiness* one of our fundamental rights, we seek happiness in everything that is perishable, in the love of a woman or in the conquest of power. . . ."[12] For Maritain we seek happiness in spite of the fact that human experience constantly frustrates the attempt--"Men seek beatitude, without believing in it."[13] If reach exceeds grasp then the response of the Christian philosopher should not be Kant's, who simply detached the motive of happiness from morality, or, as we can infer from Maritain's treatment of Sartre, the anguished cynicism of Unamuno and Solzenitzen. No, Maritain insists that "genuine Christianity does not despise the rational desire for happiness and does not reject it from the proper domain of morality but directs it to something better and more loved. . . ."[14]

Although Maritain's remarks about happiness are scattered and brief, they are illuminating. In fact, I would argue that Maritain is almost alone in his avoidance of a mistake common to most attempts at reviving and restoring the idea of happiness: Maritain realizes that the tradition of *eudaimonism*, even with it confident founding of happiness on the virtues, contains within itself unresolved problems, which led to its own gradual dissolution in the Renaissance. In other words, in order to save happiness Maritain knew it was not enough to revive Aristotle.

Obviously, a critique of classical eudaimonism cannot be completed in a short space; so I will limit myself to two important and interrelated issues, one stated explicity by Maritain, the other vaguely hinted at. Though these do not tell the whole story, taken together they can direct our effort at restoring happiness to "something better and more loved." The first issue raises a question central to the task of the Christian philosopher who takes on the issue of happiness: whether happiness is more truthfully conceived as a final end within itself or as having some good external to itself. Interestingly, Maritain praises Kant for his insight into the inherent weaknesses of Aristotle's eudaimonism--his subordination of the Good to the idea of happiness. Yet, Kant's rejection of of all finality in ethics was too extreme, and, I may add unnecessary, if he had bothered to question the purely empirical notion of happiness he had inherited from his century.

Aristotle, and Aquinas following him, clearly distinguished happiness from the pleasure that accompanies its possession. If anything characterizes the tradition of eudaimonism, even in Epicurus, it is its insistence that contentment, joy, and pleasure must be rooted in good moral character in order to qualify as the passions of a happy man or women. It is, I think, one of the great unexplored avenues of the history of Western ideas how these positive emotions became disengaged from a morally worthy and fortunate life to take the place of happiness for themselves. The emergence of what is termed "soft Epicureanism" as a substitute for eudaimonia has yet to be traced. There have been numerous protests against it: the best known of these is by someone who nearly sacrificed his mental health trying to provide the new Epicureanism with a philosophical grounding--"Better to be Socrates dissatisfied than a fool satisfied."[15] This dead end experienced by John Stuart Mill in trying to comprehend all of life in terms of the "two sovereign masters, pleasure and pain," has been ignored by the social scientists who, operating under the rubric of "eudemics," publish their studies of "subjective well-being." What better proof is there of the damage done by "pig-utilitarianism" than the still current assumption that a happy life can be described by surveys? This residuum of utilitariansim raises the second issue: how, and how closely, must we link pleasure with happiness? This may strike one as a strange question, since nothing may seem more natural than ascribing positive physical, emotional, and mental states to the happy life. And, indeed, this is what we find in most of the classical tradition. Even those Stoic and Epicurean philosophers who thought it possible to be happy "upon the rack" rested their case not merely on the stability of virtue but further on a mental *tranquility* that could remain aloof from the pain being afflicted upon the body.

For some this issue of suffering is resolved as a question of good and bad fortune. The happy life for them, as Aristotle said, is the lucky combination of acquired virtue and external goods. In Kantian terms, if a person gains the pleasure out of life he deserves he can be called happy; if not, he can be called virtuous but not happy. This no doubt is Aristotle's position but it does not solve the entire problem of pain in happiness.

But there is an important aspect left unresolved in Aristotle and the whole tradition of eudaimonia. It has to do with the suffering involved in the acquisition and maintenance of those goods that are internal and foundational to the happy life, that is, the virtues themselves. Aristotle mentions this when he remarks that a person who is virtuous will experience both pleasure and pain at the right time and at the right place. Epicurus also remarks that we must be willing to experience pain for the sake of virtue.

And, of course, Plato in the *Gorgias* makes those forever provocative remarks about the person being punished justly as being happier than one who is not.

Taken as a whole, such isolated remarks suggest more of an answer to the question than is really there. It is only with the patristic and medieval writers that the role of suffering in the happy life moves toward the center. The reason for this, and here the two questions coalesce, is that the end of the happy life--goodness itself--has moved beyond the human to the divine. In Maritain's words, happiness has taken on a "peregrinal aspect." Happiness is now broken into earthly and heavenly, temporal and eternal, imperfect and perfect; our temporal eudamonia begins to contain a looking forward (or, to be precise, a looking-over-time) into eternity.

Once God was made the final end of happiness, Maritain comments, "by the same stroke the notion of happines was transfigured."[16] God is now to be loved more than happiness and, by implication, the level of suffering now found acceptable for a praiseworthy life has increased. Aquinas, in a crucial passage from the *Summa Theologiae*, not to be found in his treatise on happiness, was forced to differ with Aristotle and the classical tradition on the relation of happiness to suffering. In his articles on Christ' passion he quotes with approval Augustine's remark that there is "no better way to cure our misery than the passion of Christ."[17] Who would have previously imagined that unhappiness could be remedied by the choice of pain? And when stating the Stoic and Aristotelian objection that the man of virtue does not suffer greatly Aquinas replies that "some sadness is praiseworthy [as] when a man is saddened over his own or another's sins."[18]

Aquinas does not protect Christ by invoking Stoic *tranquilitas* or Epicurean *ataraxia* but argues that His suffering extended to His entire soul, even the speculative intellect, which Aristotle had maintained suffering could not reach. But Christ's happiness remains intact because he is enjoying the perfect vision of the Father during death. Though Aristotle would argue that Christ's sadness must qualify his happiness, Aquinas answers that his bliss is perfect: the contrary emotions of pain and joy co-exist within his earthly beatitude. The suffering, once excluded from the happy life, has come to be seen as integral to it, part and parcel of the soul's commitment to its internal goods and final end.

Where Aquinas was willing to question the overly pure concept of happiness bequeathed to him by classicism, Maritain goes even further. In *Integral Humanism* we find the following passage:

> If it is true that the heart of man will always suffer the
> *anguish of beatitude*, it is not because man would be
> condemned always to stagnate here below; it is because
> the largest and most abounding life will always be

something very small compared with the dimensions of the human heart."[19]

That the happy life should contain pain is no accident. For Maritain temporal happiness has the full dignity of an "infravalent" end that should not be imagined along the bourgeoise lines as a "felicity of ease and repose."[20] To specify that happiness has a "peregrinal aspect" does not imply that happiness is mere resignation but rather that the heart will always be subject to a greater longing than can be satisfied by any of the world's goods, even happiness itself. In the words of Boethius, happiness is "shot through with bitterness." But if the anguish of beatitude arises from *within* the experience of happiness itself, it is not entirely visited upon it from without. Yet, insofar as our earthly happiness is inevitably visited by pain, Maritain observes within it a "law of creative conflict" that enables persons to moves to "higher forms of active peace and transfiguring integration."[21] Boethius, while writing his *Consolation* in the dungeons of Pavia in 524, came to the same conclusion: suffering belongs to the order of providence as well as that of fate and, therefore, bears within it the possibility of blessing.

I think what Maritain is suggesting here and elsewhere may be a way of reimagining happiness that could restore the dignity of happiness as eudaimonia but without falling prey to its inner faults. Maritain, in short, understands happiness as part of the demand for sanctity. And I think he is right to do so. By following in this direction we will not need to announce a Christian monopoly of the happy life any more than we would say that only professing Christians will be in heaven. If anyone had an appreciation of differing forms of sanctity it was Jacques Maritain.

Maritain picked up the happiness debate at the moment when the philosophical and theological traditions of the Renaissance began to radically diverge. The persisting empirical conception of happiness, as an enduring state of pleasure or satisfaction, was the result. When the importance of suffering was raised once again in the nineteenth century it bore little relation to happiness, but rather to the various form of unhappiness such as despair and anxiety, which, in an ironic reversal, had gained the kind of status once belonging to eudaimonia.

As Maritain tells us in *Existence and the Existent* these romantic and existentialist precursors of Unamuno and Solzenitsyn were to make a reason-destroying idol out of anguish.[22] This is not the result I recommend. Aiming at suffering destroys happiness just as much as aiming at pleasure; each belongs to happiness as an affective consequence of possessing goods. But the topic of suffering limits philosophical discourse in a special way. Philosophers, said Maritain, are rightfully "astonished" by the apparent contradiction in the behavior of the saints: on the one hand they desire suffering as one of their most precious goods, and on the other hand try so diligently to relieve others of theirs. It belongs to the "structure of the spirit," said Maritain, that the transvaluation of suffering into a superior good remains a "closed secret, valid only for the individual subjectivity" of the saint.[23] Perhaps this is the reason that Boethius called upon Lady Philosophy to offer his panegyric to the mystery of pain and providence.

How much suffering is too much to destroy happiness? What kinds of suffering can be given reasons and purposes? What about suffering people do not choose the suffering that, in Maritain's words, "falls on them like a beast"?[24] These are questions that can be resolved only in the "closed secret" of each individual soul. However, the example of the saints raises a possibility of a happiness lived outside the rational mean of pleasure and pain,[25] requiring "a perfection," Maritain said, "consisting in loving, in going through all that is unpredictable, dangerous, dark, demanding, and insensate in love."[26] Far from being natural enemies, happiness and love require one another. And if questions about suffering cannot be answered in advance by some kind of calculus it does not mean that they go unanswered. I rather think that a life that is truly praiseworthy will learn one way or another to answer them. The least we can do, in advance, is not seek to rob them of the opportunity. T.S. Eliot wrote in the *Four Quartets*:

> In order to arrive there,
> To arrive where you are, to get from where you are not,
> You must go by a way wherein there is no ecstasy.
> In order to arrive at what you do not know
> You must go by a way which is the way of ignorance.
> In order to possess what you do not possess
> You must go by the way of dispossession.
> (East Coker III.)

Mercer University, Atlanta

NOTES

1. Miguel de Unamuno, *The Tragic Sense of Life in Men and Nations*, trans. Anthony Kerrigan (Princeton, 1972), p. 225.

2. Aleksandr I. Solzhenitsyn, *Cancer Ward*, trans. Rebecca Frank (New York, 1980) p. 513.

3. Alasdair MacIntyre, *A Short History of Ethics: A history of moral philosophy from the Homeric age to the twentieth century* (New York, 1966) pp. 167, 195, 207, and especially pp. 236-238.

4. Robert N. Bellah, with Richard Madsen, William Sullivan, Ann Swidler, and Stephen Tipton, *Habits of the Heart: Individualism and Commitment in American Life* (New York, 1985) ch. 1.

5. C.H. Sisson, *Collected Poems, 1943-1983* (Manchester, 1984) p. 111.

6. Roy Fuller, *Collected Poems, 1936-61* (London, 1962) p. 34.

7. Alain, *Alain On Happiness*, trans. Robert D. Cottrell and Jane E. Cottrell (New York, 1973).

8. Bertrand Russell, *The Conquest of Happiness* (New York, 1930). John Cowper Powys, *The Art of Happiness* (New York, 1935).

9. *The Art of Happiness*, 44.

10. Jacques Maritain, *Creative Intuition in Art and Poetry* (Princeton, 1977) pp. 187-88.

11. *Ibid.*, 193.

12. Jacques Maritain, *Moral Philosophy: An historical and critical survey of the great systems* (London, 1964) p. 76.

13. *Ibid.*, p. 76.

14. *Ibid.*, p. 106.

15. John Stuart Mill, *Utilitarianism*, ed. Oskar Piest (New York, 1957) p. 14.

16. *Moral Philosophy*, p. 75.

17. *Summa Theologiae*, III, 46, 3, sed contra.

18. *Summa Theologiae*, III, 46, 6, ad 2.

19. Jacques Maritain, *Integral Humanism: Temporal and Spiritual Problems of A New Christendom*, trans. Joseph W. Evans (New York, 1968) p. 56.

20. *Ibid.*, p. 137.

21. *Ibid.*, p. 56.

22. Jacques Maritain, *Existence and the Existent*, trans. Lewis Galantière and Gerald B. Phelan (New York, 1948) p. 127.

23. *Moral Philosophy*, p. 461.

24. *Ibid.*

25. *Existence and the Existent*, p. 55.

26. *Ibid.*, pp. 49-50.

APPENDICES

THE CONTEMPORANEITY OF MARITAIN'S
EXISTENCE AND THE EXISTENT

Raymond Dennehy

I wish to emphasize but one point -- Maritain was truly a twentieth century philosopher. As one conference title expressed it, he as "A Philosopher for Our Time."

I know such titles and expressions are over-used and tired, but they could not have become so if they lacked an important application. In Maritain's case they enjoy a preeminent applicability. I can think of no other philosopher who took more seriously the philosopher's call to give witness to society. It is one thing for a philosopher to speak out *as a philosopher who is speaking out* and quite another for a philosopher to speak out *as a philosopher who is speaking out philosophically*.

There are many intellectuals who step forward to pronounce publically on some current social event or political policy, and in doing so they might even be regarded as representing the intellectual community. But frequently their pronouncements bear little or no connection with their theories. They speak out merely as "concerned" or "outraged" members of the intelligentia.

Intellectuals feel free to act this way because in their own eyes and those of society their vocation entitles them to do so. But when they simply "speak out," they are living on past glories. For the authority of the intellectual to speak out found its warrant in the connection between philosophical truth and daily life. What we have nowadays, all too frequently, are public pronouncements from members of the intelligentsia which are neither philosophical nor intellectual but ideological. (The inevitability of the replacement of philosophy by ideology has its source in relativism which never enjoys more than a brief fashionability in the aftermath of despair in the intellect's capacity to know truth. Human beings will insist upon holding some "truths" sacred even if they cannot rationally validate them.)

In contrast, Maritain was a philosopher who spoke out philosophically while steadfastly refusing to lend his support, as philosopher, to any political group or ideology. A striking feature of his philosophical witness was its conspicuous metaphysical and epistemological origins. Maritain was first and foremost a metaphysician, a metaphysician who saw the ground and application of his metaphysical theorizing in contemporary events and institutions.

As an example consider Maritain's metaphysical notion of the subject. This notion is at the very center of *Existence and the Existent:* the metaphysical and epistemological argumentation in Chapter One on behalf of the reality of essence and the primacy of the act of existing leads to the conclusion in Chapter Three that the existent is a *subject,* which is to say, a source of activity. On the level of the person, this source is transformed into a source of free, self-perfecting activity.

The socio-political ramifications of this notion immediately recommend themselves. Here we have a rationally justifiable foundation for the inherent, preeminent dignity and rights of the human person in society. I was introduced to Maritain's theory of subsistence -- which, as you know, is the crucial presupposition of his notion of the subject -- when upon reading his *The Person and the Common Good,* I came across the following sentence: "Personality is the subsistence of the spiritual soul communicated to the human composite." For some time before that moment, I had been searching for an answer to the question, "What is it about the human person that justifies his claim to inalienable rights?" The context in which the above sentence appeared suggested to me that an investigation of Maritain's writings on subsistence would reward me with the answer. I was not disappointed. His notion of subsistence furnishes the metaphysical account of the personhood of the human subject which rationally justifies his claim in *The Rights of Man and the Natural Law* that rights are due man by virtue of what he is *by nature*

What has this to do with Maritain as "a twentieth century philosopher"? The answer lies within his public witness as a metaphysician in general and in his notion of the subject in particular. Indeed, these two considerations account for the title of this address, "The Contemporaneity of Maritain's *Existence and the Existent.*"

Ours is an age of mass societies; the megapolis stands as a twentieth century phenomenon. How much has been written in the past half-century, on the one hand, about the eclipse of the self, his freedom and responsibility, in modern mass society and, on the other hand, about the need to preserve the human species! I say "on the one hand. . . and on the other" because these respective projects frequently collide with each other. The reason for the collision may be traced to a lack of the metaphysical wherewithal needed to reconcile the uniqueness and freedom of the human person with the standardization required by the general welfare of society.

Defenses of the primacy of the person have incompatible with the good of society, as laissez-faire individualist and anarchist theories demonstrated in the nineteenth century while defenses of the primacy of the human species and society have proved incompatible with the good of the person, as collectivists theories demonstrate in the present century. The attempts of German philosophy to reconcile the two, with a fusion of German romanticism and Hegelianism, in various forms of the concrete universal, have proved no more successful, owing to the pantheistic implications of claiming that the particular concretely expresses the universal. Somehow the latter manages to swallow the former. Consider, for example, Bernard Bosanquet's Philosophical Theory of the State, wherein that British admirer of Hegel writes that when the law of the state requires me to act or refrain from acting in specific ways, my freedom is not thereby diminished, for I am thereby really obeying myself since I am a particularization of the state!

What Maritain has accomplished with his elucidation of the metaphysical notion of the subject, however, is a rational justification of the dignity and rights traditionally ascribed to the human person that is at the same time compatible with the notion of him as a social being. I noted at the outset that Maritain prepared the ground for the notion of the subject by defending the reality of essence and the primacy of the act of existing. Permit me to amplify that observation.

Existence and the Existent contains emphatic warnings against the insinuation of Platonism and rationalism into Thomistic metaphysics. Maritain's point in issuing the warnings centers in the question "What exists?" His answer is that "things, subjects, existents" are what exists, not reified essences. If I may put it thus: what exists are things and things are existents, which is to say, subjects or sources of activity. The universe, Maritain accordingly observes, is entirely populated by subjects.

Now the pertinent feature of Maritain's notion of the subject unfolds in his tripartite argument. First, he explodes the Sartrean claim that the primacy of existence necessitates the denial of the reality of essence: not only do finite existents have essences, for in their finitude they exist as *this* and *that*, a specificity which means that existents are composed of the potency of essence and the reality of existence; but the vaunted freedom which Sartre would defend by denying essence would be impossible. An act springing from such an agent would amount to nothing more than a determined spontaineity, much the same as a twitch of the facial muscles or some other reflex action. Freedom of the will requires necessitation to a good which, in turn, requires the agent's formal organization towards an end. Essence confers this formal organization.

Second, in his affirmation of the primacy of existence, Maritain calls attention to the "act of all acts" which is existence. Because only a subject can exercise an act, the existent enjoys a degree of uniqueness. I say "a degree of uniqueness" since the extent of an existent's uniqueness is determined by its rank in the hierarchy if being. As Thomas Aquinas observed, "the higher a nature, the more intimate to that nature is the activity that flows from it." Thus as a unique center of conscious, autonomous being, the human person enjoys the uniqueness possessed only by a self. In material nature, man stands alone as a truly unique subject.

Third, the consequence of this notion of the subject unmasks the Platonic and rationalist error regarding essence. Universality cannot be the inevitable quality of essence; it is only so when it inhabits the intellect as an intentional being, for then it has been de-individualized by abstraction. Essence in itself is neither universal nor particular, but is either the one or the other depending on the conditions of its existence: as it exists in things, i.e., subjects, it is particular.

The subject is accordingly a unique composition of essence and existence. Recall the remarkable second chapter in *Existence and the Existent* where, anticipating the discussion of the subject's ontological foundation conferred by the mode of subsistence, Maritain investigates the meaning of the moral life of the human subject: if the moral law is a universal law, the human subject constitutes a unique embodiment of that law. By choosing to live by the law, he appropriates it to his own unique selfhood.

How does the Maritainian notion of the subject speak to the twentieth century? The answer is that it rationally grounds, in the evidence of experience, the universality and uniqueness of man. Universal because each human subject embodies what is common to all men and women at all times and in all places. Unique because existential embodiment proportions essence to the singular act of existing of the subject. This ontology furnishes the rationale for reconciling the stardardization of man required by the general welfare of political society with his need to find fulfillment in the actualization of the potentials inherent in the uniqueness of the existent that he is. In exercising his unique act of existing, he is, to be sure, specified in that exercise by what he shares in common with all human beings, the essence *man*. But his singular privilege in the spectrum of material being is to use his reason and free choice to actualize unique, and hitherto unprecedented, embodiments of that essence.

How often do we read in the pages of Maritain's books defenses of the dignity of the human person -- whether the topic of discussion be education, politics, economics, morals, or spirituality -- which either explicitly or implicitly derive their inspiration from the conception of the human person as *subject*! Consider, for example, *Freedom in the Modern World, The Person and the Common Good, Education at the Crossroads, Creative Intuition in Art and Poetry*, and *Liturgy and Contemplation*.

The future of democratic society and, indeed, of Western civilization depends on the reconciliation of the general welfare with personal autonomy and fulfillment. The twentieth century has provided us with a dramatic, and often absurd, theatre of challenges and threats both to the person and the common good. We cannot tell what the future holds. But the path to the survival, let alone the progress, of these values requires a philosophical vision of man. I am persuaded that the foundation for such a vision has been set forth by Maritain and nowhere has he done this more incisively and foundationally than in *Existence and the Existent*.

President, American Maritain Association
University of San Francisco

"Le témoignage intellectuellement manifesté"
"THE INTELLECTUALLY MANIFESTED WITNESS"

Jean-Louis Allard

Un événement d'une très grande importance vient de prendre fin à Rome, à savoir le Synode des Evêques sur la vocation et la mission du laïc dans l'Eglise et dans le monde.

A la lumière du Concile Vatican II et de l'expérience post- conciliaire, les délégué au Synode ont approfondi *la vocation chrétienne* qui découle du baptême et de la confirmation, *la dignité* fondamentale des membres du Peuple de Dieu ainsi que l'agir chrétien qui lui corresponde:

"Tout ce que vous faites trouve son sens dans ce que vous êtes", affirmait Jean-Paul II, lors de sa visite en terre canadienne, le 15 septembre 1984.

Le Cercle d'études Jacques et Raïssa Maritain (Kolbsheim) a voulu profiter de cette occasion privilégiée pour autoriser la publication d'un texte inédit de Jacques Maritain sur l'apostolat des laïcs, plus spécifiquement sur la mission spirituelle des laïcs.[1]

Dans cette brève allocution, je ferai une courte présentation du texte de Jacques Maritain, puis, je le mettrai en relation avec certains extraits du *Court traité de l'existence et de l'existant*, portant sur la question de la philosophie chrétienne; enfin je soumettrai à votre attention quelques-unes des questions qui me sont venues à l'esprit à la lecture de ces textes.

I

May I, first of all, recall the circumstances which have led Maritain to the writing of this text on lay apostolate. In presenting the text, Professor Bernard Doering explains:

> The following text, previously unpublished, is a memorandum written by Maritain at the request of Paul VI and presented to the Pope in the early months of 1965. It was composed following an interview on December 27, 1964 with Jean Guitton and the private secretary of Paul

VI, Monsignor Macchi (with whose authorization this text
is being made public), who had been sent by the Pope in
the course of the Council expressly to consult Maritain.
These pages then are posterior to the promulgation of the
dogmatic Constitution "*De Ecclesia*" (*Lumen Centium*),
which is dated November 21, 1964, and whose fourth
chapter concerns the laity.[2]

Those who are familiar with Maritain's writings are aware that he has
given much attention to the temporal mission of the Christians, more
particularly in *Integral Humanism*, a "prophetic book" in which he describes
the ideal of a new Christendom "as a temporal regime or as an age of
civilization whose animated form would be Christian and which would
correspond to the historical climate of the epoch into which we are
entering."[3]

Such an ideal will be realized only through deep changes resulting from
"making a real *refraction* of the Gospel pass into the cultural and temporal
order. It is a question of changes in the regime of human life which are at
once internal and external, which are to be accomplished in the hearts of
men and in the body politic and in its institutions, and which affect together,
though by different titles, the social and visible domain and the spiritual,
moral, and invisible one; and first of all, the spiritual domain."[4]

This means that the mission of the laity is both temporal and spiritual,
and these cannot be dissociated; they flow from the same source.
Consequently, the theme of the spiritual mission of the laity has been for
Jacques and Raïssa Maritain an object of reflection and a constant subject of
experience. The Foreword to *Le Journal de Ra ssa*, the *Carnet de notes*, the
Paysan de la Garonne contain many thoughts on this subject.

The memorandum of Jacques Maritain to Pope Paul VI on lay
apostolate seems to flow directly from the very doctrine of Vatican II. It
treats specifically of "the spiritual mission of the laity in the Church", an
expression which Maritain prefers to the usual expression "lay apostolate."

The following quotation indicates quite clearly Maritain's perspective:

> The Christian laity as such, - independently of any
> participation, in certain given cadres, in the apostolate
> proper to the hierarchy, - has a *witness* to render and a
> *spiritual mission* in the Church. And those who share the
> common condition of the laity receive this mission, not
> from a special call or a special mandate from the
> hierarchy; they receive it from their baptism and their
> confirmation, in other words from the very fact that they
> are *members of Christ*.[5]

In relation with this spiritual mission of the laity, Maritain mentions three different levels of commitments: the intellectually manifest witness, the level of family life and Christian marriage, and the organizing of social groups.

The first level, a very special one, says Maritain, refers to the *intellectually manifest witness*: the Christian intellectuals (writers, artists, scholars, etc...) who, without any particular mandate, had a profound influence in the expression of their personal experience; among those mentioned by Maritain, we find Pascal, Bach, Rouault, Tolstoy, Bloy, Claudel, Chesterton, T.S. Eliot. To this incomplete but impressive list we could certainly add Jacques and Raïssa Maritain, Yves Simon, Charles De Koninck and many others we have known.

This raises again the complex problem of Christian philosophy which will be the object of the followings part of this paper.

A more general level of Christian commitment, "at the foundation of the life of the faithful people of God" is found in family life and Christian marriage:

> A marriage is a sacred community where the spouses should mutually help each other to strive toward *the perfection of charity*. (...) Even on the level of sexual life and the perpetuation of the human species, that vocation of bearing witness to which marriage and domestic society are essentially called with regard to eternal life - to eternal life already begun here below, - is, I believe, the primary mission, in the midst of storms and high tides, with which the layman *as a Christian*, as constituting an essential part of the Mystical Body, is charged above all else"[6]

A detailed analysis of what Maritain has written concerning the spiritual mission of the family would lead us beyond the limits of this paper. But I cannot resist the temptation of bringing to your attention a part of the text in which he describes the kind of equality that exists between parents and their children within the realm of spiritual growth, an equality which situates them in the same psychological universe:

> In this context a number of things should be noted: on the one hand, the transcendence of our Heavenly Father is such that in the presence of this transcendence, and of His divine mercy, parents and children are pretty much on the same level. On the other hand adults have been told that in order to enter the Kingdom of Heaven they must become like little children. Finally the intuitivity of childhood makes contemplative prayer easily accessible to

children, and with regard to the mysteries of the faith, childhood often (without reflex conceptualization) enjoys astonishing illuminations that adults may very well envy. The result of all this is that not only should parents and children strive to establish an exchange of thoughts and feelings, a mutual openness and communication, but there should develop naturally between them even a kind of equality - which is impossible anywhere else - in their progress toward union with God and the perfection of love.[7]

The third level of witness Maritain refers to, concerns the initiatives of layman, in the spiritual order, in organizing groups "for the service of souls and of the Church"; he mentions, in particular the "Equipes sociales" of Robert Garric, the groups who bring aid to the underdeveloped countries; he includes in this level of witness the founding by Etienne Gilson of the Institute of Mediaeval Studies of Toronto; may I suggest that groups like ours (The American Maritain Association and the Canadian Jacques Maritain Association) are, in their limited way, humble efforts in the same direction.

The first and the third levels of witness mentioned by Maritain include the spiritual mission of the Christian intellectuals, either as individuals or in groups, and this leads us to a very important question: as Christian philosophers, can we acknowledge that we have such a mission without betraying the very specific task of philosophizing.

We are confronted again with the problem of Christian philosophy which Maritain has discussed lengthily in his works and to which he refers in the last chapter of *Existence and the Existent*.[8]

II

C'est donc dire que le texte de Maritain sur l'apostolat des laïcs nous renvoie à la question de la philosophie chétienne et qu'il est ainsi vitalement relié au *Court traité de l'existence et de l'existant* dont quelques pages résument d'une façon saisissante sa pensée à cet égard?[9]

Il serait téméraire de vouloir traiter ici d'une façon quelque peu approfondie de cette question complexe mais combien vitale pour nous. Qu'il me soit permis toutefois d'en évoquer les grandes lignes pour ensuite réfléchir avec vous sur quelques- unes des interrogations qui ont germé à mon esprit à la lecture comparée du texte sur *La mission spirituelle des laics* et du *Court traité*.

"Distinguer pour unir," tels sont les deux versants d'une vision réaliste de cette question: distinguer nettement la philosophie de la foi chrétienne et de la théologie pour ensuite montrer comment ces "habitus" sont dynamiquement reliés dans la vie de l'esprit.

Ainsi, Maritain affirme en premier lieu *l'autonomie de la philosophie*; le renouveau de la philosophie dépend de cette autonomie, de l'authenticité de l'oeuvre philosophique, tant en principe qu'en pratique. D'ailleurs, cette autonomie implique la reconnaissance de la valeur propre de la théologie comme sagesse supérieure.

Or, "jusqu'à présent, - en ce qui concerne la pensée chrtienne, - ni en métaphysique ni surtout en morale les thomistes ne se sont appliqués avec beaucoup de zèle à dégager pleinement la structure propre de leur philosophie des voies d'approche et de la problématique de la théologie."[10]

D'autre part, si l'on tient compte des conditions existentielles du philosophe chrétien, les principes qui l'inspirent "nous obligent à voir comment, au noeud immatériel des énergies de l'âme, la sagesse mystique et la sagesse théologique vivifient et fortifient la sagesse métaphysique de la même façon que celle-ci vivifie et fortifie les activités philosophiques de rang moins élevé."[11]

Maritain ne fait que réaffirmer sa position relative à la philosophie chrétienne, position qu'il avait déjà amplement expliquée à plusieurs reprises.[12]

Disons tout d'abord que l'expression *philosophie chrétienne* lui semble équivoque: "J'emploie ce mot de philosophie chrétienne, et comment faire autrement? A vrai dire il ne m'enchante guère, il arrive au moment où tous les mots semblent trahir, et celui-là risque d'évoquer dans les esprits - dans les esprits prévenus (et nous sommes tous) - je ne sais quelle hybridation ou atténuation de la philosophie par le christianisme, je ne sais quel enrôlement de la philosophie dans une confrérie pieuse ou dans un parti dévot."[13] En effet cette expression ne peut être employée que dans un "sens matériel" pour signifier la philosophie occidentale même lorsqu'elle trahit la pensée chrétienne car ses thèmes s'inspirent de cette pensée. Si l'on considère la philosophie dans son "sens formel," elle est proprement une activité de la raison naturelle et elle n'est pas plus chrétienne que païenne; dans sa nature propre, la philosophie "ne dépend que des évidences et des critères de la raison naturelle."[14]

Cependant, l'acte philosophique est l'acte d'une personne humaine qui, de fait, peut être pré-chrétienne, chrétienne, a-chrétienne; par voie de conséquence et sans changer sa nature intrinsèque, cet acte philosophique est dans un "état" pré-chrétien, chrétien, a-chrétien selon le cas. De cette situation concrète peuvent résulter des tensions. Par exemple, le philosophe chrétien peut et même doit philosopher en tenant compte de l'apport de sa foi; il doit en même temps respecter les exigences de la philosophie. Des tensions peuvent également surgir entre philosophes chrétiens et philosophes non-chrétiens; il faut tenter de diminuer ces tensions, de surmonter la suspicion mutuelle qu'elles recèlent sans oublier que l'accord entre philosophes ne sera jamais complètement réalisé, car "the natural condition of any philosopher seems to imply that he can be in agreement only with himself. Even this kind of agreement seems rather difficult and due to some infrequent kind of luck."[15]

S'inspirant de la pensée de Thomas d'Aquin selon laquelle "la grâce ne détruit pas la nature; elle la suppose et la perfectionne", Maritain peut affirmer l'authenticité de la philosophie même lorsqu'elle est vitalement jointe "aux lumières supérieures de la sagesse théologique et de la sagesse des saints."[16]

III

As mentioned in the preceding part, my intention, here, is not to initiate a new debate on the problem of Christian philosophy. I would simply propose to your reflection some of the interrogations that have come to my mind concerning the spiritual mission of the Christian philosophers, as described by Maritain, and within the context of his views on Christian philosophy.

1. A first question of great importance can be raised: How do we achieve the dynamic unity between our Christian beliefs (and values) and the specific demands of philosophy? How can we be authentically Christian while authentically philosophizing?

It seems to me that this is a question of maturity. A mature person, according to psychology, is the one in which there is a growing unification of the driving forces of human nature. Aren't we accepting too easily the kind of intellectual schizophrenia the functionalized and pragmatic civilization of ours seems to impose upon us?

Isn't it true that the situation of the Christian philosopher is, on that score, in an analogous situation with the so-called non-believer: both live by *a faith* which vitally affect their philosophical acts. Nevertheless, Christian philosophers seem to have, at times, hidden so to say their faith in order to appear *at par* with their non Christian colleagues...

One cannot underestimate the deep influence of his faith and of the values he lives by, on his philosophizing; to be unaware of this fact might be a way to be unfaithful to the very demands of philosophy as well as to the exigencies of a living faith.

2. The second question concerns the decline of philosophy and of the teaching of philosophy in the contemporary Christian world.

Philosophy as a discipline has lost much of its importance in University programs in general, and in Catholic universities in particular.

Psychology, sociology, etc... have become, in many instances, the new "wisdom" replacing philosophy, even in relation with theology.

Maritain has expressed great concern about the tragic situation of modern civilization which does not come from the prodigious developments of science which is a definite progress, but from the fact that our civilization prefers science to wisdom.[17]

What is the responsibility of Christian philosophers in this regard?

3. Thirdly, has the Christian philosopher a particular responsibility to be present to the many debates of our times?

The crisis of our western civilization appears to be a metaphysical crisis and a moral crisis more than an economic one.

Do Christian philosophers have something to contribute for the "salvation of the intellect"?

4. As philosophers of being, of analogy are we as vitally opened to the given of our faith, to the Documents of the Church, as hypotheses to reflect upon, as we are (and should be) to the acquisitions of science, history, art, etc...?

Many other questions could be raised in relation with this paper of Maritain on the Mission of the Christian intellectuals and of the Christian philosophers. May I say, in concluding my address, that the debate on Christian philosophy appears to be of a crucial actuality, and that beyond the theoretical debate, it presents itself as a challenge to the Christian philosophers.

If the Christian philosopher wants to philosophize without a mask, he does not have any other alternative than to philosophize "dans la foi", and to show through his acts of philosophizing that the "Christian state of philosophy" might mean something valuable for himself, for the Church, and for the world. Could this not be his proper manner to fulfill his "spiritual mission"?

In *Integral Humanism*, Maritain calls for the transformation of a "decoratively Christian society into a vitally Christian society." Maritain himself has given us the example of a vitally Christian philosopher.

If our Associations contribute somehow in helping us become more and more vitally Christian philosophers, they would have achieved a worthwhile purpose.

président
Association canadienne Jacques Maritain
Université D'Ottawa

NOTES

1. Au Canada, le texte a paru en français dans *Eglise et Théologie,* Vol. 18, no 3, octobre 1987, p. 305-313 sous le titre "L'apostolat des laics" et dans *L'Eglise canadienne,* Vol. 21, no 3, 1er octobre 1987, p. 83-87, sous le titre "La mission spirituelle des *baptisés dans l'Eglise.*"

   In the United States, the same text has appeared in English (Translation and Notes by Bernard E. Doering) in *Communio,* Vol. XIV, Number 2, Summer 1987, p. 183-202, under the title "The Spiritual Mission of the Laity."

2. *Communio,* Vol. XIV, No 2, p. 193.

3. Jacques Maritain, *Integral Humanism,* newly translated by Joseph W. Evans, New York, Charles Scribner's Sons, 1968, p. 132.

4. *Ibidem,* p. 213.

5. In *Communio,* Summer 1987, p. 196.

6. *Ibidem,* p. 197.

7. *Ibidem,* p. 198.

8. *Existence and the Existent.* (English version by Lewis Galantière and Gerald B. Phelan). N.Y., Pantheon Books Inc., 1948, p. 136-141.

9. *Court traité de l'existence et de l'existant,* Paris, Paul Hartmann Editeur, 1947, p. 217-226.

10. *Ibidem,* p. 220-221.

11. *Ibidem,* p. 224.

12. Voir surtout *De la philosophie chrétienne,* Paris, Desclée de Brouwer, 1933. 166p. et *Science et sagesse,* Paris, Labergerie, 1935, 393p.

13. Science et sagesse, p. 136.

14. *Ibidem,* p. 138.

15. *About Christian Philosophy,* dans Barduin V. Schwarz, éditeur, *The Human Person and the World of Values,* N.Y., Fordham University Press, 1960, p. 10.

16. *Court traité de l'existence et de l'existant,* p. 225.

17. See *Quatre essais sur l'esprit dans sa condition charnelle,* Paris, Alsatia, 1956, p. 170.